THE DAILY STOIC

The DAILY STOIC

366 Meditations on Wisdom,
Perseverance, and the Art of Living

RYAN HOLIDAY
AND STEPHEN HANSELMAN

Memento Mori:

THE
PAINTED
PORCH

PORTFOLIO / PENGUIN

BOOKSHOP

Portfolio/Penguin
An imprint of Penguin Random House LLC
375 Hudson Street
New York, New York 10014

Translations by Stephen Hanselman

LIBRARY OF CONGRESS CATALOGING-IN-PUBLICATION DATA
Names: Holiday, Ryan, author. Hanselman, Stephen, author.
Title: The daily stoic : 366 meditations on wisdom, perseverance,
    and the art of living / Ryan Holiday and Stephen Hanselman.
Description: New York : Portfolio, 2016.
Identifiers: LCCN 2016030358 | ISBN 9780735211735 (hardcover)
    | ISBN 9780735211742 (e-book) Subjects: LCSH: Stoics.
Classification: LCC B528 .H65 2016 | DDC 188—dc23 LC record
    available at https://lccn.loc.gov/2016030358

Printed in the United States of America
25th Printing

Set in Sabon with Humanist 521
Book design by Daniel Lagin

From Stephen to my beloved Julia, who helped me find joy.

"Of all people only those are at leisure who make time for philosophy, only they truly live. Not satisfied to merely keep good watch over their own days, they annex every age to their own. All the harvest of the past is added to their store. Only an ingrate would fail to see that these great architects of venerable thoughts were born for us and have designed a way of life for us."

—Seneca

CONTENTS

INTRODUCTION

The private diaries of one of Rome's greatest emperors, the personal letters of one of Rome's best playwrights and wisest power brokers, the lectures of a former slave and exile, turned influential teacher. Against all odds and the passing of some two millennia, these incredible documents survive.

What do they say? Could these ancient and obscure pages really contain anything relevant to modern life? The answer, it turns out, is yes. They contain some of the greatest wisdom in the history of the world.

Together these documents constitute the bedrock of what is known as Stoicism, an ancient philosophy that was once one of the most popular civic disciplines in the West, practiced by the rich and the impoverished, the powerful and the struggling alike in the pursuit of the Good Life. But over the centuries, knowledge of this way of thinking, once essential to so many, slowly faded from view.

Except to the most avid seekers of wisdom, Stoicism is either unknown or misunderstood. Indeed, it would be hard to find a word dealt a greater injustice at the hands of the English language than "Stoic." To the average person, this vibrant, action-oriented, and paradigm-shifting way of living has become shorthand for "emotionlessness." Given the fact that the mere mention of philosophy makes most nervous or bored, "Stoic philosophy" on the surface sounds like the last thing anyone would want to learn about, let alone urgently *need* in the course of daily life.

What a sad fate for a philosophy that even one of its occasional critics, Arthur Schopenhauer, would describe as "the highest point to which man can attain by the mere use of his faculty of reason."

Our goal with this book is to restore Stoicism to its rightful place as a tool in the pursuit of self-mastery, perseverance, and wisdom: something one uses to live a great life, rather than some esoteric field of academic inquiry.

Certainly, many of history's great minds not only understood Stoicism for what it truly is, they sought it out: George Washington, Walt Whitman, Frederick the Great, Eugène Delacroix, Adam Smith, Immanuel Kant, Thomas Jefferson, Matthew Arnold, Ambrose Bierce, Theodore Roosevelt, William Alexander Percy, Ralph Waldo Emerson. Each read, studied, quoted, or admired the Stoics.

The ancient Stoics themselves were no slouches. The names you encounter in this book—Marcus Aurelius, Epictetus, Seneca—belonged to, respectively, a Roman emperor, a former slave who triumphed to become an influential lecturer and friend of the emperor Hadrian, and a famous playwright and political adviser. There were Stoics like Cato the Younger, who was an admired politician; Zeno was a prosperous merchant (as several Stoics were); Cleanthes was a former boxer and worked as a water carrier to put himself through school; Chrysippus, whose writings are now completely lost but tallied more than seven hundred books, trained as a long-distance runner; Posidonius served as an ambassador; Musonius Rufus was a teacher; and many others.

Today (especially since the recent publication of *The Obstacle Is the Way*), Stoicism has found a new and diverse audience, ranging from the coaching staffs of the New England Patriots and Seattle Seahawks to rapper LL Cool J and broadcaster Michele Tafoya as well as many professional athletes, CEOs, hedge fund managers, artists, executives, and public men and women.

What have all these great men and women found within Stoicism that others missed?

A great deal. While academics often see Stoicism as an antiquated methodology of minor interest, it has been the *doers* of the world who found that it provides much needed strength and stamina for their challenging lives. When journalist and Civil War veteran Ambrose Bierce advised a young writer that studying the Stoics would teach him "how to be a worthy guest at the table of the gods," or when the painter Eugène Delacroix (famous for his painting *Liberty Leading the People*) called Stoicism his "consoling religion," they were speaking from experience. So was the brave abolitionist and colonel Thomas Wentworth Higginson, who led the first all-black regiment in the U.S. Civil War and produced one of the more memorable translations of Epictetus.

The Southern planter and writer William Alexander Percy, who led the rescue efforts in the Great Flood of 1927, had a unique reference point when he said of Stoicism that "when all is lost, it stands fast." As would the author and angel investor Tim Ferriss, when he referred to Stoicism as the ideal "personal operating system" (other high-powered executives like Jonathan Newhouse, CEO of Condé Nast International, have agreed).

But it's for the field of battle that Stoicism seems to have been particularly well designed. In 1965, as Captain James Stockdale (future Medal of Honor recipient) parachuted from his shot-up plane over Vietnam into what would ultimately be a half decade of torture and imprisonment, whose name was on his lips? Epictetus. Just as Frederick the Great reportedly rode into battle with the works of the Stoics in his saddlebags, so too did marine and NATO commander General James "Mad Dog" Mattis, who carried the *Meditations* of Marcus Aurelius with him on deployments in the Persian Gulf, Afghanistan, and Iraq. Again, these weren't professors but practitioners, and as a practical philosophy they found Stoicism perfectly suited to their purposes.

FROM GREECE TO ROME TO TODAY

Stoicism was a school of philosophy founded in Athens by Zeno of Citium in the early third century BC. Its name is derived from the Greek *stoa*, meaning porch, because that's where Zeno first taught his students. The philosophy asserts that virtue (meaning, chiefly, the four cardinal virtues of self-control, courage, justice, and wisdom) is happiness, and it is our perceptions of things—rather than the things themselves—that cause most of our trouble. Stoicism teaches that we can't control or rely on anything outside what Epictetus called our "reasoned choice"—our ability to use our reason to choose how we categorize, respond, and reorient ourselves to external events.

Early Stoicism was much closer to a comprehensive philosophy like other ancient schools whose names might be vaguely familiar: Epicureanism, Cynicism, Platonism, Skepticism. Proponents spoke of diverse topics, including physics, logic, cosmology, and many others. One of the analogies favored by the Stoics to describe their philosophy was that of a fertile field. Logic was the protective fence, physics was the field, and the crop that all this produced was ethics—or *how to live*.

As Stoicism progressed, however, it focused primarily on two of these topics—logic and ethics. Making its way from Greece to Rome, Stoicism became much more practical to fit the active, pragmatic lives of the industrious Romans. As Marcus Aurelius would later observe, "I was blessed when I set my heart on philosophy that I didn't fall into the sophist's trap, nor remove myself to the writer's desk, or chop logic, or busy myself with studying the heavens."

Instead, he (and Epictetus and Seneca) focused on a series of questions not unlike the ones we continue to ask ourselves today: "What is the best way to live?" "What do I do about my anger?" "What are my obligations to my fellow human beings?" "I'm afraid to die; why is that?" "How can I deal with the difficult situations I face?" "How should I handle the success or power I hold?"

These weren't abstract questions. In their writings—often private letters or diaries—and in their lectures, the Stoics struggled to come up with real, actionable answers. They ultimately framed their work around a series of exercises in three critical disciplines:

The Discipline of Perception (how we see and perceive the world around us)

The Discipline of Action (the decisions and actions we take—and to what end)

The Discipline of Will (how we deal with the things we cannot change, attain clear and convincing judgment, and come to a true *understanding* of our place in the world)

By controlling our perceptions, the Stoics tell us, we can find mental clarity. In directing our actions properly and justly, we'll be effective. In utilizing and aligning our will, we will find the wisdom and perspective to deal with anything the world puts before us. It was their belief that by strengthening themselves and their fellow citizens in these disciplines, they could cultivate resilience, purpose, and even joy.

Born in the tumultuous ancient world, Stoicism took aim at the unpredictable nature of everyday life and offered a set of practical tools meant for daily use. Our modern world may seem radically different than the painted porch (Stoa Poikilê) of the Athenian Agora and the Forum and court of Rome. But the Stoics took great pains to remind themselves (see November 10th) that they weren't facing things any different than their own forebears did, and that the future wouldn't radically alter the nature and end of human existence. One day is as all days, as the Stoics liked to say. And it's still true.

Which brings us to where we are right now.

A PHILOSOPHICAL BOOK FOR THE PHILOSOPHICAL LIFE

Some of us are stressed. Others are overworked. Perhaps you're struggling with the new responsibilities of parenthood. Or the chaos of a new venture. Or are you already successful and grappling with the duties of power or influence? Wrestling with an addiction? Deeply in love? Or moving from one flawed relationship to another? Are you approaching your golden years? Or enjoying the spoils of youth? Busy and active? Or bored out of your mind?

Whatever it is, whatever you're going through, there is wisdom from the Stoics that can help. In fact, in many cases they have addressed it explicitly in terms that feel shockingly modern. That's what we're going to focus on in this book.

Drawing directly from the Stoic canon, we present a selection of original translations of the greatest passages from the three major figures of late Stoicism—Seneca, Epictetus, and Marcus Aurelius—along with a few assorted sayings from their Stoic predecessors (Zeno, Cleanthes, Chrysippus, Musonius, Hecato). Accompanying each quotation is our attempt to tell a story, provide context, ask a question, prompt an exercise, or explain the perspective of the Stoic who said it so that you may find deeper understanding of whatever answers you are seeking.

The works of the Stoics have always been fresh and current, regardless of the historical ebb and flow of their popularity. It was not our intention with this book to fix them or modernize them or freshen them up (there are many excellent translations out there). Instead, we sought to organize and present the vast collective wisdom of the Stoics into as digestible, accessible, and coherent a form as possible. One can—and should—pick up the original works of the Stoics in whole form (see Suggestions for Further Reading in the back of this book). In the meantime, here, for the busy and active reader, we have attempted to produce a daily devotional that is as functional and to the point as the philosophers behind it. And in the Stoic tradition, we've added material to provoke and facilitate the asking of big questions.

Organized along the lines of the three disciplines (Perception, Action, and Will) and then further divided into important themes within those disciplines, you'll find that each month will stress a particular trait and each day will offer a new way to think or act. The areas of great interest to the Stoics all make an appearance here: virtue, mortality, emotions, self-awareness, fortitude, right action, problem solving, acceptance, mental clarity, pragmatism, unbiased thought, and duty.

The Stoics were pioneers of the morning and nightly rituals: preparation in the morning, reflection in the evening. We've written this book to be helpful with both. One meditation per day for every day of the year (including an extra day for leap years!). If you feel so inclined, pair it with a notebook to record and articulate your thoughts and reactions (see January 21st and 22nd and December 22nd), just as the Stoics often did. We've also created a durable companion to this book for daily diarists, *The Daily Stoic Journal*.

We recommend that you begin on the page with the date you are presently reading this book and continue to read the corresponding entry for each date as you move through the year, returning to the beginning of the book at the New Year. Many readers report reading all the way through first, and then savoring each day at a time on their second reading—how you read the book won't change its power.

The aim of this hands-on approach to philosophy is to help you live a better life. It is our hope that there is not a word in this book that can't or shouldn't, to paraphrase Seneca, be turned into works.

To that end, we offer this book.

PART I

The DISCIPLINE *of* PERCEPTION

JANUARY

CLARITY

January 1st
CONTROL AND CHOICE

"The chief task in life is simply this: to identify and separate matters so that I can say clearly to myself which are externals not under my control, and which have to do with the choices I actually control. Where then do I look for good and evil? Not to uncontrollable externals, but within myself to the choices that are my own . . ."

—EPICTETUS, *DISCOURSES*, 2.5.4–5

The single most important practice in Stoic philosophy is differentiating between what we can change and what we can't. What we have influence over and what we do not. A flight is delayed because of weather—no amount of yelling at an airline representative will end a storm. No amount of wishing will make you taller or shorter or born in a different country. No matter how hard you try, you can't *make* someone like you. And on top of that, time spent hurling yourself at these immovable objects is time not spent on the things we *can* change.

The recovery community practices something called the Serenity Prayer: "God, grant me the serenity to accept the things I cannot change, the courage to change the things I can, and the wisdom to know the difference." Addicts cannot change the abuse suffered in childhood. They cannot undo the choices they have made or the hurt they have caused. But they *can* change the future—through the power they have in the present moment. As Epictetus said, they can control the choices they make right now.

The same is true for us today. If we can focus on making clear what parts of our day are within our control and what parts are not, we will not only be happier, we will have a distinct advantage over other people who fail to realize they are fighting an unwinnable battle.

January 2nd
EDUCATION IS FREEDOM

"What is the fruit of these teachings? Only the most beautiful and proper harvest of the truly educated—tranquility, fearlessness, and freedom. We should not trust the masses who say only the free can be educated, but rather the lovers of wisdom who say that only the educated are free."

—EPICTETUS, *DISCOURSES*, 2.1.21–23a

Why did you pick up this book? Why pick up any book? Not to seem smarter, not to pass time on the plane, not to hear what you want to hear—there are plenty of easier choices than reading.

No, you picked up this book because you are learning how to live. Because you want to be freer, fear less, and achieve a state of peace. Education—reading and meditating on the wisdom of great minds—is not to be done for its own sake. It has a purpose.

Remember that imperative on the days you start to feel distracted, when watching television or having a snack seems like a better use of your time than reading or studying philosophy. Knowledge—self-knowledge in particular—is freedom.

January 3rd
BE RUTHLESS TO THE THINGS THAT DON'T MATTER

"How many have laid waste to your life when you weren't aware of what you were losing, how much was wasted in pointless grief, foolish joy, greedy desire, and social amusements—how little of your own was left to you. You will realize you are dying before your time!"

—SENECA, *ON THE BREVITY OF LIFE*, 3.3b

One of the hardest things to do in life is to say "No." To invitations, to requests, to obligations, to the stuff that everyone else is doing. Even harder is saying no to certain time-consuming emotions: anger, excitement, distraction, obsession, lust. None of these impulses feels like a big deal by itself, but run amok, they become a commitment like anything else.

If you're not careful, these are precisely the impositions that will overwhelm and consume your life. Do you ever wonder how you can get some of your time back, how you can feel less busy? Start by learning the power of "No!"—as in "No, thank you," and "No, I'm not going to get caught up in that," and "No, I just can't right now." It may hurt some feelings. It may turn people off. It may take some hard work. But the more you say no to the things that don't matter, the more you can say yes to the things that do. This will let you live and enjoy your life—the life that *you* want.

January 4th
THE BIG THREE

"All you need are these: certainty of judgment in the present moment;
action for the common good in the present moment;
and an attitude of gratitude in the present moment for anything
that comes your way."

—MARCUS AURELIUS, *MEDITATIONS*, 9.6

Perception, Action, Will. Those are the three overlapping but critical disciplines of Stoicism (as well as the organization of this book and yearlong journey you've just begun). There's more to the philosophy certainly—and we could spend all day talking about the unique beliefs of the various Stoics: "This is what Heraclitus thought . . ." "Zeno is from Citium, a city in Cyprus, and he believed . . ." But would such facts really help you day to day? What clarity does trivia provide?

Instead, the following little reminder sums up the three most essential parts of Stoic philosophy worth carrying with you every day, into every decision:

Control your perceptions.
Direct your actions properly.
Willingly accept what's outside your control.

That's all we need to do.

January 5th
CLARIFY YOUR INTENTIONS

"Let all your efforts be directed to something, let it keep that end
in view. It's not activity that disturbs people, but false conceptions
of things that drive them mad."

—SENECA, *ON TRANQUILITY OF MIND*, 12.5

Law 29 of *The 48 Laws of Power* is: Plan All The Way To The End.
Robert Greene writes, "By planning to the end you will not be overwhelmed by circumstances and you will know when to stop. Gently
guide fortune and help determine the future by thinking far ahead."
The second habit in *The 7 Habits of Highly Effective People* is: begin
with an end in mind.

Having an end in mind is no guarantee that you'll reach it—no Stoic
would tolerate that assumption—but *not* having an end in mind is a
guarantee you won't. To the Stoics, *oiêsis* (false conceptions) are responsible not just for disturbances in the soul but for chaotic and dysfunctional lives and operations. When your efforts are not directed at a cause
or a purpose, how will you know what to do day in and day out? How
will you know what to say no to and what to say yes to? How will you
know when you've had enough, when you've reached your goal, when
you've gotten off track, if you've never defined what those things are?

The answer is that you cannot. And so you are driven into failure—
or worse, into madness by the oblivion of directionlessness.

January 6th
WHERE, WHO, WHAT, AND WHY

"A person who doesn't know what the universe is, doesn't know where they are. A person who doesn't know their purpose in life doesn't know who they are or what the universe is. A person who doesn't know any one of these things doesn't know why they are here. So what to make of people who seek or avoid the praise of those who have no knowledge of where or who they are?"

—MARCUS AURELIUS, *MEDITATIONS*, 8.52

The late comedian Mitch Hedberg had a funny story he told in his act. Sitting down for an on-air interview, a radio DJ asked him, "So, who are you?" In that moment, he had to think, *Is this guy really deep or did I drive to the wrong station?*

How often are we asked a simple question like "Who are you?" or "What do you do?" or "Where are you from?" Considering it a superficial question—if we even consider it at all—we don't bother with more than a superficial answer.

But, gun to their head, most people couldn't give much in the way of a substantive answer. Could you? Have you taken the time to get clarity about who you are and what you stand for? Or are you too busy chasing unimportant things, mimicking the wrong influences, and following disappointing or unfulfilling or nonexistent paths?

January 7th
SEVEN CLEAR FUNCTIONS OF THE MIND

"The proper work of the mind is the exercise of choice, refusal, yearning, repulsion, preparation, purpose, and assent. What then can pollute and clog the mind's proper functioning? Nothing but its own corrupt decisions."

—EPICTETUS, *DISCOURSES*, 4.11.6–7

Let's break down each one of those tasks:

Choice—to do and think right
Refusal—of temptation
Yearning—to be better
Repulsion—of negativity, of bad influences, of what isn't true
Preparation—for what lies ahead or whatever may happen
Purpose—our guiding principle and highest priority
Assent—to be free of deception about what's inside and outside our
    control (and be ready to accept the latter)

This is what the mind is here to do. We must make sure that it does—and see everything else as pollution or a corruption.

January 8th
SEEING OUR ADDICTIONS

> "We must give up many things to which we are addicted, considering them to be good. Otherwise, courage will vanish, which should continually test itself. Greatness of soul will be lost, which can't stand out unless it disdains as petty what the mob regards as most desirable.
>
> —SENECA, *MORAL LETTERS*, 74.12b–13

What we consider to be harmless indulgences can easily become full-blown addictions. We start with coffee in the morning, and soon enough we can't start the day without it. We check our email because it's part of our job, and soon enough we feel the phantom buzz of the phone in our pocket every few seconds. Soon enough, these harmless habits are running our lives.

The little compulsions and drives we have not only chip away at our freedom and sovereignty, they cloud our clarity. We think we're in control—but are we really? As one addict put it, addiction is when we've "lost the freedom to abstain." Let us reclaim that freedom.

What that addiction is for you can vary: Soda? Drugs? Complaining? Gossip? The Internet? Biting your nails? But you must reclaim the ability to abstain because within it is your clarity and self-control.

January 9th
WHAT WE CONTROL AND WHAT WE DON'T

"Some things are in our control, while others are not. We control our opinion, choice, desire, aversion, and, in a word, everything of our own doing. We don't control our body, property, reputation, position, and, in a word, everything not of our own doing. Even more, the things in our control are by nature free, unhindered, and unobstructed, while those not in our control are weak, slavish, can be hindered, and are not our own."

—EPICTETUS, *ENCHIRIDION*, 1.1–2

Today, you won't control the external events that happen. Is that scary? A little, but it's balanced when we see that we can control our opinion *about* those events. You decide whether they're good or bad, whether they're fair or unfair. You don't control the situation, but you control what you *think* about it.

See how that works? Every single thing that is outside your control—the outside world, other people, luck, karma, whatever—still presents a corresponding area that *is* in your control. This alone gives us plenty to manage, plenty of power.

Best of all, an honest understanding of what is within our control provides real clarity about the world: all we have is our own mind. Remember that today when you try to extend your reach outward—that it's much better and more appropriately directed *inward*.

January 10th
IF YOU WANT TO BE STEADY

"The essence of good is a certain kind of reasoned choice; just as the essence of evil is another kind. What about externals, then? They are only the raw material for our reasoned choice, which finds its own good or evil in working with them. How will it find the good? Not by marveling at the material! For if judgments about the material are straight that makes our choices good, but if those judgments are twisted, our choices turn bad."

—EPICTETUS, *DISCOURSES*, 1.29.1–3

The Stoics seek steadiness, stability, and tranquility—traits most of us aspire to but seem to experience only fleetingly. How do they accomplish this elusive goal? How does one embody *eustatheia* (the word Arrian used to describe this teaching of Epictetus)?

Well, it's not luck. It's not by eliminating outside influences or running away to quiet and solitude. Instead, it's about filtering the outside world through the straightener of our judgment. That's what our reason can do—it can take the crooked, confusing, and overwhelming nature of external events and make them orderly.

However, if our judgments are crooked because we don't use reason, then everything that follows will be crooked, and we will lose our ability to steady ourselves in the chaos and rush of life. If you want to be steady, if you want clarity, proper judgment is the best way.

January 11th
IF YOU WANT TO BE UNSTEADY

"For if a person shifts their caution to their own reasoned choices and the acts of those choices, they will at the same time gain the will to avoid, but if they shift their caution away from their own reasoned choices to things not under their control, seeking to avoid what is controlled by others, they will then be agitated, fearful, and unstable."

—EPICTETUS, *DISCOURSES*, 2.1.12

The image of the Zen philosopher is the monk up in the green, quiet hills, or in a beautiful temple on some rocky cliff. The Stoics are the antithesis of this idea. Instead, they are the man in the marketplace, the senator in the Forum, the brave wife waiting for her soldier to return from battle, the sculptor busy in her studio. Still, the Stoic is equally at peace.

Epictetus is reminding you that serenity and stability are results of your choices and judgment, not your environment. If you seek to avoid all disruptions to tranquility—other people, external events, stress—you will never be successful. Your problems will follow you wherever you run and hide. But if you seek to avoid the harmful and disruptive *judgments* that cause those problems, then you will be stable and steady wherever you happen to be.

January 12th
THE ONE PATH TO SERENITY

"Keep this thought at the ready at daybreak, and through the day and night—there is only one path to happiness, and that is in giving up all outside of your sphere of choice, regarding nothing else as your possession, surrendering all else to God and Fortune."

—EPICTETUS, *DISCOURSES*, 4.4.39

This morning, remind yourself of what is in your control and what's not in your control. Remind yourself to focus on the former and not the latter.

Before lunch, remind yourself that the only thing you truly possess is your ability to make choices (and to use reason and judgment when doing so). This is the only thing that can never be taken from you completely.

In the afternoon, remind yourself that aside from the choices you make, your fate is not entirely up to you. The world is spinning and we spin along with it—whichever direction, good or bad.

In the evening, remind yourself again how much is outside of your control and where your choices begin and end.

As you lie in bed, remember that sleep is a form of surrender and trust and how easily it comes. And prepare to start the whole cycle over again tomorrow.

January 13th
CIRCLE OF CONTROL

"We control our reasoned choice and all acts that depend on that moral will. What's not under our control are the body and any of its parts, our possessions, parents, siblings, children, or country— anything with which we might associate."

—EPICTETUS, *DISCOURSES*, 1.22.10

This is important enough that it bears repeating: a wise person knows what's inside their circle of control and what is outside of it.

The good news is that it's pretty easy to remember what is inside our control. According to the Stoics, the circle of control contains just one thing: YOUR MIND. That's right, even your physical body isn't completely within the circle. After all, you could be struck with a physical illness or impairment at any moment. You could be traveling in a foreign country and be thrown in jail.

But this is all good news because it drastically reduces the amount of things that you need to think about. There is clarity in simplicity. While everyone else is running around with a list of responsibilities a mile long—things they're not actually responsible for—you've got just that one-item list. You've got just one thing to manage: your choices, your will, your mind.

So mind it.

January 14th
CUT THE STRINGS THAT PULL YOUR MIND

> "Understand at last that you have something in you more powerful and divine than what causes the bodily passions and pulls you like a mere puppet. What thoughts now occupy my mind? Is it not fear, suspicion, desire, or something like that?"
> —MARCUS AURELIUS, *MEDITATIONS*, 12.19

Think of all the interests vying for a share of your wallet or for a second of your attention. Food scientists are engineering products to exploit your taste buds. Silicon Valley engineers are designing applications as addictive as gambling. The media is manufacturing stories to provoke outrage and anger.

These are just a small slice of the temptations and forces acting on us—distracting us and pulling us away from the things that truly matter. Marcus, thankfully, was not exposed to these extreme parts of our modern culture. But he knew plenty of distracting sinkholes too: gossip, the endless call of work, as well as fear, suspicion, lust. Every human being is pulled by these internal and external forces that are increasingly more powerful and harder to resist.

Philosophy is simply asking us to pay careful attention and to strive to be more than a pawn. As Viktor Frankl puts it in *The Will to Meaning*, "Man is pushed by drives but pulled by values." These values and inner awareness prevent us from being puppets. Sure, paying attention requires work and awareness, but isn't that better than being jerked about on a string?

22

CLARITY

January 15th
PEACE IS IN STAYING THE COURSE

"Tranquility can't be grasped except by those who have reached an unwavering and firm power of judgment—the rest constantly fall and rise in their decisions, wavering in a state of alternately rejecting and accepting things. What is the cause of this back and forth? It's because nothing is clear and they rely on the most uncertain guide—common opinion."

—SENECA, *MORAL LETTERS*, 95.57b–58a

In Seneca's essay on tranquility, he uses the Greek word *euthymia*, which he defines as "believing in yourself and trusting that you are on the right path, and not being in doubt by following the myriad footpaths of those wandering in every direction." It is this state of mind, he says, that produces tranquility.

Clarity of vision allows us to have this belief. That's not to say we're always going to be 100 percent certain of everything, or that we even should be. Rather, it's that we can rest assured we're heading generally in the right direction—that we don't need to constantly compare ourselves with other people or change our mind every three seconds based on new information.

Instead, tranquility and peace are found in identifying *our* path and in sticking to it: staying the course—making adjustments here and there, naturally—but ignoring the distracting sirens who beckon us to turn toward the rocks.

January 16th
NEVER DO ANYTHING OUT OF HABIT

"So in the majority of other things, we address circumstances not in accordance with the right assumptions, but mostly by following wretched habit. Since all that I've said is the case, the person in training must seek to rise above, so as to stop seeking out pleasure and steering away from pain; to stop clinging to living and abhorring death; and in the case of property and money, to stop valuing receiving over giving."

—MUSONIUS RUFUS, *LECTURES*, 6.25.5–11

A worker is asked: "Why did you do it this way?" The answer, "Because that's the way we've always done things." The answer frustrates every good boss and sets the mouth of every entrepreneur watering. The worker has stopped thinking and is mindlessly operating out of habit. The business is ripe for disruption by a competitor, and the worker will probably get fired by any thinking boss.

We should apply the same ruthlessness to our own habits. In fact, we are studying philosophy precisely to break ourselves of rote behavior. Find what you do out of rote memory or routine. Ask yourself: *Is this really the best way to do it?* Know why you do what you do—do it for the right reasons.

January 17th
REBOOT THE REAL WORK

"I am your teacher and you are learning in my school. My aim is to bring you to completion, unhindered, free from compulsive behavior, unrestrained, without shame, free, flourishing, and happy, looking to God in things great and small—your aim is to learn and diligently practice all these things. Why then don't you complete the work, if you have the right aim and I have both the right aim and right preparation? What is missing? . . . The work is quite feasible, and is the only thing in our power. . . . Let go of the past. We must only begin. Believe me and you will see."

—EPICTETUS, *DISCOURSES*, 2.19.29–34

Do you remember, in school or early in your life, being afraid to try something because you feared you might fail at it? Most teenagers choose to fool around rather than exert themselves. Halfhearted, lazy effort gives them a ready-made excuse: "It doesn't matter. I wasn't even trying."

As we get older, failure is not so inconsequential anymore. What's at stake is not some arbitrary grade or intramural sports trophy, but the quality of your life and your ability to deal with the world around you.

Don't let that intimidate you, though. You have the best teachers in the world: the wisest philosophers who ever lived. And not only are you capable, the professor is asking for something very simple: just begin the work. The rest follows.

January 18th
SEE THE WORLD LIKE A POET AND AN ARTIST

"Pass through this brief patch of time in harmony with nature, and come to your final resting place gracefully, just as a ripened olive might drop, praising the earth that nourished it and grateful to the tree that gave it growth."

—MARCUS AURELIUS, *MEDITATIONS*, 4.48.2

There are some stunningly beautiful turns of phrase in Marcus's *Meditations*—a surprising treat considering the intended audience (just himself). In one passage, he praises the "charm and allure" of nature's process, the "stalks of ripe grain bending low, the frowning brow of the lion, the foam dripping from the boar's mouth." We should thank private rhetoric teacher Marcus Cornelius Fronto for the imagery in these vivid passages. Fronto, widely considered to be Rome's best orator besides Cicero, was chosen by Marcus's adopted father to teach Marcus to think and write and speak.

More than just pretty phrases, they gave him—and now us—a powerful perspective on ordinary or seemingly *un*beautiful events. It takes an artist's eye to see that the end of life is not unlike a ripe fruit falling from its tree. It takes a poet to notice the way "baking bread splits in places and those cracks, while not intended in the baker's art, catch our eye and serve to stir our appetite" and find a metaphor in them.

There is clarity (and joy) in seeing what others can't see, in finding grace and harmony in places others overlook. Isn't that far better than seeing the world as some dark place?

January 19th
WHEREVER YOU GO, THERE YOUR CHOICE IS

"A podium and a prison is each a place, one high and the other low, but in either place your freedom of choice can be maintained if you so wish."

—EPICTETUS, *DISCOURSES*, 2.6.25

The Stoics all held vastly different stations in life. Some were rich, some were born at the bottom of Rome's rigid hierarchy. Some had it easy, and others had it unimaginably hard. This is true for us as well—we all come to philosophy from different backgrounds, and even within our own lives we experience bouts of good fortune and bad fortune.

But in all circumstances—adversity or advantage—we really have just one thing we need to do: focus on what is in our control as opposed to what is not. Right now we might be laid low with struggles, whereas just a few years ago we might have lived high on the hog, and in just a few days we might be doing so well that success is actually a burden. One thing will stay constant: our freedom of choice—both in the big picture and small picture.

Ultimately, this is clarity. Whoever we are, wherever we are—what matters is our choices. What are they? How will we evaluate them? How will we make the most of them? Those are the questions life asks us, regardless of our station. How will you answer?

January 20th
REIGNITE YOUR THOUGHTS

"Your principles can't be extinguished unless you snuff out the thoughts that feed them, for it's continually in your power to reignite new ones. . . . It's possible to start living again! See things anew as you once did—that is how to restart life!"

—MARCUS AURELIUS, *MEDITATIONS*, 7.2

Have you had a bad couple of weeks? Have you been drifting away from the principles and beliefs that you hold dear? It's perfectly fine. It happens to all of us.

In fact, it probably happened to Marcus—that may be why he scribbled this note to himself. Perhaps he'd been dealing with difficult senators or having difficulties with his troubled son. Perhaps in these scenarios he'd lost his temper, became depressed, or stopped checking in with himself. Who wouldn't?

But the reminder here is that no matter what happens, no matter how disappointing our behavior has been in the past, the principles themselves remain unchanged. We can return and embrace them at any moment. What happened yesterday—what happened five minutes ago—is the past. We can reignite and restart whenever we like.

Why not do it right now?

January 21st
A MORNING RITUAL

"Ask yourself the following first thing in the morning:

- What am I lacking in attaining freedom from passion?
- What for tranquility?
- What am I? A mere body, estate-holder, or reputation? None of these things.
- What, then? A rational being.
- What then is demanded of me? Meditate on your actions.
- How did I steer away from serenity?
- What did I do that was unfriendly, unsocial, or uncaring?
- What did I fail to do in all these things?"

—EPICTETUS, *DISCOURSES*, 4.6.34–35

Many successful people have a morning ritual. For some, it's meditation. For others, it's exercise. For many, it's journaling—just a few pages where they write down their thoughts, fears, hopes. In these cases, the point is not so much the activity itself as it is the ritualized reflection. The idea is to take some time to look inward and examine.

Taking that time is what Stoics advocated more than almost anything else. We don't know whether Marcus Aurelius wrote his *Meditations* in the morning or at night, but we know he carved out moments of quiet alone time—and that he wrote for himself, not for anyone else. If you're looking for a place to start your own ritual, you could do worse than Marcus's example and Epictetus's checklist.

Every day, starting today, ask yourself these same tough questions. Let philosophy and hard work guide you to better answers, one morning at a time, over the course of a life.

January 22nd
THE DAY IN REVIEW

"I will keep constant watch over myself and—most usefully—will put each day up for review. For this is what makes us evil—that none of us looks back upon our own lives. We reflect upon only that which we are about to do. And yet our plans for the future descend from the past."

—SENECA, *MORAL LETTERS*, 83.2

In a letter to his older brother Novatus, Seneca describes a beneficial exercise he borrowed from another prominent philosopher. At the end of each day he would ask himself variations of the following questions: *What bad habit did I curb today? How am I better? Were my actions just? How can I improve?*

At the beginning or end of each day, the Stoic sits down with his journal and reviews: what he did, what he thought, what could be improved. It's for this reason that Marcus Aurelius's *Meditations* is a somewhat inscrutable book—it was for personal clarity and not public benefit. Writing down Stoic exercises was and is also a form of practicing them, just as repeating a prayer or hymn might be.

Keep your own journal, whether it's saved on a computer or in a little notebook. Take time to consciously recall the events of the previous day. Be unflinching in your assessments. Notice what contributed to your happiness and what detracted from it. Write down what you'd like to work on or quotes that you like. By making the effort to record such thoughts, you're less likely to forget them. An added bonus: you'll have a running tally to track your progress too.

January 23rd
THE TRUTH ABOUT MONEY

"Let's pass over to the really rich—how often the occasions they look just like the poor! When they travel abroad they must restrict their baggage, and when haste is necessary, they dismiss their entourage. And those who are in the army, how few of their possessions they get to keep . . ."

—SENECA, *ON CONSOLATION TO HELVIA*, 12. 1.b–2

The author F. Scott Fitzgerald, who often glamorized the lifestyles of the rich and famous in books like *The Great Gatsby*, opens one of his short stories with the now classic lines: "Let me tell you about the very rich. They are different from you and me." A few years after this story was published, his friend Ernest Hemingway teased Fitzgerald by writing, "Yes, they have more money."

That's what Seneca is reminding us. As someone who was one of the richest men in Rome, he knew firsthand that money only marginally changes life. It doesn't solve the problems that people without it seem to think it will. In fact, no material possession will. External things can't fix internal issues.

We constantly forget this—and it causes us so much confusion and pain. As Hemingway would later write of Fitzgerald, "He thought [the rich] were a special glamorous race and when he found they weren't it wrecked him as much as any other thing that wrecked him." Without a change the same will be true for us.

January 24th
PUSH FOR DEEP UNDERSTANDING

"From Rusticus . . . I learned to read carefully and not be satisfied
with a rough understanding of the whole, and not to agree too
quickly with those who have a lot to say about something."
—MARCUS AURELIUS, *MEDITATIONS*, 1.7.3

The first book of Marcus Aurelius's *Meditations* begins with a catalog of gratitude. He thanks, one by one, the leading influences in his
life. One of the people he thanks is Quintus Junius Rusticus, a teacher
who developed in his student a love of deep clarity and understanding—
a desire to not just stop at the surface when it comes to learning.

It was also from Rusticus that Marcus was introduced to Epictetus.
In fact, Rusticus loaned Marcus his personal copy of Epictetus's lectures. Marcus clearly wasn't satisfied with just getting the gist of these
lectures and didn't simply accept them on his teacher's recommenda-
tion. Paul Johnson once joked that Edmund Wilson read books "as
though the author was on trial for his life." That's how Marcus read
Epictetus—and when the lessons passed muster, he *absorbed* them.
They became part of his DNA as a human being. He quoted them at
length over the course of his life, finding real clarity and strength in
words, even amid the immense luxury and power he would come to
possess.

That's the kind of deep reading and study we need to cultivate as
well, which is why we're reading just one page a day instead of a chapter at a time. So we can take the time to read attentively and deeply.

January 25th
THE ONLY PRIZE

"What's left to be prized? This, I think—to limit our action or inaction to only what's in keeping with the needs of our own preparation . . . it's what the exertions of education and teaching are all about—here is the thing to be prized! If you hold this firmly, you'll stop trying to get yourself all the other things. . . . If you don't, you won't be free, self-sufficient, or liberated from passion, but necessarily full of envy, jealousy, and suspicion for any who have the power to take them, and you'll plot against those who do have what you prize. . . . But by having some self-respect for your own mind and prizing it, you will please yourself and be in better harmony with your fellow human beings, and more in tune with the gods—praising everything they have set in order and allotted you."

—MARCUS AURELIUS, *MEDITATIONS*, 6.16.2b–4a

Warren Buffett, whose net worth is approximately $65 billion, lives in the same house he bought in 1958 for $31,500. John Urschel, a lineman for the Baltimore Ravens, makes millions but manages to live on $25,000 a year. San Antonio Spurs star Kawhi Leonard gets around in the 1997 Chevy Tahoe he's had since he was a teenager, even with a contract worth some $94 million. Why? It's not because these men are cheap. It's because the things *that matter to them are cheap.*

Neither Buffett nor Urschel nor Leonard ended up this way by accident. Their lifestyle is the result of prioritizing. They cultivate interests that are decidedly below their financial means, and as a result, *any* income would allow them freedom to pursue the things they most care about. It just happens that they became wealthy beyond any expectation. This kind of clarity—about what they love most in the world—means they can enjoy their lives. It means they'd still be happy even if the markets were to turn or their careers were cut short by injury.

The more things we desire and the more we have to do to earn or attain those achievements, the less we actually enjoy our lives—and the less free we are.

January 26th
THE POWER OF A MANTRA

"Erase the false impressions from your mind by constantly saying to yourself, I have it in my soul to keep out any evil, desire or any kind of disturbance—instead, seeing the true nature of things, I will give them only their due. Always remember this power that nature gave you."

—MARCUS AURELIUS, *MEDITATIONS*, 8.29

Anyone who has taken a yoga class or been exposed to Hindu or Buddhist thought has probably heard of the concept of a mantra. In Sanskrit, it means "sacred utterance"—essentially a word, a phrase, a thought, even a sound—intended to provide clarity or spiritual guidance. A mantra can be especially helpful in the meditative process because it allows us to block out everything else while we focus.

It's fitting, then, that Marcus Aurelius would suggest this Stoic mantra—a reminder or watch phrase to use when we feel false impressions, distractions, or the crush of everyday life upon us. It says, essentially, "I have the power within me to keep that out. I can see the truth."

Change the wording as you like. That part is up to you. But have a mantra and use it to find the clarity you crave.

January 27th
THE THREE AREAS OF TRAINING

"There are three areas in which the person who would be wise and good must be trained. The first has to do with desires and aversions—that a person may never miss the mark in desires nor fall into what repels them. The second has to do with impulses to act and not to act—and more broadly, with duty—that a person may act deliberately for good reasons and not carelessly. The third has to do with freedom from deception and composure and the whole area of judgment, the assent our mind gives to its perceptions. Of these areas, the chief and most urgent is the first which has to do with the passions, for strong emotions arise only when we fail in our desires and aversions."

—EPICTETUS, *DISCOURSES*, 3.2.1–3a

Today, let's focus on the three areas of training that Epictetus laid out for us.

First, we must consider what we should desire and what we should be averse to. Why? So that we want what is good and avoid what is bad. It's not enough to just listen to your body—because our attractions often lead us astray.

Next, we must examine our impulses to act—that is, our *motivations*. Are we doing things for the right reasons? Or do we act because we haven't stopped to think? Or do we believe that we *have* to do something?

Finally, there is our judgment. Our ability to see things clearly and properly comes when we use our great gift from nature: *reason*.

These are three distinct areas of training, but in practice they are inextricably intertwined. Our judgment affects what we desire, our desires affect how we act, just as our judgment determines how we act. But we can't just expect this to happen. We must put real thought and energy into each area of our lives. If we do, we'll find real clarity and success.

January 28th
WATCHING THE WISE

"Take a good hard look at people's ruling principle, especially of
the wise, what they run away from and what they seek out."

—MARCUS AURELIUS, *MEDITATIONS*, 4.38

Seneca has said, "Without a ruler to do it against, you can't make
crooked straight." That is the role of wise people in our lives—to
serve as model and inspiration. To bounce our ideas off and test our
presumptions.

Who that person will be for you is up to you. Perhaps it's your father
or your mother. Maybe it's a philosopher or a writer or a thinker. Perhaps WWJD (What would Jesus do?) is the right model for you.

But pick someone, watch what they do (and what they *don't* do),
and do your best to do the same.

January 29th
KEEP IT SIMPLE

"At every moment keep a sturdy mind on the task at hand, as a Roman and human being, doing it with strict and simple dignity, affection, freedom, and justice—giving yourself a break from all other considerations. You can do this if you approach each task as if it is your last, giving up every distraction, emotional subversion of reason, and all drama, vanity, and complaint over your fair share. You can see how mastery over a few things makes it possible to live an abundant and devout life—for, if you keep watch over these things, the gods won't ask for more."

—MARCUS AURELIUS, *MEDITATIONS*, 2.5

Each day presents the chance to overthink things. What should I wear? Do they like me? Am I eating well enough? What's next for me in life? Is my boss happy with my work?

Today, let's focus just on what's in front of us. We'll follow the dictum that New England Patriots coach Bill Belichick gives his players: "Do your job." Like a Roman, like a good soldier, like a master of our craft. We don't need to get lost in a thousand other distractions or in other people's business.

Marcus says to approach each task as if it were your last, because it very well could be. And even if it isn't, botching what's right in front of you doesn't help anything. Find clarity in the simplicity of doing your job today.

January 30th
YOU DON'T HAVE TO STAY ON TOP OF EVERYTHING

"If you wish to improve, be content to appear clueless or stupid in extraneous matters—don't wish to seem knowledgeable. And if some regard you as important, distrust yourself."

—EPICTETUS, *ENCHIRIDION*, 13a

One of the most powerful things you can do as a human being in our hyperconnected, 24/7 media world is say: "I don't know." Or, more provocatively: "I don't care." Most of society seems to have taken it as a commandment that one must know about every single current event, watch every episode of every critically acclaimed television series, follow the news religiously, and present themselves to others as an informed and worldly individual.

But where is the evidence that this is actually necessary? Is the obligation enforced by the police? Or is it that you're just afraid of seeming silly at a dinner party? Yes, you owe it to your country and your family to know generally about events that may directly affect them, but that's about all.

How much more time, energy, and pure brainpower would you have available if you drastically cut your media consumption? How much more rested and present would you feel if you were no longer excited and outraged by every scandal, breaking story, and potential crisis (many of which never come to pass anyway)?

January 31st
PHILOSOPHY AS MEDICINE OF THE SOUL

"Don't return to philosophy as a task-master, but as patients seek out relief in a treatment of sore eyes, or a dressing for a burn, or from an ointment. Regarding it this way, you'll obey reason without putting it on display and rest easy in its care."

—MARCUS AURELIUS, *MEDITATIONS*, 5.9

The busier we get, the more we work and learn and read, the further we may drift. We get in a rhythm. We're making money, being creative, and we're stimulated and busy. It seems like everything is going well. But we drift further and further from philosophy.

Eventually this neglect will contribute to a problem—the stress builds up, our mind gets cloudy, we forget what's important—and result in an injury of some kind. When that happens, it's important that we tap the brakes—put aside all the momentum and the moment. Return to the regimen and practices that we know are rooted in clarity, good judgment, good principles, and *good health.*

Stoicism is designed to be medicine for the soul. It relieves us of the vulnerabilities of modern life. It restores us with the vigor we need to thrive in life. Check in with it today, and let it do its healing.

FEBRUARY

PASSIONS AND EMOTIONS

February 1st
FOR THE HOT-HEADED MAN

"Keep this thought handy when you feel a fit of rage coming on—
it isn't manly to be enraged. Rather, gentleness and civility are
more human, and therefore manlier. A real man doesn't give way
to anger and discontent, and such a person has strength, courage,
and endurance—unlike the angry and complaining. The nearer a
man comes to a calm mind, the closer he is to strength."
—MARCUS AURELIUS, *MEDITATIONS*, 11.18.5b

Why do athletes talk trash to each other? Why do they deliberately
say offensive and nasty things to their competitors when the refs
aren't looking? To provoke a reaction. Distracting and angering opponents is an easy way to knock them off their game.

Try to remember that when you find yourself getting mad. Anger is
not impressive or tough—it's a mistake. It's *weakness*. Depending on
what you're doing, it might even be a trap that someone laid for you.

Fans and opponents called boxer Joe Louis the "Ring Robot" because
he was utterly unemotional—his cold, calm demeanor was far more ter-
rifying than any crazed look or emotional outburst would have been.

Strength is the ability to maintain a hold of oneself. It's being the
person who never gets mad, who cannot be rattled, because they are in
control of their passions—rather than controlled *by* their passions.

February 2nd
A PROPER FRAME OF MIND

"Frame your thoughts like this—you are an old person, you won't let yourself be enslaved by this any longer, no longer pulled like a puppet by every impulse, and you'll stop complaining about your present fortune or dreading the future."

—MARCUS AURELIUS, *MEDITATIONS*, 2.2

We resent the person who comes in and tries to boss us around. *Don't tell me how to dress, how to think, how to do my job, how to live.* This is because we are independent, self-sufficient people.

Or at least that's what we tell ourselves.

Yet if someone says something we disagree with, something inside us tells us we *have* to argue with them. If there's a plate of cookies in front of us, we *have* to eat them. If someone does something we dislike, we *have* to get mad about it. When something bad happens, we *have* to be sad, depressed, or worried. But if something good happens a few minutes later, all of a sudden we're happy, excited, and want more.

We would never let another person jerk us around the way we let our impulses do. It's time we start seeing it that way—that we're not puppets that can be made to dance this way or that way just because we feel like it. We should be the ones in control, not our emotions, because we are independent, self-sufficient people.

February 3rd
THE SOURCE OF YOUR ANXIETY

"When I see an anxious person, I ask myself, what do they want? For if a person wasn't wanting something outside of their own control, why would they be stricken by anxiety?"

—EPICTETUS, *DISCOURSES*, 2.13.1

The anxious father, worried about his children. What does he want? A world that is always safe. A frenzied traveler—what does she want? For the weather to hold and for traffic to part so she can make her flight. A nervous investor? That the market will turn around and an investment will pay off.

All of these scenarios hold the same thing in common. As Epictetus says, it's wanting something outside our control. Getting worked up, getting excited, nervously pacing—these intense, pained, and anxious moments show us at our most futile and servile. Staring at the clock, at the ticker, at the next checkout lane over, at the sky—it's as if we all belong to a religious cult that believes the gods of fate will only give us what we want if we sacrifice our peace of mind.

Today, when you find yourself getting anxious, ask yourself: *Why are my insides twisted into knots? Am I in control here or is my anxiety?* And most important: *Is my anxiety doing me any good?*

February 4th
ON BEING INVINCIBLE

"Who then is invincible? The one who cannot be upset by anything outside their reasoned choice."

—EPICTETUS, *DISCOURSES*, 1.18.21

Have you ever watched a seasoned pro handle the media? No question is too tough, no tone too pointed or insulting. They parry every blow with humor, poise, and patience. Even when stung or provoked, they *choose* not to flinch or react. They're able to do this not only because of training and experience, but because they understand that reacting emotionally will only make the situation worse. The media is waiting for them to slip up or get upset, so to successfully navigate press events they have internalized the importance of keeping themselves under calm control.

It's unlikely you'll face a horde of probing reporters bombarding you with insensitive questions today. But it might be helpful—whatever stresses or frustrations or overload that do come your way—to picture that image and use it as your model for dealing with them. Our reasoned choice—our *prohairesis*, as the Stoics called it—is a kind of invincibility that we can cultivate. We can shrug off hostile attacks and breeze through pressure or problems. And, like our model, when we finish, we can point back into the crowd and say, "Next!"

February 5th
STEADY YOUR IMPULSES

"Don't be bounced around, but submit every impulse to the claims
of justice, and protect your clear conviction in every appearance."
—MARCUS AURELIUS, *MEDITATIONS*, 4.22

Think of the manic people in your life. Not the ones suffering from
an unfortunate disorder, but the ones whose lives and choices are
in disorder. Everything is soaring highs or crushing lows; the day is
either amazing or awful. Aren't those people exhausting? Don't you wish
they just had a filter through which they could test the good impulses
versus the bad ones?

There is such a filter. Justice. Reason. Philosophy. If there's a central
message of Stoic thought, it's this: impulses of all kinds are going to
come, and your work is to control them, like bringing a dog to heel.
Put more simply: think before you act. Ask: *Who is in control here?*
What principles are guiding me?

February 6th
DON'T SEEK OUT STRIFE

"I don't agree with those who plunge headlong into the middle of the flood and who, accepting a turbulent life, struggle daily in great spirit with difficult circumstances. The wise person will endure that, but won't choose it—choosing to be at peace, rather than at war."

—SENECA, *MORAL LETTERS*, 28.7

It has become a cliché to quote Theodore Roosevelt's "Man in the Arena" speech, which lionizes "the one whose face is marred by dust and sweat and blood; who strives valiantly . . ." compared with the critic who sits on the sidelines. Roosevelt gave that speech shortly after he left office, at the height of his popularity. In a few years, he would run against his former protégé in an attempt to retake the White House, losing badly and nearly assassinated in the process. He would also nearly die exploring a river in the Amazon, kill thousands of animals in African safaris, and then beg Woodrow Wilson to allow him to enlist in World War I despite being 59 years old. He would do a *lot* of things that seem somewhat baffling in retrospect.

Theodore Roosevelt was a truly great man. But he was also driven by a compulsion, a work and activity addiction that was seemingly without end. Many of us share this affliction—being driven by something we can't control. We're afraid of being still, so we seek out strife and action as a distraction. We choose to be at war—in some cases, literally—when peace is in fact the more honorable and fitting choice.

Yes, the man in the arena is admirable. As is the soldier and the politician and the businesswoman and all the other occupations. But, and this is a big *but*, only if we're in the arena for the right reasons.

February 7th
FEAR IS A SELF-FULFILLING PROPHECY

"Many are harmed by fear itself, and many may have come to their fate while dreading fate."

—SENECA, *OEDIPUS*, 992

"Only the paranoid survive," Andy Grove, a former CEO of Intel, famously said. It might be true. But we also know that the paranoid often destroy themselves quicker and more spectacularly than any enemy. Seneca, with his access and insight into the most powerful elite in Rome, would have seen this dynamic play out quite vividly. Nero, the student whose excesses Seneca tried to curb, killed not only his own mother and wife but eventually turned on Seneca, his mentor, too.

The combination of power, fear, and mania can be deadly. The leader, convinced that he might be betrayed, acts first and betrays others first. Afraid that he's not well liked, he works so hard to get others to like him that it has the opposite effect. Convinced of mismanagement, he micromanages and becomes the source of the mismanagement. And on and on—the things we fear or dread, we blindly inflict on ourselves.

The next time you are afraid of some supposedly disastrous outcome, remember that if you don't control your impulses, if you lose your self-control, you may be the very source of the disaster you so fear. It has happened to smarter and more powerful and more successful people. It can happen to us too.

February 8th
DID THAT MAKE YOU FEEL BETTER?

"You cry, I'm suffering severe pain! Are you then relieved from feeling it, if you bear it in an unmanly way?"

—SENECA, *MORAL LETTERS*, 78.17

The next time someone gets upset near you—crying, yelling, breaking something, being pointed or cruel—watch how quickly this statement will stop them cold: "I hope this is making you feel better." Because, of course, it isn't. Only in the bubble of extreme emotion can we justify any of that kind of behavior—and when called to account for it, we usually feel sheepish or embarrassed.

It's worth applying that standard to yourself. The next time you find yourself in the middle of a freakout, or moaning and groaning with flulike symptoms, or crying tears of regret, just ask: *Is this actually making me feel better? Is this actually relieving* any *of the symptoms I wish were gone?*

February 9th
YOU DON'T HAVE TO HAVE AN OPINION

"We have the power to hold no opinion about a thing and to not
let it upset our state of mind—for things have no natural power
to shape our judgments."

—MARCUS AURELIUS, *MEDITATIONS*, 6.52

Here's a funny exercise: think about all the upsetting things you *don't*
know about—stuff people might have said about you behind your
back, mistakes you might have made that never came to your attention,
things you dropped or lost without even realizing it. What's your reaction? You don't have one because you don't know about it.

In other words, it *is* possible to hold no opinion about a negative
thing. You just need to cultivate that power instead of wielding it accidentally. Especially when having an opinion is likely to make us aggravated. Practice the ability of having absolutely no thoughts about
something—act as if you had no idea it ever occurred. Or that you've
never heard of it before. Let it become irrelevant or nonexistent to you.
It'll be a lot less powerful this way.

February 10th
ANGER IS BAD FUEL

"There is no more stupefying thing than anger, nothing more bent
on its own strength. If successful, none more arrogant, if foiled,
none more insane—since it's not driven back by weariness even
in defeat, when fortune removes its adversary it turns its teeth on
itself."

—SENECA, *ON ANGER*, 3.1.5

As the Stoics have said many times, getting angry almost never
solves anything. Usually, it makes things worse. We get upset, then
the other person gets upset—now everyone is upset, and the problem
is no closer to getting solved.

Many successful people will try to tell you that anger is a powerful
fuel in their lives. The desire to "prove them all wrong" or "shove it in
their faces" has made many a millionaire. The anger at being called fat
or stupid has created fine physical specimens and brilliant minds. The
anger at being rejected has motivated many to carve their own path.

But that's shortsighted. Such stories ignore the pollution produced
as a side effect and the wear and tear it put on the engine. It ignores what
happens when that initial anger runs out—and how now more and more
must be generated to keep the machine going (until, eventually, the only
source left is anger at oneself). "Hate is too great a burden to bear,"
Martin Luther King Jr. warned his fellow civil rights leaders in 1967,
even though they had every reason to respond to hate with hate.

The same is true for anger—in fact, it's true for most extreme emotions. They are toxic fuel. There's plenty of it out in the world, no
question, but never worth the costs that come along with it.

February 11th
HERO OR NERO?

"Our soul is sometimes a king, and sometimes a tyrant. A king, by attending to what is honorable, protects the good health of the body in its care, and gives it no base or sordid command. But an uncontrolled, desire-fueled, over-indulged soul is turned from a king into that most feared and detested thing—a tyrant."

—SENECA, *MORAL LETTERS*, 114.24

There is that saying that absolute power corrupts absolutely. At first glance, that's true. Seneca's pupil Nero and his litany of crimes and murders is a perfect example. Another emperor, Domitian, arbitrarily banished all philosophers from Rome (Epictetus was forced to flee as a result). Many of Rome's emperors were tyrants. Yet, not many years later, Epictetus would become a close friend of another emperor, Hadrian, who would help Marcus Aurelius to the throne, one of the truest examples of a wise philosopher king.

So it's not so clear that power *always* corrupts. In fact, it looks like it comes down, in many ways, to the inner strength and self-awareness of individuals—what they value, what desires they keep in check, whether their understanding of fairness and justice can counteract the temptations of unlimited wealth and deference.

The same is true for you. Both personally and professionally. Tyrant or king? Hero or Nero? Which will you be?

February 12th
PROTECT YOUR PEACE OF MIND

"Keep constant guard over your perceptions, for it is no small thing you are protecting, but your respect, trustworthiness and steadiness, peace of mind, freedom from pain and fear, in a word your freedom. For what would you sell these things?"

—EPICTETUS, *DISCOURSES*, 4.3.6b–8

The dysfunctional job that stresses you out, a contentious relationship, life in the spotlight. Stoicism, because it helps us manage and think through our emotional reactions, can make these kinds of situations easier to bear. It can help you manage and mitigate the triggers that seem to be so constantly tripped.

But here's a question: Why are you subjecting yourself to this? Is this really the environment you were made for? To be provoked by nasty emails and an endless parade of workplace problems? Our adrenal glands can handle only so much before they become exhausted. Shouldn't you preserve them for life-and-death situations?

So yes, use Stoicism to manage these difficulties. But don't forget to ask: *Is this really the life I want?* Every time you get upset, a little bit of life leaves the body. Are these really the things on which you want to spend that priceless resource? Don't be afraid to make a change—a big one.

February 13th
PLEASURE CAN BECOME PUNISHMENT

"Whenever you get an impression of some pleasure, as with any impression, guard yourself from being carried away by it, let it await your action, give yourself a pause. After that, bring to mind both times, first when you have enjoyed the pleasure and later when you will regret it and hate yourself. Then compare to those the joy and satisfaction you'd feel for abstaining altogether. However, if a seemingly appropriate time arises to act on it, don't be overcome by its comfort, pleasantness, and allure—but against all of this, how much better the consciousness of conquering it."

—EPICTETUS, *ENCHIRIDION*, 34

Self-control is a difficult thing, no question. Which is why a popular trick from dieting might be helpful. Some diets allow a "cheat day"—one day per week in which dieters can eat anything and everything they want. Indeed, they're encouraged to write a list during the week of all the foods they craved so they can enjoy them all at once as a treat (the thinking being that if you're eating healthy six out of seven days, you're still ahead).

At first, this sounds like a dream, but anyone who has actually done this knows the truth: each cheat day you eat yourself sick and hate yourself afterward. Soon enough, you're willingly abstaining from cheating at all. Because you don't need it, and you definitely don't want it. It's not unlike a parent catching her child with cigarettes and forcing him to smoke the whole pack.

It's important to connect the so-called temptation with its actual effects. Once you understand that indulging might actually be worse than resisting, the urge begins to lose its appeal. In this way, self-control becomes the real pleasure, and the temptation becomes the regret.

February 14th
THINK BEFORE YOU ACT

"For to be wise is only one thing—to fix our attention on our intelligence, which guides all things everywhere."

—HERACLITUS, QUOTED IN DIOGENES LAERTIUS,
LIVES OF THE EMINENT PHILOSOPHERS, 9.1

Why did I do that? you've probably asked yourself. We all have. *How could I have been so stupid? What was I thinking?*

You weren't. That's the problem. Within that head of yours is all the reason and intelligence you need. It's making sure that it's deferred to and utilized that's the tough part. It's making sure that your mind is in charge, not your emotions, not your immediate physical sensations, not your surging hormones.

Fix your attention on your intelligence. Let it do its thing.

February 15th
ONLY BAD DREAMS

"Clear your mind and get a hold on yourself and, as when awakened from sleep and realizing it was only a bad dream upsetting you, wake up and see that what's there is just like those dreams."
—MARCUS AURELIUS, *MEDITATIONS*, 6.31

The author Raymond Chandler was describing most of us when he wrote in a letter to his publisher, "I never looked back, although I had many uneasy periods looking forward." Thomas Jefferson once joked in a letter to John Adams, "How much pain have cost us the evils which have never happened!" And Seneca would put it best: "There is nothing so certain in our fears that's not yet more certain in the fact that most of what we dread comes to nothing."

Many of the things that upset us, the Stoics believed, are a product of the imagination, not reality. Like dreams, they are vivid and realistic at the time but preposterous once we come out of it. In a dream, we never stop to think and say: "Does this make any sense?" No, we go along with it. The same goes with our flights of anger or fear or other extreme emotions.

Getting upset is like continuing the dream while you're awake. The thing that provoked you wasn't real—but your reaction was. And so from the fake comes real consequences. Which is why you need to wake up right now instead of creating a nightmare.

February 16th
DON'T MAKE THINGS HARDER THAN THEY NEED TO BE

"If someone asks you how to write your name, would you bark out each letter? And if they get angry, would you then return the anger? Wouldn't you rather gently spell out each letter for them? So then, remember in life that your duties are the sum of individual acts. Pay attention to each of these as you do your duty . . . just methodically complete your task."

—MARCUS AURELIUS, *MEDITATIONS*, 6.26

Here's a common scenario. You're working with a frustrating coworker or a difficult boss. They ask you to do something and, because you dislike the messenger, you immediately object. There's this problem or that one, or their request is obnoxious and rude. So you tell them, "No, I'm not going to do it." Then they retaliate by not doing something that you had previously asked of them. And so the conflict escalates.

Meanwhile, if you could step back and see it objectively, you'd probably see that not *everything* they're asking for is unreasonable. In fact, some of it is pretty easy to do or is, at least, agreeable. And if you did it, it might make the rest of the tasks a bit more tolerable too. Pretty soon, you've done the entire thing.

Life (and our job) is difficult enough. Let's not make it harder by getting emotional about insignificant matters or digging in for battles we don't actually care about. Let's not let emotion get in the way of *kathêkon*, the simple, appropriate actions on the path to virtue.

February 17th
THE ENEMY OF HAPPINESS

"It is quite impossible to unite happiness with a yearning for what we don't have. Happiness has all that it wants, and resembling the well-fed, there shouldn't be hunger or thirst."

—EPICTETUS, *DISCOURSES*, 3.24.17

I'll be happy when I graduate, we tell ourselves. *I'll be happy when I get this promotion, when this diet pays off, when I have the money that my parents never had.* Conditional happiness is what psychologists call this kind of thinking. Like the horizon, you can walk for miles and miles and never reach it. You won't even get any closer.

Eagerly anticipating some future event, passionately imagining something you desire, looking forward to some happy scenario—as pleasurable as these activities might seem, they ruin your chance at happiness here and now. Locate that yearning for *more, better, someday* and see it for what it is: the enemy of your contentment. Choose it or your happiness. As Epictetus says, the two are not compatible.

February 18th
PREPARE FOR THE STORM

"This is the true athlete—the person in rigorous training against
false impressions. Remain firm, you who suffer, don't be kidnapped
by your impressions! The struggle is great, the task divine—to gain
mastery, freedom, happiness, and tranquility."

—EPICTETUS, *DISCOURSES*, 2.18.27–28

Epictetus also used the metaphor of a storm, saying that our impressions are not unlike extreme weather that can catch us and whirl us about. When we get worked up or passionate about an issue, we can relate.

But let's think about the role of the weather in modern times. Today, we have forecasters and experts who can fairly accurately predict storm patterns. Today, we're defenseless against a hurricane only if we refuse to prepare or heed the warnings.

If we don't have a plan, if we never learned how to put up the storm windows, we will be at the mercy of these external—and internal—elements. We're still puny human beings compared with one-hundred-mile-per-hour winds, but we have the advantage of being able to prepare—being able to struggle against them in a new way.

February 19th
THE BANQUET OF LIFE

"Remember to conduct yourself in life as if at a banquet. As something being passed around comes to you, reach out your hand and take a moderate helping. Does it pass you by? Don't stop it. It hasn't yet come? Don't burn in desire for it, but wait until it arrives in front of you. Act this way with children, a spouse, toward position, with wealth—one day it will make you worthy of a banquet with the gods."

—EPICTETUS, *ENCHIRIDION*, 15

The next time you see something you want, remember Epictetus's metaphor of life's banquet. As you find yourself getting excited, ready to do anything and everything to get it—the equivalent of reaching across the table and grabbing a dish out of someone's hands—just remind yourself: that's bad manners and unnecessary. Then wait patiently for your turn.

This metaphor has other interpretations too. For instance, we might reflect that we're lucky to have been invited to such a wonderful feast (gratitude). Or that we should take our time and savor the taste of what's on offer (enjoying the present moment) but that to stuff ourselves sick with food and drink serves no one, least of all our health (gluttony is a deadly sin, after all). That at the end of the meal, it's rude not to help the host clean up and do the dishes (selflessness). And finally, that next time, it's our turn to host and treat others just as we had been treated (charity).

Enjoy the meal!

February 20th
THE GRAND PARADE OF DESIRE

"Robbers, perverts, killers, and tyrants—gather for your inspection their so-called pleasures!"

—MARCUS AURELIUS, *MEDITATIONS*, 6.34

It's never great to judge other people, but it's worth taking a second to investigate how a life dedicated to indulging every whim actually works out. The writer Anne Lamott jokes in *Bird by Bird*, "Ever wonder what God thinks of money? Just look at the people he gives it to." The same goes for pleasure. Look at the dictator and his harem filled with plotting, manipulative mistresses. Look how quickly the partying of a young starlet turns to drug addiction and a stalled career.

Ask yourself: *Is that really worth it? Is it really that pleasurable?*

Consider that when you crave something or contemplate indulging in a "harmless" vice.

February 21st
WISH NOT, WANT NOT

> "Remember that it's not only the desire for wealth and position that debases and subjugates us, but also the desire for peace, leisure, travel, and learning. It doesn't matter what the external thing is, the value we place on it subjugates us to another . . . where our heart is set, there our impediment lies."
>
> —EPICTETUS, *DISCOURSES*, 4.4.1–2; 15

Surely, Epictetus isn't saying that peace, leisure, travel, and learning are bad, is he? Thankfully, no. But ceaseless, ardent *desire*—if not bad in and of itself—is fraught with potential complications. What we desire makes us vulnerable. Whether it's an opportunity to travel the world or to be the president or for five minutes of peace and quiet, when we pine for something, when we hope against hope, we set ourselves up for disappointment. Because fate can always intervene and then we'll likely lose our self-control in response.

As Diogenes, the famous Cynic, once said, "It is the privilege of the gods to want nothing, and of godlike men to want little." To want nothing makes one invincible—because nothing lies outside your control. This doesn't just go for not wanting the easy-to-criticize things like wealth or fame—the kinds of folly that we see illustrated in some of our most classic plays and fables. That green light that Gatsby strove for can represent seemingly good things too, like love or a noble cause. But it can wreck someone all the same.

When it comes to your goals and the things you strive for, ask yourself: *Am I in control of them or they in control of me?*

February 22nd
WHAT'S BETTER LEFT UNSAID

> "Cato practiced the kind of public speech capable of moving the masses, believing proper political philosophy takes care like any great city to maintain the warlike element. But he was never seen practicing in front of others, and no one ever heard him rehearse a speech. When he was told that people blamed him for his silence, he replied, 'Better they not blame my life. I begin to speak only when I'm certain what I'll say isn't better left unsaid.'"
>
> —PLUTARCH, *CATO THE YOUNGER*, 4

It's easy to act—to just dive in. It's harder to stop, to pause, to think: *No, I'm not sure I need to do that yet. I'm not sure I am ready.* As Cato entered politics, many expected swift and great things from him—stirring speeches, roaring condemnations, wise analyses. He was aware of this pressure—a pressure that exists on all of us at all times—and resisted. It's easy to pander to the mob (and to our ego).

Instead, he waited and *prepared*. He parsed his own thoughts, made sure he was not reacting emotionally, selfishly, ignorantly, or prematurely. Only then would he speak—when he was confident that his words were worthy of being heard.

To do this requires awareness. It requires us to stop and evaluate ourselves honestly. Can you do that?

February 23rd
CIRCUMSTANCES HAVE NO CARE FOR OUR FEELINGS

"You shouldn't give circumstances the power to rouse anger, for they don't care at all."

—MARCUS AURELIUS, *MEDITATIONS*, 7.38

A significant chunk of Marcus Aurelius's *Meditations* is made up of short quotes and passages from other writers. This is because Marcus wasn't necessarily trying to produce an original work—instead he was *practicing*, reminding himself here and there of important lessons, and sometimes these lessons were things he had read.

This particular quote is special because it comes from a play by Euripides, which, except for a handful of quoted fragments like this, is lost to us. From what we can gather about the play, Bellerophon, the hero, comes to doubt the existence of the gods. But in this line, he is saying: Why bother getting mad at causes and forces far bigger than us? Why do we take these things personally? After all, external events are not sentient beings—they cannot respond to our shouts and cries—and neither can the mostly indifferent gods.

That's what Marcus was reminding himself of here: circumstances are incapable of considering or caring for your feelings, your anxiety, or your excitement. They don't care about your reaction. They are not people. So stop acting like getting worked up is having an impact on a given situation. Situations don't care at all.

February 24th
THE REAL SOURCE OF HARM

"Keep in mind that it isn't the one who has it in for you and takes a swipe that harms you, but rather the harm comes from your own belief about the abuse. So when someone arouses your anger, know that it's really your own opinion fueling it. Instead, make it your first response not to be carried away by such impressions, for with time and distance self-mastery is more easily achieved."

—EPICTETUS, *ENCHIRIDION*, 20

The Stoics remind us that there really is no such thing as an objectively good or bad occurrence. When a billionaire loses $1 million in market fluctuation, it's not the same as when you or I lose a million dollars. Criticism from your worst enemy is received differently than negative words from a spouse. If someone sends you an angry email but you never see it, did it actually happen? In other words, these situations require our participation, context, and categorization in order to be "bad."

Our reaction is what actually decides whether harm has occurred. If we feel that we've been wronged and get angry, of course that's how it will seem. If we raise our voice because we feel we're being confronted, naturally a confrontation will ensue.

But if we retain control of ourselves, we decide whether to label something good or bad. In fact, if that same event happened to us at different points in our lifetime, we might have very different reactions. So why not choose now to *not* apply these labels? Why not choose *not* to react?

February 25th
THE SMOKE AND DUST OF MYTH

"Keep a list before your mind of those who burned with anger and resentment about something, of even the most renowned for success, misfortune, evil deeds, or any special distinction. Then ask yourself, how did that work out? Smoke and dust, the stuff of simple myth trying to be legend . . ."

—MARCUS AURELIUS, *MEDITATIONS*, 12.27

In Marcus Aurelius's writings, he constantly points out how the emperors who came before him were barely remembered just a few years later. To him, this was a reminder that no matter how much he conquered, no matter how much he inflicted his will on the world, it would be like building a castle in the sand—soon to be erased by the winds of time.

The same goes for those driven to the heights of hate or anger or obsession or perfectionism. Marcus liked to point out that Alexander the Great—one of the most passionate and ambitious men who ever lived—was buried in the same ground as his mule driver. Eventually, all of us will pass away and slowly be forgotten. We should enjoy this brief time we have on earth—not be enslaved to emotions that make us miserable and dissatisfied.

February 26th
TO EACH HIS OWN

"Another has done me wrong? Let him see to it. He has his own tendencies, and his own affairs. What I have now is what the common nature has willed, and what I endeavor to accomplish now is what my nature wills."

—Marcus Aurelius, *Meditations*, 5.25

Abraham Lincoln occasionally got fuming mad with a subordinate, one of his generals, even a friend. Rather than taking it out on that person directly, he'd write a long letter, outlining his case why they were wrong and what he wanted them to know. Then Lincoln would fold it up, put the letter in the desk drawer, and never send it. Many of these letters survive only by chance.

He knew, as the former emperor of Rome knew, that it's easy to fight back. It's tempting to give them a piece of your mind. But you almost always end up with regret. You almost always wish you *hadn't* sent the letter. Think of the last time you flew off the handle. What was the outcome? Was there any benefit?

February 27th
CULTIVATING INDIFFERENCE WHERE OTHERS GROW PASSION

"Of all the things that are, some are good, others bad, and yet others indifferent. The good are virtues and all that share in them; the bad are the vices and all that indulge them; the indifferent lie in between virtue and vice and include wealth, health, life, death, pleasure, and pain."

—EPICTETUS, *DISCOURSES*, 2.19.12b–13

Imagine the power you'd have in your life and relationships if all the things that trouble everyone else—how thin they are, how much money they have, how long they have left to live, how they will die—didn't matter so much. What if, where others were upset, envious, excited, possessive, or greedy, you were objective, calm, and clearheaded? Can you envision that? Imagine what it would do for your relationships at work, or for your love life, or your friendships.

Seneca was an incredibly wealthy, even famous, man—yet he was a Stoic. He had many material things, yet, as the Stoics say, he was also indifferent to them. He enjoyed them while they were there, but he accepted that they might someday disappear. What a better attitude than desperately craving *more* or fearfully dreading losing even one penny. Indifference is solid middle ground.

It's not about avoidance or shunning, but rather not giving any possible outcome more power or preference than is appropriate. This is not easy to do, certainly, but if you could manage, how much more relaxed would you be?

February 28th
WHEN YOU LOSE CONTROL

"The soul is like a bowl of water, and our impressions are like the ray of light falling upon the water. When the water is troubled, it appears that the light itself is moved too, but it isn't. So, when a person loses their composure it isn't their skills and virtues that are troubled, but the spirit in which they exist, and when that spirit calms down so do those things."

—EPICTETUS, *DISCOURSES*, 3.3.20–22

You messed up a little. Or maybe you messed up *a lot*.

So? That doesn't change the philosophy that you know. It's not as if your reasoned choice has permanently abandoned you. Rather, it was you who temporarily abandoned it.

Remember that the tools and aims of our training are unaffected by the turbulence of the moment. Stop. Regain your composure. It's waiting for you.

February 29th
YOU CAN'T ALWAYS (BE) GET(TING) WHAT YOU WANT

"When children stick their hand down a narrow goody jar they can't get their full fist out and start crying. Drop a few treats and you will get it out! Curb your desire—don't set your heart on so many things and you will get what you need."

—EPICTETUS, *DISCOURSES*, 3.9.22

"We can have it all" is the mantra of our modern lives. Work, family, purpose, success, leisure time—we want all of this, at the same time (right now, to boot).

In Greece, the lecture hall (*scholeion*) was a leisure center where students contemplated the higher things (the good, true, and beautiful) for the purpose of living a better life. It was about prioritization, about questioning the priorities of the outside world. Today, we're too busy getting things, just like kids jamming their hand down a jar of goodies, to do much of this questioning.

"Don't set your heart on so many things," says Epictetus. Focus. Prioritize. Train your mind to ask: *Do I need this thing? What will happen if I do not get it? Can I make do without it?*

The answers to these questions will help you relax, help you cut out all the needless things that make you busy—too busy to be balanced or happy.

MARCH

AWARENESS

March 1st
WHERE PHILOSOPHY BEGINS

"An important place to begin in philosophy is this: a clear perception of one's own ruling principle."

—EPICTETUS, *DISCOURSES*, 1.26.15

Philosophy is intimidating. Where does one start? With books? With lectures? With the sale of your worldly possessions?

None of these things. Epictetus is saying that one becomes a philosopher when they begin to exercise their guiding reason and start to question the emotions and beliefs and even language that others take for granted. It is thought that an animal has self-awareness when it is able to fully recognize itself in a mirror. Perhaps we could say that we begin our journey into philosophy when we become aware of the ability to analyze our own minds.

Can you start with that step today? When you do, you'll find that from it we really come alive, that we live lives—to paraphrase Socrates—that are actually worth living.

March 2nd
ACCURATE SELF-ASSESSMENT

"Above all, it is necessary for a person to have a true self-estimate,
for we commonly think we can do more than we really can."
—SENECA, *ON TRANQUILITY OF MIND*, 5.2

Most people resist the idea of a true self-estimate, probably because they fear it might mean *downgrading* some of their beliefs about who they are and what they're capable of. As Goethe's maxim goes, it is a great failing "to see yourself as more than you are." How could you really be considered self-aware if you refuse to consider your weaknesses?

Don't fear self-assessment because you're worried you might have to admit some things about yourself. The second half of Goethe's maxim is important too. He states that it is equally damaging to "value yourself at less than your true worth." Is it not equally common to be surprised at how well we're able to handle a previously feared scenario? The way that we're able to put aside the grief for a loved one and care for others—though we always thought we'd be wrecked if something were to happen to our parents or a sibling. The way we're able to rise to the occasion in a stressful situation or a life-changing opportunity.

We underestimate our capabilities just as much and just as dangerously as we overestimate other abilities. Cultivate the ability to judge yourself accurately and honestly. Look inward to discern what you're capable of and what it will take to unlock that potential.

· March 3rd
(DIS)INTEGRATION

"These things don't go together. You must be a unified human being, either good or bad. You must diligently work either on your own reasoning or on things out of your control—take great care with the inside and not what's outside, which is to say, stand with the philosopher, or else with the mob!"

—EPICTETUS, *DISCOURSES*, 3.15.13

We're all complicated people. We have multiple sides to ourselves—conflicting wants, desires, and fears. The outside world is no less confusing and contradictory. If we're not careful, all these forces—pushing and pulling—will eventually tear us apart. We can't live as both Jekyll and Hyde. Not for long, anyway.

We have a choice: to stand with the philosopher and focus strenuously on the inside, or to behave like a leader of a mob, becoming whatever the crowd needs at a given moment.

If we do not focus on our internal integration—on self-awareness—we risk external disintegration.

March 4th
AWARENESS IS FREEDOM

"The person is free who lives as they wish, neither compelled, nor hindered, nor limited—whose choices aren't hampered, whose desires succeed, and who don't fall into what repels them. Who wishes to live in deception—tripped up, mistaken, undisciplined, complaining, in a rut? No one. These are base people who don't live as they wish; and so, no base person is free."

—EPICTETUS, *DISCOURSES*, 4.1.1–3a

It is sad to consider how much time many people spend in the course of a day doing things they "have" to do—not necessary obligations like work or family, but the obligations we needlessly accept out of vanity or ignorance. Consider the actions we take in order to impress other people or the lengths we'll go to fulfill urges or sate desires we don't even question. In one of his famous letters, Seneca observes how often powerful people are slaves to their money, to their positions, to their mistresses, even—as was legal in Rome—to their slaves. "No slavery is more disgraceful," he quipped, "than one which is self-imposed."

We see this slavery all the time—a codependent person who can't help but clean up after a dysfunctional friend, a boss who micromanages employees and sweats every penny. The countless causes, events, and get-togethers we're too busy to attend but agree to anyway.

Take an inventory of your obligations from time to time. How many of these are self-imposed? How many of them are truly necessary? Are you as free as you think?

March 5th
CUTTING BACK ON THE COSTLY

"So, concerning the things we pursue, and for which we vigorously exert ourselves, we owe this consideration—either there is nothing useful in them, or most aren't useful. Some of them are superfluous, while others aren't worth that much. But we don't discern this and see them as free, when they cost us dearly."

—SENECA, *MORAL LETTERS*, 42.6

Of Seneca's many letters, this is probably one of the most important—and one of the least understood. He's making a point that goes unheard in a society of ever-bigger houses and ever more possessions: that there's a hidden cost to all that accumulating. And the sooner we're aware of it, the better.

Remember: even what we get for free has a cost, if only in what we pay to store it—in our garages and in our minds. As you walk past your possessions today, ask yourself: *Do I need this? Is it superfluous? What's this actually worth? What is it costing me?*

You might be surprised by the answers and how much we've been paying without even knowing it.

March 6th
DON'T TELL YOURSELF STORIES

"In public avoid talking often and excessively about your accomplishments and dangers, for however much you enjoy recounting your dangers, it's not so pleasant for others to hear about your affairs."

—EPICTETUS, *ENCHIRIDION*, 33.14

Modern philosopher Nassim Taleb has warned of the "narrative fallacy"—the tendency to assemble unrelated events of the past into stories. These stories, however gratifying to create, are inherently misleading. They lead to a sense of cohesion and certainty that isn't real.

If that's too heady, remember that as Epictetus points out, there is another reason not to tell stories about your past. It's boring, annoying, and self-absorbed. It might make you feel good to dominate the conversation and make it all about you, but how do you think it is for everyone else? Do you think people are really enjoying the highlights of your high school football days? Is this really the time for another exaggerated tale of your sexual prowess?

Try your best not to create this fantasy bubble—live in what's real. *Listen* and *connect* with people, don't perform for them.

March 7th
DON'T TRUST THE SENSES

"Heraclitus called self-deception an awful disease and eyesight a lying sense."

—DIOGENES LAERTIUS,
LIVES OF THE EMINENT PHILOSOPHERS, 9.7

Self-awareness is the ability to objectively evaluate the self. It's the ability to question our own instincts, patterns, and assumptions. *Oiêsis*, self-deception or arrogant and unchallenged opinion, requires that we hold all our opinions up to hard scrutiny; even our eyes deceive us.

On the one hand, that's alarming. *I can't even trust my own senses?!* Sure, you could think about it that way. Or you could take it another way: because our senses are often wrong, our emotions overly alarmed, our projections overly optimistic, we're better off not rushing into conclusions about anything. We can take a beat with everything we do and become aware of everything that's going on so we can make the right decision.

March 8th
DON'T UNINTENTIONALLY HAND OVER YOUR FREEDOM

> "If a person gave away your body to some passerby, you'd be furious. Yet you hand over your mind to anyone who comes along, so they may abuse you, leaving it disturbed and troubled—have you no shame in that?"
>
> —EPICTETUS, *ENCHIRIDION*, 28

Instinctively, we protect our physical selves. We don't let people touch us, push us around, control where we go. But when it comes to the mind, we're less disciplined. We hand it over willingly to social media, to television, to what other people are doing, thinking, or saying. We sit down to work and the next thing you know, we're browsing the Internet. We sit down with our families, but within minutes we have our phones out. We sit down peacefully in a park, but instead of looking inward, we're judging people as they pass by.

We don't even know that we're doing this. We don't realize how much waste is in it, how inefficient and distracted it makes us. And what's worse—no one is *making* this happen. It's totally self-inflicted.

To the Stoics, this is an abomination. They know that the world can control our bodies—we can be thrown in jail or be tossed about by the weather. But the mind? That's ours. We *must* protect it. Maintain control over your mind and perceptions, they'd say. It's your most prized possession.

March 9th
FIND THE RIGHT SCENE

"Above all, keep a close watch on this—that you are never so tied to your former acquaintances and friends that you are pulled down to their level. If you don't, you'll be ruined. . . . You must choose whether to be loved by these friends and remain the same person, or to become a better person at the cost of those friends . . . if you try to have it both ways you will neither make progress nor keep what you once had."

—EPICTETUS, *DISCOURSES*, 4.2.1; 4–5

"From good people you'll learn good, but if you mingle with the bad you'll destroy such soul as you had."

—MUSONIUS RUFUS, QUOTING THEOGNIS
OF MEGARA, *LECTURES*, 11.53.21–22

Jim Rohn's widely quoted line is: "You are the average of the five people you spend the most time with." James Altucher advises young writers and entrepreneurs to find their "scene"—a group of peers who push them to be better. Your father might have given you a warning when he saw you spending time with some bad kids: "Remember, you become like your friends." One of Goethe's maxims captures it better: "Tell me with whom you consort and I will tell you who you are."

Consciously consider whom you allow into your life—not like some snobby elitist but like someone who is trying to cultivate the best life possible. Ask yourself about the people you meet and spend time with: *Are they making me better? Do they encourage me to push forward and hold me accountable? Or do they drag me down to their level?* Now, with this in mind, ask the most important question: *Should I spend more or less time with these folks?*

The second part of Goethe's quote tells us the stakes of this choice: "If I know how you spend your time," he said, "then I know what might become of you."

March 10th
FIND YOURSELF A CATO

"We can remove most sins if we have a witness standing by as we are about to go wrong. The soul should have someone it can respect, by whose example it can make its inner sanctum more inviolable. Happy is the person who can improve others, not only when present, but even when in their thoughts!"

—SENECA, *MORAL LETTERS*, 11.9

Cato the Younger, a Roman politician best known for his self-discipline and for his heroic defense of the Republic against Julius Caesar, appears constantly throughout Stoic literature—which is interesting because he didn't write anything down. He taught no classes. He gave no interviews. His bold and brave example is what made him such a commonly cited and quoted philosopher.

Seneca tells us that we should each have our own Cato—a great and noble person we can allow into our minds and use to guide our actions, even when they're not physically present. The economist Adam Smith had a similar concept, which he called the indifferent spectator. It doesn't have to be an actual person, just someone who, like Seneca said, can stand witness to our behavior. Someone who can quietly admonish us if we are considering doing something lazy, dishonest, or selfish.

And if we do it right, and live our lives in such a way, perhaps we can serve as someone else's Cato or indifferent spectator when they need it.

March 11th
LIVING WITHOUT RESTRICTION

"The unrestricted person, who has in hand what they will in all events, is free. But anyone who can be restricted, coerced, or pushed into something against what they will is a slave."

—EPICTETUS, *DISCOURSES*, 4.1.128b–129a

Take a look at some of the most powerful, rich, and famous people in the world. Ignore the trappings of their success and what they're able to buy. Look instead at what they're forced to trade in return—look at what success has cost them.

Mostly? Freedom. Their work demands they wear a suit. Their success depends on attending certain parties, kissing up to people they don't like. It will require—inevitably—realizing they are unable to say what they actually think. Worse, it demands that they become a different type of person or do bad things.

Sure, it might pay well—but they haven't truly examined the transaction. As Seneca put it, "Slavery resides under marble and gold." Too many successful people are prisoners in jails of their own making. Is that what you want? Is that what you're working hard toward? Let's hope not.

March 12th
SEEING THINGS AS THE PERSON AT FAULT DOES

"Whenever someone has done wrong by you, immediately consider what notion of good or evil they had in doing it. For when
you see that, you'll feel compassion, instead of astonishment or
rage. For you may yourself have the same notions of good and
evil, or similar ones, in which case you'll make an allowance for
what they've done. But if you no longer hold the same notions,
you'll be more readily gracious for their error."

—MARCUS AURELIUS, *MEDITATIONS*, 7.26

Socrates, perhaps the wisest person to ever live, used to say that "nobody
does wrong willingly." Meaning that no one is wrong on purpose
either. Nobody *thinks* they're wrong, even when they are. They think
they're right, they're just mistaken. Otherwise, they wouldn't think it
anymore!

Could it be that the slights you've experienced or the harm that
others have done to you was not inflicted intentionally? What if they
simply thought they were doing the right thing—for them, even for
you? It's like the memorial for Confederate soldiers at Arlington (obviously a cause that was wrongly fought for by people doing wrong), which
states, in part, that the Confederate soldiers served "in simple obedience to duty, as they understood it." Again—they understood wrongly,
but it was their genuine understanding, just as Lincoln was genuine
when he ended his famous Cooper Union speech by saying, "Let us, to
the end, dare to do our duty as we understand it."

How much more tolerant and understanding would you be today if
you could see the actions of other people as attempts to do the right
thing? Whether you agree or not, how radically would this lens change
your perspective on otherwise offensive or belligerent actions?

March 13th
ONE DAY IT WILL ALL MAKE SENSE

"Whenever you find yourself blaming providence, turn it around in your mind and you will see that what has happened is in keeping with reason."

—EPICTETUS, *DISCOURSES*, 3.17.1

Part of the reason we fight against the things that happen is that we're so focused on *our* plan that we forget that there might be a bigger plan we don't know about. Is it not the case that plenty of times something we thought was a disaster turned out to be, with the passage of time, a lucky break? We also forget that we're not the only people who matter and that our loss might be someone else's gain.

This sense of being wronged is a simple awareness problem. We need to remember that all things are guided by reason—but that it is a vast and universal reason that we cannot always see. That the surprise hurricane was the result of a butterfly flapping its wings a hemisphere away or that misfortune we have experienced is simply the prelude to a pleasant and enviable future.

March 14th
SELF-DECEPTION IS OUR ENEMY

"Zeno would also say that nothing is more hostile to a firm grasp on knowledge than self-deception."

—DIOGENES LAERTIUS,
LIVES OF THE EMINENT PHILOSOPHERS, 7.23

Self-deception, delusions of grandeur—these aren't just annoying personality traits. Ego is more than just off-putting and obnoxious. Instead, it's the sworn enemy of our ability to learn and grow.

As Epictetus put it, "It is impossible for a person to begin to learn what he thinks he already knows." Today, we will be unable to improve, unable to learn, unable to earn the respect of others if we think we're already perfect, a genius admired far and wide. In this sense, ego and self-deception are the enemies of the things we wish to have because we delude ourselves into believing that we already possess them.

So we must meet ego with the hostility and contempt that it insidiously deploys against us—to keep it away, if only for twenty-four hours at a time.

March 15th
THE PRESENT IS ALL WE POSSESS

"Were you to live three thousand years, or even a countless multiple of that, keep in mind that no one ever loses a life other than the one they are living, and no one ever lives a life other than the one they are losing. The longest and the shortest life, then, amount to the same, for the present moment lasts the same for all and is all anyone possesses. No one can lose either the past or the future, for how can someone be deprived of what's not theirs?"

—MARCUS AURELIUS, *MEDITATIONS*, 2.14

Today, notice how often you look for more. That is, wanting the past to be more than what it was (different, better, still here, etc.) or wanting the future to unfold exactly as you expect (with hardly a thought as to how that might affect other people).

When you do this, you're neglecting the present moment. Talk about ungrateful! There's a saying—attributed to Bil Keane, the cartoonist—worth remembering: "Yesterday's the past, tomorrow's the future, but today is a gift. That's why it's called the present." This present is in our possession—but it has an expiration date, a quickly approaching one. If you enjoy all of it, it will be enough. It can last a whole lifetime.

March 16th
THAT SACRED PART OF YOU

"Hold sacred your capacity for understanding. For in it is all, that our ruling principle won't allow anything to enter that is either inconsistent with nature or with the constitution of a logical creature. It's what demands due diligence, care for others, and obedience to God."

—MARCUS AURELIUS, *MEDITATIONS*, 3.9

The fact that you can think, the fact that you can read this book, the fact that you are able to reason in and out of situations—all of this is what gives you the ability to improve your circumstances and become better. It's important to appreciate this ability, because it's a genuine ability. Not everyone is so lucky.

Seriously—what you take for granted, others wouldn't even think to dream of.

Take a little time today to remember that you're blessed with the capacity to use logic and reason to navigate situations and circumstances. This gives you unthinkable power to alter your circumstances and the circumstances of others. And remember that with power comes responsibility.

March 17th
THE BEAUTY OF CHOICE

"You are not your body and hair-style, but your capacity for choosing well. If your choices are beautiful, so too will you be."
—EPICTETUS, *DISCOURSES*, 3.1.39b–40a

It's that line in the movie *Fight Club*: "You are not your job, you're not how much money you have in the bank. You are not the car you drive. You're not the contents of your wallet." Obviously our friend Epictetus never saw that movie or read the book—but apparently the consumerism of the 1990s existed in ancient Rome too.

It's easy to confuse the image we present to the world for who we actually are, especially when media messaging deliberately blurs that distinction.

You might *look* beautiful today, but if that was the result of vain obsession in the mirror this morning, the Stoics would ask, are you *actually* beautiful? A body built from hard work is admirable. A body built to impress gym rats is not.

That's what the Stoics urge us to consider. Not how things appear, but what effort, activity, and choices they are a result of.

March 18th
IMPOSSIBLE WITHOUT YOUR CONSENT

"Today I escaped from the crush of circumstances, or better put, I threw them out, for the crush wasn't from outside me but in my own assumptions."

—MARCUS AURELIUS, *MEDITATIONS*, 9.13

On tough days we might say, "My work is overwhelming," or "My boss is really frustrating." If only we could understand that this is impossible. Someone can't frustrate *you*, work can't overwhelm *you*—these are external objects, and they have no access to your mind. Those emotions you feel, as real as they are, come from the inside, not the outside.

The Stoics use the word *hypolêpsis*, which means "taking up"—of perceptions, thoughts, and judgments by our mind. What we assume, what we willingly generate in our mind, that's on us. We can't blame other people for making us feel stressed or frustrated any more than we can blame them for our jealousy. The cause is within us. They're just the target.

March 19th
TIMELESS WISDOM

> "For there are two rules to keep at the ready—that there is nothing good or bad outside my own reasoned choice, and that we shouldn't try to lead events but to follow them."
>
> —EPICTETUS, *DISCOURSES*, 3.10.18

In the mid-twentieth century, there was an Indian Jesuit priest named Anthony de Mello. Born in Bombay when it was still under British control, de Mello was an amalgam of many different cultures and perspectives: East, West; he even trained as a psychotherapist. It's interesting when one sees timeless wisdom develop across schools, across epochs and ideas. Here is a quote from de Mello's book, *The Way to Love*, that sounds almost exactly like Epictetus:

> "The cause of my irritation is not in this person but in me."

Remember, each individual has a choice. You are always the one in control. The cause of irritation—or our notion that something is bad—that comes from us, from our labels or our expectations. Just as easily, we can change those labels; we can change our entitlement and decide to accept and love what's happening around us. And this wisdom has been repeated and independently discovered in every century and every country since time began.

March 20th
READY AND AT HOME

"I may wish to be free from torture, but if the time comes for me to endure it, I'll wish to bear it courageously with bravery and honor. Wouldn't I prefer not to fall into war? But if war does befall me, I'll wish to carry nobly the wounds, starvation, and other necessities of war. Neither am I so crazy as to desire illness, but if I must suffer illness, I'll wish to do nothing rash or dishonorable. The point is not to wish for these adversities, but for the virtue that makes adversities bearable."

—SENECA, *MORAL LETTERS*, 67.4

President James Garfield was a great man—raised in humble circumstances, self-educated, and eventually a Civil War hero—whose presidency was cut short by an assassin's bullet. In his brief time in office, he faced a bitterly divided country as well as a bitterly and internally divided Republican Party. During one fight, which challenged the very authority of his office, he stood firm, telling an adviser: "Of course I deprecate war, but if it is brought to my door the bringer will find me at home."

That's what Seneca is saying here. We'd be crazy to *want* to face difficulty in life. But we'd be equally crazy to pretend that it isn't going to happen. Which is why when it knocks on our door—as it very well may this morning—let's make sure we're prepared to answer. Not the way we are when a surprise visitor comes late at night, but the way we are when we're waiting for an important guest: dressed, in the right head space, ready to go.

March 21st
THE BEST RETREAT IS IN HERE, NOT OUT THERE

"People seek retreats for themselves in the country, by the sea, or in the mountains. You are very much in the habit of yearning for those same things. But this is entirely the trait of a base person, when you can, at any moment, find such a retreat in yourself. For nowhere can you find a more peaceful and less busy retreat than in your own soul—especially if on close inspection it is filled with ease, which I say is nothing more than being well-ordered. Treat yourself often to this retreat and be renewed."

—MARCUS AURELIUS, *MEDITATIONS*, 4.3.1

D o you have a vacation coming up? Are you looking forward to the weekend so you can have some peace and quiet? *Maybe,* you think, *after things settle down* or *after I get this over with.* But how often has that ever actually worked?

The Zen meditation teacher Jon Kabat-Zinn coined a famous expression: "Wherever you go, there you are." We can find a retreat at any time by looking inward. We can sit with our eyes closed and feel our breath go in and out. We can turn on some music and tune out the world. We can turn off technology or shut off those rampant thoughts in our head. *That* will provide us peace. Nothing else.

March 22nd
THE SIGN OF TRUE EDUCATION

"What is it then to be properly educated? It is learning to apply our natural preconceptions to the right things according to Nature, and beyond that to separate the things that lie within our power from those that don't."

—EPICTETUS, *DISCOURSES*, 1.22.9–10a

A degree on a wall means you're educated as much as shoes on your feet mean you're walking. It's a start, but hardly sufficient.

Otherwise, how could so many "educated" people make unreasonable decisions? Or miss so many obvious things? Partly it's because they forget that they ought to focus only on that which lies within their power to control. A surviving fragment from the philosopher Heraclitus expresses that reality:

"Many who have learned
  from Hesiod the countless names
  of gods and monsters
  never understand
  that night and day are one."

Just as you can walk plenty well without shoes, you don't need to step into a classroom to understand the basic, fundamental reality of nature and of our proper role in it. Begin with awareness and reflection. Not just once, but every single second of every single day.

AWARENESS

March 23rd
THE STRAITJACKETED SOUL

"The diseases of the rational soul are long-standing and hardened vices, such as greed and ambition—they have put the soul in a straitjacket and have begun to be permanent evils inside it. To put it briefly, this sickness is an unrelenting distortion of judgment, so things that are only mildly desirable are vigorously sought after."

—SENECA, *MORAL LETTERS*, 75.11

In the financial disaster of the late 2000s, hundreds of smart, rational people lost trillions of dollars' worth of wealth. How could such smart people have been so foolish? These people knew the system, knew how the markets were supposed to work, and had managed billions, if not trillions, of dollars. And yet, almost to a person, they were wrong—and wrong to the tune of global market havoc.

It's not hard to look at that situation and understand that greed was some part of the problem. Greed was what led people to create complex markets that no one understood in the hope of making a quick buck. Greed caused other people to make trades on strange pools of debt. Greed prevented anyone from calling out this situation for what it was—a house of cards just waiting for the slightest breeze to knock it all down.

It doesn't do you much good to criticize those folks after the fact. It's better to look at how greed and vices might be having a similar effect in your own life. What lapses in judgment might your vices be causing you? What "sicknesses" might you have?

And how can your rational mind step in and regulate them?

March 24th
THERE IS PHILOSOPHY IN EVERYTHING

"Eat like a human being, drink like a human being, dress up, marry, have children, get politically active—suffer abuse, bear with a headstrong brother, father, son, neighbor, or companion. Show us these things so we can see that you truly have learned from the philosophers."

—EPICTETUS, *DISCOURSES*, 3.21.5–6

Plutarch, a Roman biographer as well as an admirer of the Stoics, didn't begin his study of the greats of Roman literature until late in life. But, as he recounts in his biography of Demosthenes, he was surprised at how quickly it all came to him. He wrote, "It wasn't so much that the words brought me into a full understanding of events, as that, somehow, I had a personal experience of the events that allowed me to follow closely the meaning of the words."

This is what Epictetus means about the study of philosophy. Study, yes, but go live your life as well. It's the only way that you'll actually understand what any of it means. And more important, it's only from your actions and choices over time that it will be possible to see whether you took any of the teachings to heart.

Be aware of that today when you're going to work, going on a date, deciding whom to vote for, calling your parents in the evening, waving to your neighbor as you walk to your door, tipping the delivery man, saying goodnight to someone you love. All of that is philosophy. All of it is experience that brings meaning to the words.

March 25th
WEALTH AND FREEDOM ARE FREE

"... freedom isn't secured by filling up on your heart's desire but by removing your desire."

—EPICTETUS, *DISCOURSES*, 4.1.175

There are two ways to be wealthy—to get everything you want or to want everything you have. Which is easier right here and right now? The same goes for freedom. If you chafe and fight and struggle for more, you will never be free. If you could find and focus on the pockets of freedom you already have? Well, then you'd be free right here, right now.

March 26th
WHAT RULES YOUR RULING REASON?

"How does your ruling reason manage itself? For in that is the key to everything. Whatever else remains, be it in the power of your choice or not, is but a corpse and smoke."

—MARCUS AURELIUS, *MEDITATIONS*, 12.33

The Roman satirist Juvenal is famous for this question: *Quis custodiet ipsos custodes?* (Who watches the watchmen?) In a way, this is what Marcus is asking himself—and what you might ask yourself throughout the day. What influences the ruling reason that guides your life?

This means an exploration of subjects like evolutionary biology, psychology, neurology, and even the subconscious. Because these deeper forces shape even the most disciplined, rational minds. You can be the most patient person in the world, but if science shows we make poor decisions on an empty stomach—what good is all that patience?

So don't stop at Stoicism, but explore the forces that drive and make Stoicism possible. Learn what underpins this philosophy you're studying, how the body and mind tick. Understand not only your ruling reason—the watchmen—but whoever and whatever rules that too.

March 27th
PAY WHAT THINGS ARE WORTH

"Diogenes of Sinope said we sell things of great value for things of very little, and vice versa."

—DIOGENES LAERTIUS,
LIVES OF THE EMINENT PHILOSOPHERS, 6.2.35b

You can buy a Plume Blanche diamond-encrusted sofa for close to two hundred thousand dollars. It's also possible to hire one person to kill another person for five hundred dollars. Remember that next time you hear someone ramble on about how the market decides what things are worth. The market might be rational . . . but the people who comprise it are not.

Diogenes, who founded the Cynic school, emphasized the true worth (*axia*) of things, a theme that persisted in Stoicism and was strongly reflected in both Epictetus and Marcus. It's easy to lose track. When the people around you dump a fortune into trinkets they can't take with them when they die, it might seem like a good investment for you to make too.

But of course it isn't. The good things in life cost what they cost. The unnecessary things are not worth it at any price. The key is being aware of the difference.

March 28th
COWARDICE AS A DESIGN PROBLEM

"Life without a design is erratic. As soon as one is in place, principles become necessary. I think you'll concede that nothing is more
shameful than uncertain and wavering conduct, and beating a
cowardly retreat. This will happen in all our affairs unless we
remove the faults that seize and detain our spirits, preventing
them from pushing forward and making an all-out effort."

—SENECA, *MORAL LETTERS*, 95.46

The opposing team comes out strong, establishes an early lead, and
you never had time to recover. You walk into a business meeting,
are caught off guard, and the whole thing goes poorly. A delicate conversation escalates into a shouting match. You switched majors halfway
through college and had to start your coursework over and graduate
late. Sound familiar?

It's the chaos that ensues from not having a plan. Not because plans
are perfect, but because people without plans—like a line of infantrymen without a strong leader—are much more likely to get overwhelmed
and fall apart. The Super Bowl–winning coach Bill Walsh used to avoid
this risk by scripting the beginning of his games. "If you want to sleep
at night before the game," he said in a lecture on game planning, "have
your first 25 plays established in your own mind the night before that.
You can walk into the stadium and you can start the game without that
stress factor." You'll also be able to ignore a couple of early points or a
surprise from your opponent. It's irrelevant to you—you already have
your marching orders.

Don't try to make it up on the fly. Have a plan.

March 29th
WHY DO YOU NEED TO IMPRESS THESE PEOPLE AGAIN?

"If you should ever turn your will to things outside your control in order to impress someone, be sure that you have wrecked your whole purpose in life. Be content, then, to be a philosopher in all that you do, and if you wish also to be seen as one, show yourself first that you are and you will succeed."

—EPICTETUS, *ENCHIRIDION*, 23

Is there anything sadder than the immense lengths we'll go to impress someone? The things we'll do to earn someone's approval can seem, when examined in retrospect, like the result of some temporary form of insanity. Suddenly we're wearing uncomfortable, ridiculous clothes we've been told are cool, eating differently, talking differently, eagerly waiting for a call or text. If we did these things because *we* liked it, that would be one thing. But that's not what it is. It's just a means to an end—to get someone to give us the nod.

The irony, as Marcus Aurelius points out repeatedly, is that the people whose opinion we covet are not all that great. They're flawed—they're distracted and wowed by all sorts of silly things themselves. We know this and yet we don't want to think about it. To quote *Fight Club* again, "We buy things we don't need, to impress people we don't like."

Doesn't that sound pretty ridiculous? But more than that, isn't it about as far as possible as you can get from the serenity and security that philosophy can provide?

March 30th
REASON IN ALL THINGS

"Hurry to your own ruling reason, to the reason of the Whole, and to your neighbor's. To your own mind to make it just; to the mind of the Whole to remember your place in it; and to your neighbor's mind to learn whether it's ignorant or of sound knowledge—while recognizing it's like yours."

—MARCUS AURELIUS, *MEDITATIONS*, 9.22

If our lives are not ruled by reason, what are they ruled by? Impulse? Whim? Mimicry? Unthinking habit? As we examine our past behavior, it's sad how often we find this to be the case—that we were not acting consciously or deliberately but instead by forces we did not bother to evaluate. It also happens that these are the instances that we're mostly likely to regret.

March 31st
YOU'RE A PRODUCT OF YOUR TRAINING

"Chasing what can't be done is madness. But the base person is unable to do anything else."

—MARCUS AURELIUS, *MEDITATIONS*, 5.17

A dog that's allowed to chase cars will chase cars. A child who is never given any boundaries will become spoiled. An investor without discipline is not an investor—he's a gambler. A mind that isn't in control of itself, that doesn't understand its power to regulate itself, will be jerked around by external events and unquestioned impulses.

That can't be how you'd like tomorrow to go. So you must be aware of that. You must put in place training and habits now to replace ignorance and ill discipline. Only then will you begin to behave and act differently. Only then will you stop seeking the impossible, the short-sighted, and the unnecessary.

APRIL

UNBIASED THOUGHT

April 1st
THE COLOR OF YOUR THOUGHTS

"Your mind will take the shape of what you frequently hold in thought, for the human spirit is colored by such impressions."

—MARCUS AURELIUS, *MEDITATIONS*, 5.16

If you bend your body into a sitting position every day for a long enough period of time, the curvature of your spine changes. A doctor can tell from a radiograph (or an autopsy) whether someone sat at a desk for a living. If you shove your feet into tiny, narrow dress shoes each day, your feet begin to take on that form as well.

The same is true for our mind. If you hold a perpetually negative outlook, soon enough everything you encounter will seem negative. Close it off and you'll become closed-minded. Color it with the wrong thoughts and your life will be dyed the same.

April 2nd
BE WARY OF WHAT YOU LET IN

"Drama, combat, terror, numbness, and subservience—every day
these things wipe out your sacred principles, whenever your mind
entertains them uncritically or lets them slip in."

—MARCUS AURELIUS, *MEDITATIONS*, 10.9

How much harder is it to do the right thing when you're surrounded
by people with low standards? How much harder is it to be positive and empathetic inside the negativity bubble of television chatter?
How much harder is it to focus on your own issues when you're distracted with other people's drama and conflict?

We'll inevitably be exposed to these influences at some point, no
matter how much we try to avoid them. But when we are, there is nothing that says we have to allow those influences to penetrate our minds.
We have the ability to put our guard up and decide what we actually
allow in. Uninvited guests might arrive at your home, but you don't have
to ask them to stay for dinner. You don't have to let them into your mind.

April 3rd
DECEIVED AND DIVIDED

> "Circumstances are what deceive us—you must be discerning in them. We embrace evil before good. We desire the opposite of what we once desired. Our prayers are at war with our prayers, our plans with our plans."
>
> —SENECA, *MORAL LETTERS*, 45.6

A woman says she wants to meet a nice guy and get married—yet she spends all her time around jerks. A man says that he wishes he could find a great job, but he hasn't actually bothered to do the looking. Business executives try to pursue two different strategies at the same time—straddling it's called—and they are shocked when they succeed at neither.

All of these people, just as is often true for us too, are deceived and divided. One hand is working against the other. As Martin Luther King Jr. once put it, "There is something of a civil war going on within all of our lives," a war inside each individual between the good parts of their soul and the bad.

The Stoics say that that war is usually a result of our conflicting desires, our screwed-up judgments or biased thoughts. We don't stop and ask: *OK, what do I really want? What am I actually after here?* If we did, we'd notice the contradictory and inconsistent wishes that we have. And then we'd stop working against ourselves.

April 4th
DON'T LET THIS GO TO YOUR HEAD

"Make sure you're not made 'Emperor,' avoid that imperial stain. It can happen to you, so keep yourself simple, good, pure, saintly, plain, a friend of justice, god-fearing, gracious, affectionate, and strong for your proper work. Fight to remain the person that philosophy wished to make you. Revere the gods, and look after each other. Life is short—the fruit of this life is a good character and acts for the common good."

—MARCUS AURELIUS, *MEDITATIONS*, 6.30

It is difficult even to conceive of what life must have been like for Marcus Aurelius—he wasn't born emperor, nor did he obtain the position deliberately. It was simply thrust upon him. Nevertheless, he was suddenly the richest man in the world, head of the most powerful army on earth, ruling over the largest empire in history, considered a god among men.

It's no wonder he wrote little messages like this one to remind himself not to spin off the planet. Without them, he might have lost his sense of what was important—falling prey to the lies from all the people who needed things from him. And here we are, whatever we happen to be doing, at risk of spinning off ourselves.

When we experience success, we must make sure that it doesn't change us—that we continue to maintain our character despite the temptation not to. Reason must lead the way no matter what good fortune comes along.

April 5th
TRUST, BUT VERIFY

"First off, don't let the force of the impression carry you away. Say to it, 'hold up a bit and let me see who you are and where you are from—let me put you to the test' . . ."

—EPICTETUS, *DISCOURSES*, 2.18.24

One of the wonders of your mind is the quickness with which it can comprehend and categorize things. As Malcolm Gladwell wrote in *Blink*, we are constantly making split-second decisions based on years of experience and knowledge as well as using the same skill to confirm prejudices, stereotypes, and assumptions. Clearly, the former thinking is a source of strength, whereas the latter is a great weakness.

We lose very little by taking a beat to consider our own thoughts. *Is this really so bad? What do I really know about this person? Why do I have such strong feelings here? Is anxiety really adding much to the situation? What's so special about _____?*

By asking these questions—by putting our impressions to the test as Epictetus recommends—we're less likely to be carried away by them or make a move on a mistaken or biased one. We're still free to use our instincts, but we should always, as the Russian proverb says, "trust, but verify."

April 6th
PREPARE YOURSELF FOR NEGATIVITY

"When you first rise in the morning tell yourself: I will encounter busybodies, ingrates, egomaniacs, liars, the jealous and cranks. They are all stricken with these afflictions because they don't know the difference between good and evil. Because I have understood the beauty of good and the ugliness of evil, I know that these wrong-doers are still akin to me . . . and that none can do me harm, or implicate me in ugliness—nor can I be angry at my relatives or hate them. For we are made for cooperation."

—MARCUS AURELIUS, *MEDITATIONS*, 2.1

You can be certain as clockwork that at some point today you're going to interact with someone who seems like a jerk (as we all have been). The question is: Are you going to be ready for it?

This exercise calls to mind a joke from the eighteenth-century writer and witticist Nicolas Chamfort, who remarked that if you "swallow a toad every morning," you'll be fortified against anything else disgusting that might happen the rest of the day. Might it not be better to understand up front—right when you wake up—that other people often behave in selfish or ignorant ways (the toad) than it is to nibble it throughout the day?

But there is a second part to this, just as there is a second half of Marcus's quote: "No one can implicate me in ugliness—nor can I be angry at my relative or hate him." The point of this preparation is not to write off everyone in advance. It's that, maybe, because you've prepared for it, you'll be able to act with patience, forgiveness, and understanding.

April 7th
EXPECT TO CHANGE YOUR OPINIONS

"There are two things that must be rooted out in human beings—arrogant opinion and mistrust. Arrogant opinion expects that there is nothing further needed, and mistrust assumes that under the torrent of circumstance there can be no happiness."

—EPICTETUS, *DISCOURSES*, 3.14.8

How often do we begin some project certain we know exactly how it will go? How often do we meet people and think we know exactly who and what they are? And how often are these assumptions proved to be completely and utterly wrong?

This is why we must fight our biases and preconceptions: because they are a liability. Ask yourself: *What haven't I considered? Why is this thing the way it is? Am I part of the problem here or the solution? Could I be wrong here?* Be doubly careful to honor what you do not know, and then set that against the knowledge you actually have.

Remember, if there is one core teaching at the heart of this philosophy, it's that we're not as smart and as wise as we'd like to think we are. If we ever do want to become wise, it comes from the questioning and from humility—not, as many would like to think, from certainty, mistrust, and arrogance.

April 8th
THE COST OF ACCEPTING COUNTERFEITS

"When it comes to money, where we feel our clear interest, we have an entire art where the tester uses many means to discover the worth . . . just as we give great attention to judging things that might steer us badly. But when it comes to our own ruling principle, we yawn and doze off, accepting any appearance that flashes by without counting the cost."

—EPICTETUS, *DISCOURSES*, 1.20.8; 11

When coins were much more rudimentary, people had to spend a lot of time testing them to confirm the currency they'd just received was genuine. The Greek word *dokimazein* means "to assay" or check the quality of a mineral ore. Merchants were often skilled enough that they could test coinage by throwing it against a hard surface and listen to the note it rang. Even today, though, if someone were to hand you a hundred-dollar bill, you might rub it between your fingers or hold it up to the light, just to confirm it wasn't a fake.

All this for an imaginary currency, an invention of society. The point of this metaphor is to highlight how much effort we put into making sure money is real, whereas we accept potentially life-changing thoughts or assumptions without so much as a question. One ironic assumption along these lines: that having a lot of money makes you wealthy. Or that because a lot of people believe something, it must be true.

Really, we should be testing these notions as vigilantly as a money changer. For, as Epictetus reminds us, "the first and greatest task of the philosopher is to test and separate appearances, and to act on nothing that is untested."

April 9th
TEST YOUR IMPRESSIONS

"From the very beginning, make it your practice to say to every harsh impression, 'you are an impression and not at all what you appear to be.' Next, examine and test it by the rules you possess, the first and greatest of which is this—whether it belongs to the things in our control or not in our control, and if the latter, be prepared to respond, 'It is nothing to me.'"

—EPICTETUS, *ENCHIRIDION*, 1.5

In an overly quantified world of policies and processes, some are swinging back in the other direction. Bold leaders will "trust their gut." A spiritual guru will say that it's important to "let your body guide you." A friend trying to help us with a difficult decision might ask, "What *feels* right here?"

These approaches to decision making contradict voluminous case studies in which people's instincts have led them right into trouble. Our senses are wrong all the time! As animals subjected to the slow force of evolution, we have developed all sorts of heuristics, biases, and emotional responses that might have worked well on the savannah but are totally counterproductive in today's world.

Part of Stoicism is cultivating the awareness that allows you to step back and analyze your own senses, question their accuracy, and proceed only with the positive and constructive ones. Sure, it's tempting to throw discipline and order to the wind and go with what feels right—but if our many youthful regrets are any indication, what *feels* right *right now* doesn't always stand up well over time. Hold your senses suspect. Again, trust, but always verify.

April 10th
JUDGMENTS CAUSE DISTURBANCE

"It isn't events themselves that disturb people, but only their judgments about them."

—EPICTETUS, *ENCHIRIDION*, 5

The samurai swordsman Musashi made a distinction between our "perceiving eye" and our "observing eye." The observing eye sees what is. The perceiving eye sees what things supposedly mean. Which one do you think causes us the most anguish?

An event is inanimate. It's objective. It simply is what it is. That's what our observing eye sees.

This will ruin me. How could this have happened? Ugh! It's so-and-so's fault. That's our perceiving eye at work. Bringing disturbance with it and then blaming it on the event.

April 11th
IF YOU WANT TO LEARN, BE HUMBLE

"Throw out your conceited opinions, for it is impossible for a person to begin to learn what he thinks he already knows."

—EPICTETUS, *DISCOURSES*, 2.17.1

Of all the Stoics, Epictetus is the closest one to a true teacher. He had a school. He hosted classes. In fact, his wisdom is passed down to us through a student who took really good lecture notes. One of the things that frustrated Epictetus about philosophy students—and has frustrated all college professors since time began—is how students claim to want to be taught but really secretly believe they already know everything.

The reality is that we're all guilty of thinking we know it all, and we'd all learn more if we could set that attitude aside. As smart or successful as we may be, there is always someone who is smarter, more successful, and wiser than us. Emerson put it well: "Every man I meet is my master in some point, and in that I learn of him."

If you want to learn, if you want to improve your life, seeking out teachers, philosophers, and great books is a good start. But this approach will only be effective if you're humble and ready to let go of opinions you already have.

April 12th
REJECT TANTALIZING GIFTS

"Atreus: Who would reject the flood of fortune's gifts?
Thyestes: Anyone who has experienced how easily they flow back."
—SENECA, *THYESTES*, 536

Thyestes is one of Seneca's darkest and most disturbing plays. Even two thousand years later it remains a classic of the revenge genre. Without spoiling it, the quote above comes from the scene in which Atreus is attempting to lure his hated brother Thyestes into a cruel trap by offering him tempting and generous gifts. At first, Thyestes declines, to the complete bafflement of his enemy.

We are typically surprised when someone turns down an expensive gift or a position of honor or success. General William T. Sherman emphatically rejected offers to run for president of the United States, saying at one point: "I will not accept if nominated and will not serve if elected." If his friend Ulysses S. Grant had made such a "Sherman-esque statement" (as such rejections are now known), Grant certainly would have preserved his own legacy from the disastrous turn of events it suffered.

Despite his initial misgivings, Thyestes is ultimately tempted and persuaded to accept "fortune's gifts," . . . which turned out to be a ruse hiding devastating tragedy. Not every opportunity is fraught with danger, but the play was intended to remind us that our attraction toward what is new and shiny can lead us into serious trouble.

April 13th
LESS IS MORE

"Don't act grudgingly, selfishly, without due diligence, or to be a contrarian. Don't overdress your thought in fine language. Don't be a person of too many words and too many deeds. . . . Be cheerful, not wanting outside help or the relief others might bring. A person needs to stand on their own, not be propped up."

—MARCUS AURELIUS, *MEDITATIONS*, 3.5

In most areas of life, the saying "Less is more" stands true. For instance, the writers we admire tend to be masters of economy and brevity. What they leave out is just as important—sometimes more important—than what they leave in. There is a poem by Philip Levine titled "He Would Never Use One Word Where None Would Do." And from *Hamlet*, the best of all—the retort from Queen Gertrude after a long, rhetorical speech from Polonius: "More matter with less art," she tells him. Get to the point!

Imagine the emperor of Rome, with his captive audience and unlimited power, telling himself not to be a person of "too many words and too many deeds." Let that be a reminder the next time you feel self-indulgent or a little full of yourself, the next time you feel like impressing people.

April 14th
BECOMING AN EXPERT IN WHAT MATTERS

"Believe me, it's better to produce the balance-sheet of your own
life than that of the grain market."

—SENECA, *ON THE BREVITY OF LIFE*, 18.3b

The things that some people manage to be experts in: fantasy sports, celebrity trivia, derivatives and commodities markets, thirteenth-century hygiene habits of the clergy.

We can get very good at what we're *paid* to do, or adept at a hobby we wish we could be paid to do. Yet our own lives, habits, and tendencies might be a mystery to us.

Seneca was writing this important reminder to his father-in-law, who, as it happened, was for a time in charge of Rome's granary. But then his position was revoked for political purposes. Who really cares, Seneca was saying, now you can focus that energy on your inner life.

At the end of your time on this planet, what expertise is going to be more valuable—your understanding of matters of living and dying, or your knowledge of the '87 Bears? Which will help your children more—your insight into happiness and meaning, or that you followed breaking political news every day for thirty years?

April 15th
PAY YOUR TAXES

> "Nothing will ever befall me that I will receive with gloom or a bad disposition. I will pay my taxes gladly. Now, all the things which cause complaint or dread are like the taxes of life—things from which, my dear Lucilius, you should never hope for exemption or seek escape."
>
> —SENECA, *MORAL LETTERS*, 96.2

As your income taxes come due, you might be like many people—complaining at what you have to fork over to the government. Forty percent of everything I make goes to these people? And for what?!

First off, taxes go to a lot of programs and services you almost certainly take for granted. Second, you think you're so special? People have been complaining about their taxes for thousands of years, and now they're dead. Get over it. Third, this is a good problem to have. Far better than, say, making so little there is nothing left to pay the government or living in an anarchy and having to pay for every basic service in a struggle against nature.

But more important, income taxes are not the only taxes you pay in life. They are just the financial form. Everything we do has a toll attached to it. Waiting around is a tax on traveling. Rumors and gossip are the taxes that come from acquiring a public persona. Disagreements and occasional frustration are taxes placed on even the happiest of relationships. Theft is a tax on abundance and having things that other people want. Stress and problems are tariffs that come attached to success. And on and on and on.

There are many forms of taxes in life. You can argue with them, you can go to great—but ultimately futile—lengths to evade them, or you can simply pay them and enjoy the fruits of what you get to keep.

April 16th
OBSERVE CAUSE AND EFFECT

"Pay close attention in conversation to what is being said, and to what follows from any action. In the action, immediately look for the target, in words, listen closely to what's being signaled."

—MARCUS AURELIUS, *MEDITATIONS*, 7.4

Through the work of the psychologist Albert Ellis, Stoicism has reached millions of people through what's known as cognitive-behavioral therapy (CBT). As a form of a therapy, CBT helps patients identify destructive patterns in their thoughts and behavior so they can, over time, direct and influence them in a more positive direction.

Of course, Marcus Aurelius had no formal training in psychology, but his words here are as important as any doctor's. He's asking you to become an observer of your own thoughts and the actions those thoughts provoke. Where do they come from? What biases do they contain? Are they constructive or destructive? Do they cause you to make mistakes or engage in behavior you later regret? Look for patterns; find where cause meets effect.

Only when this is done can negative behavior patterns be broken; only then can real life improvements be made.

April 17th
NO HARM, NO FOUL

"Do away with the opinion I am harmed, and the harm is cast away too. Do away with being harmed, and harm disappears."

—MARCUS AURELIUS, *MEDITATIONS*, 4.7

A word can have multiple meanings. One usage can be harsh and another might be completely innocent. The same word can mean a cruel slur or a pile of sticks. In the same way, something said sarcastically differs drastically from something that was pointed and mean.

The interpretation of a remark or a word has an immense amount of power. It's the difference between a laugh and hurt feelings. The difference between a fight breaking out and two people connecting.

This is why it is so important to control the biases and lenses we bring to our interactions. When you hear or see something, which interpretation do you jump to? What is your default interpretation of someone else's intentions?

If being upset or hurt is something you'd like to experience less often, then make sure your interpretations of others' words make that possible. Choose the right inference from someone's actions or from external events, and it's a lot more likely that you'll have the right response.

April 18th
OPINIONS ARE LIKE . . .

"What is bad luck? Opinion. What are conflict, dispute, blame, accusation, irreverence, and frivolity? They are all opinions, and more than that, they are opinions that lie outside of our own reasoned choice, presented as if they were good or evil. Let a person shift their opinions only to what belongs in the field of their own choice, and I guarantee that person will have peace of mind, whatever is happening around them."

—EPICTETUS, *DISCOURSES*, 3.3.18b–19

Opinions. Everyone's got one.

Think about all the opinions you have: about whether today's weather is convenient, about what liberals and conservatives believe, about whether so-and-so's remark is rude or not, about whether you're successful (or not), and on and on. We're constantly looking at the world around us and putting our opinion on top of it. And our opinion is often shaped by dogma (religious or cultural), entitlements, expectations, and in some cases, ignorance.

No wonder we feel upset and angry so often! But what if we let these opinions go? Let's try weeding (*ekkoptein*; cutting or knocking out) them out of our lives so that things simply *are*. Not good or bad, not colored with opinion or judgment. Just *are*.

UNBIASED THOUGHT

April 19th
OUR SPHERE OF IMPULSES

"Epictetus says we must discover the missing art of assent and pay special attention to the sphere of our impulses—that they are subject to reservation, to the common good, and that they are in proportion to actual worth."

—MARCUS AURELIUS, *MEDITATIONS*, 11.37

Here we have the emperor, the most powerful man in the world, quoting in his diary the wisdom of a former slave (and from what we know, Marcus might have had direct notes from Epictetus's lectures via one of his former students). That wisdom was ultimately about surrender and serving the common good—about the limits of our power and the importance of checking our impulses—something every person in authority needs to hear.

Power and powerlessness seem so rarely to enter the same orbit—but when they do it can change the world. Think about President Abraham Lincoln meeting with, corresponding with, and learning from Frederick Douglass, another former slave of considerable wisdom and insight.

In any case, all those men lived by the principles expressed here: that in our lives—whether we're experiencing great power or powerlessness—it's critical to leave room for what may happen and keep the common good and the actual worth of things front and center. And, above all, be willing to learn from anyone and everyone, regardless of their station in life.

April 20th
REAL GOOD IS SIMPLE

"Here's a way to think about what the masses regard as being 'good' things. If you would first start by setting your mind upon things that are unquestionably good—wisdom, self-control, justice, courage—with this preconception you'll no longer be able to listen to the popular refrain that there are too many good things to experience in a lifetime."

—MARCUS AURELIUS, *MEDITATIONS*, 5.12

Is it that controversial to say that there are the things that people value (and pressure you to value as well)—and there are the things that are actually good? Or to question whether wealth and fame are all they are cracked up to be? As Seneca observed in one of his plays:

"If only the hearts of the wealthy were opened to all!
How great the fears high fortune stirs up within them."

For centuries, people have assumed that wealth would be a wonderful cure-all for their unhappiness or problems. Why else would they have worked so hard for it? But when people actually acquired the money and status they craved, they discovered it wasn't quite what they had hoped. The same is true of so many things we covet without really thinking.

On the other hand, the "good" that the Stoics advocate is simpler and more straightforward: wisdom, self-control, justice, courage. No one who achieves these quiet virtues experiences buyer's remorse.

April 21st
DON'T LET YOUR ATTENTION SLIDE

"When you let your attention slide for a bit, don't think you will get back a grip on it whenever you wish—instead, bear in mind that because of today's mistake everything that follows will be necessarily worse. . . . Is it possible to be free from error? Not by any means, but it is possible to be a person always stretching to avoid error. For we must be content to at least escape a few mistakes by never letting our attention slide."

—EPICTETUS, *DISCOURSES*, 4.12.1; 19

Winifred Gallagher, in her book *Rapt*, quotes David Meyer, a cognitive scientist at the University of Michigan: "Einstein didn't invent the theory of relativity while he was multitasking at the Swiss patent office." It came after, when he *really* had time to focus and study. Attention matters—and in an era in which our attention is being fought for by every new app, website, article, book, tweet, and post, its value has only gone up.

Part of what Epictetus is saying here is that attention is a habit, and that letting your attention slip and wander builds bad habits and enables mistakes.

You'll never complete all your tasks if you allow yourself to be distracted with every tiny interruption. Your attention is one of your most critical resources. Don't squander it!

April 22nd
THE MARKS OF A RATIONAL PERSON

"These are the characteristics of the rational soul: self-awareness, self-examination, and self-determination. It reaps its own harvest. . . . It succeeds in its own purpose . . ."

—MARCUS AURELIUS, *MEDITATIONS*, 11.1–2

To be rational today, we have to do just three things:

First, we must look inward.
Next, we must examine ourselves critically.
Finally, we must make our own decisions—uninhibited by biases or popular notions.

April 23rd
THE MIND IS ALL YOURS

"You have been formed of three parts—body, breath, and mind. Of these, the first two are yours insofar as they are only in your care. The third alone is truly yours."

—MARCUS AURELIUS, *MEDITATIONS*, 12.3

The body can be ravaged by disease or injured or disabled in a sudden accident. It can be imprisoned or subjected to torture. The breath can suddenly cease because our time has come, or because someone has taken it from us. Breathing can grow labored because of exertion or illness as well. But up until the very end, our mind is ours.

It's not that the other two parts of life that Marcus mentions—our body and our breath—don't matter. They're just less "ours" than our mind. You wouldn't spend much time fixing up a house that you rent, would you? Our mind is ours—free and clear. Let's make sure we treat it right.

April 24th
A PRODUCTIVE USE FOR CONTEMPT

"Just as when meat or other foods are set before us we think, this is a dead fish, a dead bird or pig; and also, this fine wine is only the juice of a bunch of grapes, this purple-edged robe just sheep's wool dyed in a bit of blood from a shellfish; or of sex, that it is only rubbing private parts together followed by a spasmic discharge—in the same way our impressions grab actual events and permeate them, so we see them as they really are."

—MARCUS AURELIUS, *MEDITATIONS*, 6.13

There is one Stoic exercise that might well be described as contemptuous expressions. Stoics use an almost cynical language as a way to dismantle some of the fanciest or most coveted parts of life. Marcus's joke about sex—why would he say something like that? Well, if you take a second to consider sex in such an absurd light, you may be less likely to do something shameful or embarrassing in the pursuit of it. It's a counterbalance to the natural bias we have toward something that feels really good.

We can apply this same way of thinking to a lot of things that people prize. Consider that envy-inducing photo you see on social media—imagine the person painstakingly staging it. What about that job promotion that means so much? Look at the lives of other so-called successful people. Still think it holds magical power? Money, which we want more of and are reluctant to part with—consider how covered in bacteria and filth it is. That beautiful, perfect person you're admiring from afar? Remember that if they're single, other people must have dumped them at some point. There must be *something* wrong with them.

This exercise won't turn you into a cynic. But it will provide some much-needed objectivity.

April 25th
THERE'S NOTHING WRONG WITH BEING WRONG

"If anyone can prove and show to me that I think and act in error,
I will gladly change it—for I seek the truth, by which no one has
ever been harmed. The one who is harmed is the one who abides
in deceit and ignorance."

—MARCUS AURELIUS, *MEDITATIONS*, 6.21

Someone once attempted to argue with the philosopher Cicero by
quoting something he had said or written. This person claimed
Cicero was saying one thing now but had believed something different
in the past. His response: "I live from one day to the next! If something
strikes me as probable, I say it; and that is how, unlike everyone else, I
remain a free agent."

No one should be ashamed at changing his mind—that's what the
mind is for. "A foolish consistency is the hobgoblin of little minds,"
Emerson said, "adored by little statesmen and philosophers and
divines." That's why we go to such lengths to learn and expose ourselves to wisdom. It would be embarrassing if we *didn't* end up finding
out if we were wrong in the past.

Remember: you're a free agent. When someone points out a legiti-
mate flaw in your belief or in your actions, they're not criticizing you.
They're presenting a better alternative. Accept it!

April 26th
THINGS HAPPEN IN TRAINING

"When your sparring partner scratches or head-butts you, you don't then make a show of it, or protest, or view him with suspicion or as plotting against you. And yet you keep an eye on him, not as an enemy or with suspicion, but with a healthy avoidance. You should act this way with all things in life. We should give a pass to many things with our fellow trainees. For, as I've said, it's possible to avoid without suspicion or hate."

—MARCUS AURELIUS, *MEDITATIONS*, 6.20

By seeing each day and each situation as a kind of training exercise, the stakes suddenly become a lot lower. The way you interpret your own mistakes and the mistakes of others is suddenly a lot more generous. It's certainly a more resilient attitude than going around acting like the stakes of every encounter put the championship on the line.

When you catch an elbow or an unfair blow today, shake off the pain and remind yourself: *I'm learning. My sparring partner is learning too. This is practice for both of us—that's all. I know a bit more about him or her, and from my reaction, they're going to learn a little bit more about me too.*

TURN IT INSIDE OUT

"Turn it inside out and see what it is like—what it becomes like when old, sick, or prostituting itself. How short-lived the praiser and praised, the one who remembers and the remembered. Remembered in some corner of these parts, and even there not in the same way by all, or even by one. And the whole earth is but a mere speck."

—MARCUS AURELIUS, *MEDITATIONS*, 8.21

Stoicism is about looking at things from every angle—and certain situations are easier to understand from different perspectives. In potentially negative situations, the objective, even superficial gaze might actually be superior. That view might let us see things clearly without diving too much into what they might represent or what might have caused them. In other situations, particularly those that involve something impressive or praiseworthy, another approach, like that of contemptuous expressions, is helpful. By examining situations from the inside out, we can be less daunted by them, less likely to be swayed by them.

Dig into your fear of death or obscurity, and what will you find? Turn some fancy ceremony inside out and you'll find—what?

UNBIASED THOUGHT   129

April 28th
WANTS MAKE YOU A SERVANT

"Tantalus: The highest power is—
Thyestes: No power, if you desire nothing."

—SENECA, *THYESTES*, 440

In the modern world, our interactions with tyranny are a bit more voluntary than they were in ancient times. We put up with our controlling boss, though we could probably get a different job if we wanted. We change how we dress or refrain from saying what we actually think? Because we want to fit in with some cool group. We put up with cruel critics or customers? Because we want their approval. In these cases, their power exists because of our wants. You change that, and you're free.

The late fashion photographer Bill Cunningham occasionally declined to invoice magazines for his work. When a young upstart asked him why that was, Cunningham's response was epic: "If you don't take money, they can't tell you what to do, kid."

Remember: taking the money, wanting the money—proverbially or literally—makes you a servant to the people who have it. Indifference to it, as Seneca put it, turns the highest power into *no power*, at least as far as your life is concerned.

April 29th
WASHING AWAY THE DUST OF LIFE

"Watch the stars in their courses and imagine yourself running alongside them. Think constantly on the changes of the elements into each other, for such thoughts wash away the dust of earthly life."

—MARCUS AURELIUS, *MEDITATIONS*, 7.47

It is almost impossible to stare up at the stars and not feel something. As cosmologist Neil deGrasse Tyson has explained, the cosmos fills us with complicated emotions. On the one hand, we feel an infinitesimal smallness in comparison to the vast universe; on the other, an extreme connectedness to this larger whole.

Obviously, given that we're in our bodies every day, it's tempting to think that's the most important thing in the world. But we counteract that bias by looking at nature—at things much bigger than us. A line from Seneca, which has since become a proverb, expresses Marcus's insight well: *Mundus ipse est ingens deorum omnium templum* (The world itself is a huge temple of all the gods).

Looking at the beautiful expanse of the sky is an antidote to the nagging pettiness of earthly concerns. And it is good and sobering to lose yourself in that as often as you can.

April 30th
WHAT IS IN KEEPING WITH YOUR CHARACTER?

"Just as what is considered rational or irrational differs for each person, in the same way what is good or evil and useful or useless differs for each person. This is why we need education, so that we might learn how to adjust our preconceived notions of the rational and irrational in harmony with nature. In sorting this out, we don't simply rely on our estimate of the value of external things, but also apply the rule of what is in keeping with one's character."

—EPICTETUS, *DISCOURSES*, 1.2.5–7

It is easy to get wrapped up in our own opinions of things. It's as if we're adhering to invisible scripts—following instructions or patterns we don't even understand. The more you question these scripts and the more you subject them to the rigorous test of your education, the more you'll be your own compass. You'll have convictions and thoughts that are your own and belong to no one else.

Character is a powerful defense in a world that would love to be able to seduce you, buy you, tempt you, and change you. If you know what you believe and why you believe it, you'll avoid poisonous relationships, toxic jobs, fair-weather friends, and any number of ills that afflict people who haven't thought through their deepest concerns. That's your education. That's why you do this work.

PART II

The **DISCIPLINE** *of* **ACTION**

MAY

RIGHT ACTION

May 1st
MAKE CHARACTER YOUR LOUDEST STATEMENT

"For philosophy doesn't consist in outward display, but in taking
heed to what is needed and being mindful of it."

—MUSONIUS RUFUS, *LECTURES*, 16.75.15–16

The monk dresses in his robes. A priest puts on his collar. A banker
wears an expensive suit and carries a briefcase. A Stoic has no uniform and resembles no stereotype. They are not identifiable by look or
by sight or by sound.

The only way to recognize them? By their character.

May 2nd
BE THE PERSON YOU WANT TO BE

"First tell yourself what kind of person you want to be, then do what you have to do. For in nearly every pursuit we see this to be the case. Those in athletic pursuit first choose the sport they want, and then do that work."

—EPICTETUS, *DISCOURSES*, 3.23.1–2a

An archer is highly unlikely to hit a target she did not aim for. The same goes for you, whatever your target. You are *certain* to miss the target if you don't bother to draw back and fire. Our perceptions and principles guide us in the selection of what we want—but ultimately our actions determine whether we get there or not.

So yes, spend some time—real, uninterrupted time—thinking about what's important to you, what your priorities are. Then, *work* toward that and forsake all the others. It's not enough to wish and hope. One must *act*—and act right.

May 3rd
SHOW, NOT TELL, WHAT YOU KNOW

"Those who receive the bare theories immediately want to spew them, as an upset stomach does its food. First digest your theories and you won't throw them up. Otherwise they will be raw, spoiled, and not nourishing. After you've digested them, show us the changes in your reasoned choices, just like the shoulders of gymnasts display their diet and training, and as the craft of artisans show in what they've learned."

—EPICTETUS, *DISCOURSES*, 3.21.1–3

Many of the Stoic aphorisms are simple to remember and even sound smart when quoted. But that's not what philosophy is really about. The goal is to turn these words into *works*. As Musonius Rufus put it, the justification for philosophy is when "one brings together sound teaching with sound conduct."

Today, or anytime, when you catch yourself wanting to condescendingly drop some knowledge that you have, grab it and ask: *Would I be better saying words or letting my actions and choices illustrate that knowledge for me?*

May 4th
WHAT'S TRULY IMPRESSIVE

"How much better is it to be known for doing well by many than for living extravagantly? How much more worthy than spending on sticks and stones is it to spend on people?"

—MUSONIUS RUFUS, *LECTURES*, 19.91.26–28

Think of all you know about the lifestyles of the rich and the famous. That so-and-so bought a home for so many millions. That so-and-so travels with their own barber. That so-and-so owns a pet tiger or an elephant.

The exact same gossip and notoriety was popular in Roman times. Certain Romans were known for the thousands of sesterces they spent on their koi ponds. Others were notorious for orgiastic parties and sumptuous feasts. The works of Roman poets such as Juvenal and Martial abound with tidbits about these types.

The conspicuously wealthy earn and ultimately get what they want out of spending: their reputation. But what an empty one! Is it really that impressive to spend, spend, spend? Given the funds, who *wouldn't* be able to do that?

Marcus Aurelius courageously sold off some of the imperial furnishings to pay down war debts. More recently, José Mujica, the former president of Uruguay, stood out for giving 90 percent of his presidential salary to charity and driving a twenty-five-year-old car. Who can do stuff like that? Not everyone. So who's the more impressive?

May 5th
YOU ARE THE PROJECT

"The raw material for the work of a good and excellent person is their own guiding reason, the body is that of the doctor and the physical trainer, and the farm the farmer's."

—EPICTETUS, *DISCOURSES*, 3.3.1

Professionals don't have to justify spending time training or practicing their work. It's what they do, and practice is how they get good at it. The raw materials vary from career to career, just as the locations and duration vary depending on the person and the profession. But the one constant is the working of those materials, the gradual improvements and proficiency.

According to the Stoics, your mind is the asset that must be worked on most—and understood best.

May 6th
RIGHTEOUSNESS IS BEAUTIFUL

"Then what makes a beautiful human being? Isn't it the presence of human excellence? Young friend, if you wish to be beautiful, then work diligently at human excellence. And what is that? Observe those whom you praise without prejudice. The just or the unjust? The just. The even-tempered or the undisciplined? The even-tempered. The self-controlled or the uncontrolled? The self-controlled. In making yourself that kind of person, you will become beautiful—but to the extent you ignore these qualities, you'll be ugly, even if you use every trick in the book to appear beautiful."

—EPICTETUS, *DISCOURSES*, 3.1.6b–9

Contemporary notions of beauty are ridiculous. Our standards for what's attractive are incredibly *un*-Stoic in that we prize and extol things people have almost no control over—high cheekbones, complexion, height, piercing eyes.

Is it really beautiful to win the genetic lottery? Or should beauty be contingent on the choices, actions, and attributes we develop? An even keel, a sense of justice, a commitment to duty. These are beautiful traits—and they go much deeper than appearances.

Today, you can choose to be without prejudice, to act with justice, to keep an even keel, to be in control of yourself—even when that means dedication and sacrifice. If that's not beautiful, what is?

May 7th
HOW TO HAVE A GOOD DAY

"God laid down this law, saying: if you want some good, get it from
  yourself."

—EPICTETUS, *DISCOURSES*, 1.29.4

Here is how to *guarantee* you have a good day: do good things.
  Any other source of joy is outside your control or is nonrenewable. But this one is all you, all the time, and unending. It is the ultimate form of self-reliance.

May 8th
GOOD AND EVIL? LOOK AT YOUR CHOICES

"Where is Good? In our reasoned choices. Where is Evil? In our reasoned choices. Where is that which is neither Good nor Evil? In the things outside of our own reasoned choice."

—Epictetus, *Discourses*, 2.16.1

Today, as things happen and you find yourself wondering what they all mean—as you find yourself contemplating various decisions, remember: the right thing to do always comes from our reasoned choice. Not whether something is rewarded. Not whether something will succeed, but whether it is the right *choice*.

Epictetus's dictum helps us cut through all this with clarity and confidence. Is something good or bad? Is this right or wrong?

Ignore everything else. Focus only on your choices.

May 9th
CARPE DIEM

"Let us therefore set out whole-heartedly, leaving aside our many distractions and exert ourselves in this single purpose, before we realize too late the swift and unstoppable flight of time and are left behind. As each day arises, welcome it as the very best day of all, and make it your own possession. We must seize what flees."

—SENECA, *MORAL LETTERS*, 108.27b–28a

You will only get one shot at today. You have only twenty-four hours with which to take it. And then it is gone and lost forever. Will you fully inhabit all of today? Will you call out, "I've got this," and do your very best to be your very best?

What will you manage to make of today before it slips from your fingers and becomes the past? When someone asks you what you did yesterday, do you really want the answer to be "nothing"?

May 10th
DON'T BE INSPIRED, BE INSPIRATIONAL

"Let us also produce some bold act of our own—and join the ranks of the most emulated."

—SENECA, *MORAL LETTERS*, 98.13b

It was common in Greek and Roman times, just as it is now, for politicians to pander to their audience. They would lavish effusive praise on the crowd, on their country, on inspiring military victories of the past. How many times have you heard a political candidate say, "This is the greatest country in the history of the world"? As orator Demosthenes pointed out, we'll gladly sit for hours to hear a speaker who stands in front of some famous or sacred landmark, "praising [our] ancestors, describing their exploits and enumerating their trophies."

But what does this flattery accomplish? Nothing. Worse, the admiration of shiny accolades distracts us from their true purpose. Also, as Demosthenes explains, it betrays the very ancestors who inspire us. He concluded his speech to the Athenian people with words that Seneca would later echo and still resounds centuries later. "Reflect, then," he said, "that your ancestors set up those trophies, not that you may gaze at them in wonder, but that you may also imitate the virtues of the men who set them up."

The same goes for the quotes in this book and for other inspiring words you might hear. Don't just admire them. Use them. Follow their example.

May 11th
GUILT IS WORSE THAN JAIL

"The greatest portion of peace of mind is doing nothing wrong.
Those who lack self-control live disoriented and disturbed lives."
—SENECA, *MORAL LETTERS*, 105.7

Consider the fugitives who willingly turn themselves in after years on the run. Why would they do that? They were free, one step ahead of the law, but they gave up! Because the guilt and the stress of the fugitive life eventually gets worse than the prospect of lost freedom—in fact, it was its own kind of prison.

It's the same reason why, as a child, you might have confessed to a lie to completely unsuspecting parents. It's the reason why one partner might voluntarily admit to a crushing infidelity—even though the other partner had no idea. "Why are you telling me this?!" the betrayed shouts as she walks out the door. "Because things have been going so well and I couldn't take it anymore!"

There are immense costs of doing wrong, not only to society, but to the perpetrator. Look at the lives of most people who reject ethics and discipline, and the chaos and misery that so often follows. This punishment is almost always as bad or worse than whatever society metes out.

This is why so many petty criminals confess or voluntarily surrender. They don't always stick to it, but at the lowest moment, they finally realize: this is no way to live. They want the peace of mind that comes with doing *right*. And so do you.

May 12th
KINDNESS IS ALWAYS THE RIGHT RESPONSE

"Kindness is invincible, but only when it's sincere, with no hypocrisy or faking. For what can even the most malicious person do if you keep showing kindness and, if given the chance, you gently point out where they went wrong—right as they are trying to harm you?"

—MARCUS AURELIUS, *MEDITATIONS*, 11.18.5.9a

What if the next time you were treated meanly, you didn't just restrain yourself from fighting back—what if you responded with unmitigated kindness? What if you could "love your enemies, do good to those who hate you"? What kind of effect do you think that would have?

The Bible says that when you can do something nice and caring to a hateful enemy, it is like "heap[ing] burning coals on his head." The expected reaction to hatred is more hatred. When someone says something pointed or mean today, they expect you to respond in kind—not with *kindness*. When that doesn't happen, they are embarrassed. It's a shock to their system—it makes them and you better.

Most rudeness, meanness, and cruelty are a mask for deep-seated weakness. Kindness in these situations is only possible for people of great strength. You have that strength. Use it.

FUELING THE HABIT BONFIRE

"Every habit and capability is confirmed and grows in its corresponding actions, walking by walking, and running by running . . . therefore, if you want to do something make a habit of it, if you don't want to do that, don't, but make a habit of something else instead. The same principle is at work in our state of mind. When you get angry, you've not only experienced that evil, but you've also reinforced a bad habit, adding fuel to the fire."

—EPICTETUS, *DISCOURSES*, 2.18.1–5

"We are what we repeatedly do," Aristotle said, "therefore, excellence is not an act but a habit." The Stoics add to that that we are a product of our thoughts ("Such as are your habitual thoughts, such also will be the character of your mind," Marcus Aurelius put it).

Think about your activities of the last week as well as what you have planned for today and the week that follows. The person you'd like to be, or the person you see yourself as—how closely do your actions actually correspond to him or her? Which fire are you fueling? Which person are you becoming?

May 14th
OUR WELL-BEING LIES IN OUR ACTIONS

"Those obsessed with glory attach their well-being to the regard of others, those who love pleasure tie it to feelings, but the one with true understanding seeks it only in their own actions. . . . Think on the character of the people one wishes to please, the possessions one means to gain, and the tactics one employs to such ends. How quickly time erases such things, and how many has it wiped away already."

—MARCUS AURELIUS, *MEDITATIONS*, 6:51, 59

If your happiness is dependent on accomplishing certain goals, what happens if fate intervenes? What if you're snubbed? If outside events interrupt? What if you do achieve everything but find that nobody is impressed? That's the problem with letting your happiness be determined by things you can't control. It's an insane risk.

If an actor focuses on the public reception to a project—whether critics like it or whether it's a hit, they will be constantly disappointed and hurt. But if they love their *performance*—and put everything they have into making it the best that they're capable of—they will always find satisfaction in their job. Like them, we should take pleasure from our actions—in taking the right actions—rather than the results that come from them.

Our ambition should not be to win, then, but to play with our full effort. Our intention is not to be thanked or recognized, but to help and to do what we think is right. Our focus is not on what happens to us but on how we respond. In this, we will always find contentment and resilience.

May 15th
COUNT YOUR BLESSINGS

"Don't set your mind on things you don't possess as if they were yours, but count the blessings you actually possess and think how much you would desire them if they weren't already yours. But watch yourself, that you don't value these things to the point of being troubled if you should lose them."

—MARCUS AURELIUS, *MEDITATIONS*, 7.27

We regularly covet what other people have. We desperately try to keep up with the Joneses, all the while the Joneses are miserable trying to keep up with us.

It would be funny if it weren't so sad. So today, stop trying to get what other people have. Fight your urge to gather and hoard. That's not the right way to live and act. Appreciate and take advantage of what you already do have, and let that attitude guide your actions.

May 16th
THE CHAIN METHOD

"If you don't wish to be a hot-head, don't feed your habit. Try as a first step to remain calm and count the days you haven't been angry. I used to be angry every day, now every other day, then every third or fourth . . . if you make it as far as 30 days, thank God! For habit is first weakened and then obliterated. When you can say 'I didn't lose my temper today, or the next day, or for three or four months, but kept my cool under provocation,' you will know you are in better health."

—EPICTETUS, *DISCOURSES*, 2.18.11b–14

The comedian Jerry Seinfeld once gave a young comic named Brad Isaac some advice about how to write and create material. Keep a calendar, he told him, and each day that you write jokes, put an X. Soon enough, you get a chain going—and then your job is to simply *not* break the chain. Success becomes a matter of momentum. Once you get a little, it's easier to keep it going.

Whereas Seinfeld used the chain method to build a positive habit, Epictetus was saying that it can also be used to eliminate a negative one. It's not all that different than taking sobriety "one day at a time." Start with one day doing whatever it is, be it managing your temper or wandering eyes or procrastination. Then do the same the following day and the day after that. Build a chain and then work not to break it. Don't ruin your streak.

May 17th
THE STOIC IS A WORK IN PROGRESS

"Show me someone sick and happy, in danger and happy, dying
and happy, exiled and happy, disgraced and happy. Show me! By
God, how much I'd like to see a Stoic. But since you can't show
me someone that perfectly formed, at least show me someone
actively forming themselves so, inclined in this way. . . . Show me!"

—EPICTETUS, *DISCOURSES*, 2.19.24–25a, 28

Instead of seeing philosophy as an end to which one aspires, see it as
something one *applies*. Not occasionally, but over the course of a life—
making incremental progress along the way. Sustained execution, not
shapeless epiphanies.

Epictetus loved to shake his students out of their smug satisfaction
with their own progress. He wanted to remind them—and now you—
of the constant work and serious training needed every day if we are
ever to approach that perfect form.

It's important for us to remember in our own journey to self-
improvement: one never *arrives*. The sage—the perfect Stoic who
behaves perfectly in every situation—is an ideal, not an end.

May 18th
HOW YOU DO ANYTHING IS HOW YOU DO EVERYTHING

"Pay attention to what's in front of you—the principle, the task, or what's being portrayed."

—MARCUS AURELIUS, *MEDITATIONS*, 8.22

It's fun to think about the future. It's easy to ruminate on the past. It's harder to put that energy into what's in front of us right at this moment—especially if it's something we don't want to do. We think: *This is just a job; it isn't who I am. It doesn't matter.* But it does matter. Who knows—it might be the last thing you ever do. Here lies Dave, buried alive under a mountain of unfinished business.

There is an old saying: "How you do anything is how you do everything." It's true. How you handle today is how you'll handle every day. How you handle this minute is how you'll handle every minute.

May 19th
LEARN, PRACTICE, TRAIN

"That's why the philosophers warn us not to be satisfied with mere learning, but to add practice and then training. For as time passes we forget what we learned and end up doing the opposite, and hold opinions the opposite of what we should."

—EPICTETUS, *DISCOURSES*, 2.9.13–14

Very few people can simply watch an instructional video or hear something explained and then know, backward and forward, how to do it. Most of us actually have to *do* something several times in order to truly learn. One of the hallmarks of the martial arts, military training, and athletic training of almost any kind is the hours upon hours upon hours of monotonous practice. An athlete at the highest level will train for years to perform movements that can last mere seconds—or less. The two-minute drill, how to escape from a chokehold, the perfect jumper. Simply knowing isn't enough. It must be absorbed into the muscles and the body. It must become part of us. Or we risk losing it the second that we experience stress or difficulty.

It is true with philosophical principles as well. You can't just hear something once and expect to rely on it when the world is crashing down around us. Remember, Marcus Aurelius wasn't writing his meditations for other people. He was actively meditating *for himself*. Even as a successful, wise, and experienced man, he was until the last days of his life practicing and training himself to do the right thing. Like a black belt, he was still showing up to the dojo every day to roll; like a professional athlete, he still showed up to practice each week—even though others probably thought it was unnecessary.

May 20th
QUALITY OVER QUANTITY

"What's the point of having countless books and libraries, whose
titles could hardly be read through in a lifetime. The learner is not
taught, but burdened by the sheer volume, and it's better to plant
the seeds of a few authors than to be scattered about by many."
—SENECA, *ON TRANQUILITY OF MIND*, 9.4

There is no prize for having read the most books before you die.
Even if you were the most dedicated reader in the world—a book
a day, even—your collection would probably never be bigger than a small
branch library. You'll never even come close to matching what's stored
in the servers at Google Books or keep up with the hundreds of thousands of new titles published on Amazon each year.

What if, when it came to your reading and learning, you prioritized
quality over quantity? What if you read the few great books deeply
instead of briefly skimming all the new books? Your shelves might be
emptier, but your brain and your life would be fuller.

May 21st
WHAT KIND OF BOXER ARE YOU?

"But what is philosophy? Doesn't it simply mean preparing our-selves for what may come? Don't you understand that really amounts to saying that if I would so prepare myself to endure, then let anything happen that will? Otherwise, it would be like the boxer exiting the ring because he took some punches. Actu-ally, you can leave the boxing ring without consequence, but what advantage would come from abandoning the pursuit of wisdom? So, what should each of us say to every trial we face? This is what I've trained for, for this my discipline!"

—EPICTETUS, *DISCOURSES*, 3.10.6–7

The Stoics loved to use boxing and wrestling metaphors the way we use baseball and football analogies today. This is probably because the sport of *pankration*—literally, "all strength," but a purer form of mixed martial arts than one sees today in the UFC—was integral to boy-hood and manhood in Greece and Rome. (In fact, recent analysis has found instances of "cauliflower ear," a common grappling injury, on Greek statues.) The Stoics refer to fighting because it's what they knew.

Seneca writes that unbruised prosperity is weak and easy to defeat in the ring, but "a man who has been at constant feud with misfortunes acquires a skin calloused by suffering." This man, he says, fights all the way to the ground and never gives up.

That's what Epictetus means too. What kind of boxer are you if you leave because you get hit? That's the nature of the sport! Is that going to stop you from continuing?

May 22nd
TODAY IS THE DAY

"You get what you deserve. Instead of being a good person today, you choose instead to become one tomorrow."
—Marcus Aurelius, *Meditations*, 8.22

"I don't complain about the lack of time . . . what little I have will go far enough. Today—this day—will achieve what no tomorrow will fail to speak about. I will lay siege to the gods and shake up the world."
—Seneca, *Medea*, 423–425

We almost always know *what* the right thing is. We know we should not get upset, that we shouldn't take this personally, that we should walk to the health food store instead of swinging by the drive-through, that we need to sit down and focus for an hour. The tougher part is deciding to do it in a given moment.

What stops us? The author Steven Pressfield calls this force The Resistance. As he put it in *The War of Art*, "We don't tell ourselves, 'I'm never going to write my symphony.' Instead we say, 'I'm going to write my symphony; I'm just going to start tomorrow.'"

Today, not tomorrow, is the day that we can start to be good.

May 23rd
SHOW ME HOW TO LIVE

"Show me that the good life doesn't consist in its length, but in its use, and that it is possible—no, entirely too common—for a person who has had a long life to have lived too little."

—SENECA, *MORAL LETTERS*, 49.10b

There's no need to show Seneca. Show yourself. That no matter how many years you're ultimately given, your life can be clearly and earnestly said to have been a long and full one. We all know someone like that—someone we lost too early but even now think, *If I could do half of what they did, I'll consider my life well lived.*

The best way to get there is by focusing on what is here right now, on the task you have at hand—big or small. As he says, by pouring ourselves fully and intentionally into the present, it "gentle[s] the passing of time's precipitous flight."

May 24th
MAKING YOUR OWN GOOD FORTUNE

"You say, good fortune used to meet you at every corner. But the fortunate person is the one who gives themselves a good fortune. And good fortunes are a well-tuned soul, good impulses and good actions."

—MARCUS AURELIUS, *MEDITATIONS*, 5.36

What is the more productive notion of good luck? One that is defined by totally random factors outside your control, or a matter of probability that can be increased—though not guaranteed—by the right decisions and the right preparation? Obviously, the latter. This is why successful yet mysteriously "lucky" people seem to gravitate toward it.

According to the wonderful site Quote Investigator, versions of this idea date back at least to the sixteenth century in the proverb "Diligence is the mother of good luck." In the 1920s, Coleman Cox put a modern spin on it by saying, "I am a great believer in luck. The harder I work, the more of it I seem to have." (That saying has been incorrectly attributed to Thomas Jefferson, who said nothing of the kind.) Today, we say, "Luck is where hard work meets opportunity." Or is it typically flipped?

Today, you can hope that good fortune and good luck magically come your way. Or you can prepare yourself to get lucky by focusing on doing the right thing at the right time—and, ironically, render luck mostly unnecessary in the process.

May 25th
WHERE TO FIND JOY

"Joy for human beings lies in proper human work. And proper human work consists in: acts of kindness to other human beings, disdain for the stirrings of the senses, identifying trustworthy impressions, and contemplating the natural order and all that happens in keeping with it."

—MARCUS AURELIUS, *MEDITATIONS*, 8.26

When dog trainers are brought in to work with a dysfunctional or unhappy dog, they usually start with one question: "Do you take it for walks?" They ask because dogs were bred to do certain tasks—to do work—and when deprived of this essential part of their nature, they suffer and act out. This is true no matter how spoiled and nice their life might be.

The same is true for humans. When you hear the Stoics brush aside certain emotions or material luxuries, it's not because they don't enjoy them. It's not because the Stoic life is one bereft of happiness or fun. The Stoics simply mean to help us find our essence—to experience the joy of our proper human work.

May 26th
STOP CARING WHAT PEOPLE THINK

"I'm constantly amazed by how easily we love ourselves above all
others, yet we put more stock in the opinions of others than in
our own estimation of self. . . . How much credence we give to the
opinions our peers have of us and how little to our very own!"
—MARCUS AURELIUS, *MEDITATIONS*, 12.4

How quickly we can disregard our own feelings about something
and adopt someone else's. We think a shirt looks good at the store
but will view it with shame and scorn if our spouse or a coworker makes
an offhand remark. We can be immensely happy with our own lives—
until we find out that someone we don't even like has more. Or worse
and more precariously, we don't feel good about our accomplishments
or talents until some third party validates them.

Like most Stoic exercises, this one attempts to teach us that although
we control our own opinions, we don't control what other people think—
about us least of all. For this reason, putting ourselves at the mercy of
those opinions and trying to gain the approval of others are a dangerous endeavor.

Don't spend much time thinking about what other people think.
Think about what *you* think. Think instead about the results, about
the impact, about whether *it is the right thing to do.*

May 27th
SWEAT THE SMALL STUFF

"Well-being is realized by small steps, but is truly no small thing."
—ZENO, QUOTED IN DIOGENES LAERTIUS,
LIVES OF THE EMINENT PHILOSOPHERS, 7.1.26

The famous biographer Diogenes Laertius attributes this quote to Zeno but admits that it might have also been said by Socrates, meaning that it may be a quote of a quote of a quote. But does it really matter? Truth is truth.

In this case, the truth is one we know well: the little things add up. Someone is a good person not because they say they are, but because they take good actions. One does not magically get one's act together—it is a matter of many individual choices. It's a matter of getting up at the right time, making your bed, resisting shortcuts, investing in yourself, doing your work. And make no mistake: while the individual action is small, its cumulative impact is not.

Think about all the small choices that will roll themselves out in front of you today. Do you know which are the right way and which are the easy way? Choose the right way, and watch as all these little things add up toward transformation.

May 28th
THE FIRST TWO THINGS BEFORE ACTING

"The first thing to do—don't get worked up. For everything happens according to the nature of all things, and in a short time you'll be nobody and nowhere, even as the great emperors Hadrian and Augustus are now. The next thing to do—consider carefully the task at hand for what it is, while remembering that your purpose is to be a good human being. Get straight to doing what nature requires of you, and speak as you see most just and fitting—with kindness, modesty, and sincerity."

—MARCUS AURELIUS, *MEDITATIONS*, 8.5

Imagine, for a second, what Marcus's life as an emperor must have been like. He would preside over the Senate. He would lead the troops in battle, direct the grand strategy of the army as its highest commander. He would also hear appeals—from citizens, from lawyers, from foreign governments. In other words, like most people in power, he was called on to make decisions: all day, every day, decision after decision.

His formula for decision making is a battle-tested method for doing and acting right—literally. Which is why we ought to try to use it ourselves.

First, don't get upset—because that will color your decision negatively and make it harder than it needs to be.

Second, remember the purpose and principles you value most. Running potential actions through this filter will eliminate the bad choices and highlight the right ones.

Don't get upset.

Do the right thing.

That's it.

May 29th
WORK IS THERAPY

"Work nourishes noble minds."

—SENECA, *MORAL LETTERS*, 31.5

You know that feeling you get when you haven't been to the gym in a few days? A bit doughy. Irritable. Claustrophobic. Uncertain. Others get a similar feeling when they've been on vacation for too long or right after they first retire. The mind and the body are there to be used—they begin to turn on themselves when not put to some productive end.

It's sad to think that this kind of frustration is an everyday reality for a lot of people. They leave so much of their potential unfulfilled because they have jobs where they don't really do much or because they have too much time on their hands. Worse is when we try to push these feelings away by buying things, going out, fighting, creating drama—indulging in the empty calories of existence instead of finding the real nourishment.

The solution is simple and, thankfully, always right at hand. Get out there and work.

May 30th
WORKING HARD OR HARDLY WORKING?

"I can't call a person a hard worker just because I hear they read and write, even if working at it all night. Until I know what a person is working for, I can't deem them industrious. . . . I *can* if the end they work for is their own ruling principle, having it be and remain in constant harmony with Nature."

—EPICTETUS, *DISCOURSES*, 4.4.41; 43

What are the chances that the busiest person you know is actually the most productive? We tend to associate busyness with goodness and believe that spending many hours at work should be rewarded.

Instead, evaluate *what* you are doing, *why* you are doing it, and *where* accomplishing it will take you. If you don't have a good answer, then stop.

May 31st
WE HAVE BUT ONE OBLIGATION

"What is your vocation? To be a good person."

—MARCUS AURELIUS, *MEDITATIONS*, 11.5

The Stoics believed, above all else, that our job on this earth is to be a good human being. It is a basic duty, yet we are experts at coming up with excuses for avoiding it.

To quote Belichick again: "Do your job."

JUNE

PROBLEM SOLVING

June 1st
ALWAYS HAVE A MENTAL REVERSE CLAUSE

"Indeed, no one can thwart the purposes of your mind—for they can't be touched by fire, steel, tyranny, slander, or anything."

—MARCUS AURELIUS, *MEDITATIONS*, 8.41

Obstacles are a part of life—things happen, stuff gets in our way, situations go awry. But nothing can stop the Stoic mind when it's operating properly, because in every course of action, it has retained "a reverse clause."

What's that? It's a backup option. If a friend betrays us, our reverse clause is to learn from how this happened and how to forgive this person's mistake. If we're thrown in prison, our reverse clause is that we can refuse to be broken by this change of events and try to be of service to our fellow prisoners. When a technical glitch erases our work, our reverse clause is that we can start fresh and do it better this time. Our progress can be impeded or disrupted, but the mind can always be changed—it retains the power to redirect the path.

Part of this is remembering the usual course of things—Murphy's Law states that "if anything can go wrong, it will." So we keep this reverse clause handy because we know we're probably going to have to use it. No one can thwart that.

June 2nd
PLATO'S VIEW

> "How beautifully Plato put it. Whenever you want to talk about people, it's best to take a bird's-eye view and see everything all at once—of gatherings, armies, farms, weddings and divorces, births and deaths, noisy courtrooms or silent spaces, every foreign people, holidays, memorials, markets—all blended together and arranged in a pairing of opposites."
>
> —MARCUS AURELIUS, *MEDITATIONS*, 7.48

There is a beautiful dialogue called "Icaromenippus, an Aerial Expedition" by the poet Lucian in which the narrator is given the ability to fly and sees the world from above. Turning his eyes earthward, he sees how comically small even the richest people, the biggest estates, and entire empires look from above. All their battles and concerns were made petty in perspective.

In ancient times, this exercise was only theoretical—the highest anyone could get was the top of a mountain or a building a few stories tall. But as technology has progressed, humans have been able to actually take that bird's-eye view—and greater.

Edgar Mitchell, an astronaut, was one of the first people to see the earth from outer space. As he later recounted:

> "In outer space you develop an instant global consciousness, a people orientation, an intense dissatisfaction with the state of the world, and a compulsion to do something about it. From out there on the moon, international politics look so petty. You want to grab a politician by the scruff of the neck and drag him a quarter of a million miles out and say, 'Look at that, you son of a bitch.'"

Many a problem can be solved with the perspective of Plato's view. Use it.

June 3rd
IT IS WELL TO BE FLEXIBLE

"He can't serve in the military? Let him seek public office. Must he live in the private sector? Let him be a spokesperson. Is he condemned to silence? Let him aid his fellow citizens by silent public witness. Is it dangerous to enter the Forum? Let him display himself, in private homes, at public events and gatherings, as a good associate, faithful friend, and moderate tablemate. Has he lost the duties of a citizen? Let him exercise those of a human being."

—SENECA, *ON TRANQUILITY OF MIND*, 4.3

Shortly before his death, as victory in the Civil War was finally within his grasp, Lincoln told a story to an audience of generals and admirals about a man who had approached him for a high-ranking government appointment. First, the man asked if he might be made a foreign minister. Upon being turned down, the man asked for a more modest position. Upon being turned down again, he asked for a job as a low-level customs officer. Finding he could not get even that, he finally just asked Lincoln for an old pair of trousers. "Ah," Lincoln laughed as he concluded the story, "it is well to be humble."

This story embodies the flexibility and determination of Stoicism. If we can't do *this*, then perhaps we can try *that*. And if we can't do *that*, then perhaps we can try some *other* thing. And if that thing is impossible, there is always another. Even if that final thing is just being a good human being—we always have some opportunity to practice our philosophy, to make some contribution.

June 4th
THIS IS WHAT WE'RE HERE FOR

"Why then are we offended? Why do we complain? This is what
  we're here for."

—SENECA, *ON PROVIDENCE*, 5.7b–8

No one said life was easy. No one said it would be fair.
 Don't forget, though, that you come from a long, unbroken line
of ancestors who survived unimaginable adversity, difficulty, and struggle. It's their genes and their blood that run through your body right
now. Without them, you wouldn't be here.

You're an heir to an impressive tradition—and as their viable off-
spring, you're capable of what they are capable of. You're meant for
this. Bred for it.

Just something to keep in mind if things get tough.

June 5th
BLOW YOUR OWN NOSE

"We cry to God Almighty, how can we escape this agony? Fool, don't you have hands? Or could it be God forgot to give you a pair? Sit and pray your nose doesn't run! Or, rather just wipe your nose and stop seeking a scapegoat."

—EPICTETUS, *DISCOURSES*, 2.16.13

The world is unfair. The game is rigged. So-and-so has it out for you. Maybe these theories are true, but practically speaking—for the right here and now—what good are they to you? That government report or that sympathetic news article isn't going to pay the bills or rehab your broken leg or find that bridge loan you need. Succumbing to the self-pity and "woe is me" narrative accomplishes nothing—nothing except sapping you of the energy and motivation you need to *do something about your problem.*

We have a choice: Do we focus on the ways we have been wronged, or do we use what we've been given and get to work? Will we wait for someone to save us, or will we listen to Marcus Aurelius's empowering call to "get active in your own rescue—if you care for yourself at all— and do it while you can." That's better than just blowing your own nose (which is a step forward in itself).

June 6th
WHEN TO STICK AND WHEN TO QUIT

"Think of those who, not by fault of inconsistency but by lack of
effort, are too unstable to live as they wish, but only live as they
have begun."

—Seneca, *On Tranquility of Mind*, 2.6b

In *The Dip*, Seth Godin draws an interesting analogy from the three
types of people you see in line at the supermarket. One gets in a short
line and sticks to it no matter how slow it is or how much faster the
others seem to be going. Another changes lines repeatedly based on
whatever he thinks might save a few seconds. And a third switches only
once—when it's clear her line is delayed and there is a clear alternative—
and then continues with her day. He's urging you to ask: Which type
are you?

Seneca is also advising us to be this third type. Just because you've
begun down one path doesn't mean you're committed to it *forever*, especially if that path turns out to be flawed or impeded. At that same time,
this is not an excuse to be flighty or incessantly noncommittal. It takes
courage to decide to do things differently and to make a change, as well
as discipline and awareness to know that the notion of "Oh, but this
looks *even* better" is a temptation that cannot be endlessly indulged
either.

June 7th
FINDING THE RIGHT MENTORS

"We like to say that we don't get to choose our parents, that they were given by chance—yet we can truly choose whose children we'd like to be."

—SENECA, *ON THE BREVITY OF LIFE*, 15.3a

We are fortunate enough that some of the greatest men and women in history have recorded their wisdom (and folly) in books and journals. Many others have had their lives chronicled by a careful biographer—from Plutarch to Boswell to Robert Caro. The literature available at your average library amounts to millions of pages and thousands of years of knowledge, insight, and experience.

Maybe your parents were poor role models, or you lacked a great mentor. Yet if we choose to, we can easily access the wisdom of those who came before us—those whom we aspire to be like.

We not only owe it to ourselves to seek out this hard-won knowledge, we owe it to the people who took the time to record their experiences to try to carry on the traditions and follow their examples—to be the promising children of these noble parents.

June 8th
BRICK BY BORING BRICK

"You must build up your life action by action, and be content if each one achieves its goal as far as possible—and no one can keep you from this. But there will be some external obstacle! Perhaps, but no obstacle to acting with justice, self-control, and wisdom. But what if some other area of my action is thwarted? Well, gladly accept the obstacle for what it is and shift your attention to what is given, and another action will immediately take its place, one that better fits the life you are building."

—MARCUS AURELIUS, *MEDITATIONS*, 8.32

Elite athletes in collegiate and professional sports increasingly follow a philosophy known as "The Process." It's a philosophy created by University of Alabama coach Nick Saban, who taught his players to ignore the big picture—important games, winning championships, the opponent's enormous lead—and focus instead on doing the absolutely smallest things well—practicing with full effort, finishing a specific play, converting on a single possession. A season lasts months, a game lasts hours, catching up might be four touchdowns away, but a single play is only a few seconds. And games and seasons are *constituted* by seconds.

If teams follow The Process, they tend to win. They overcome obstacles and eventually make their way to the top without ever having focused on the obstacles directly. If you follow The Process in your life—assembling the right actions in the right order, one right after another—you too will do well. Not only that, you will be better equipped to make quick work of the obstacles along that path. You'll be too busy putting one foot in front of the next to even notice the obstacles were there.

June 9th
SOLVE PROBLEMS EARLY

"There is no vice which lacks a defense, none that at the outset isn't modest and easily intervened—but after this the trouble spreads widely. If you allow it to get started you won't be able to control when it stops. Every emotion is at first weak. Later it rouses itself and gathers strength as it moves along—it's easier to slow it down than to supplant it."

—SENECA, *MORAL LETTERS*, 116.2b–3a

"Rivers," Publilius Syrus reminds us with an epigram, "are easiest to cross at their source." That's what Seneca means too. The raging waters and deadly currents of bad habits, ill discipline, chaos, and dysfunction—somewhere they began as no more than just a slight trickle. Somewhere they are a placid lake or pond, even a bubbling underground spring.

Which would you rather do—nearly drown in a dangerous crossing in a few weeks or cross now while it's still easy? It's up to you.

June 10th
YOU CAN DO IT

"If you find something very difficult to achieve yourself, don't imagine it impossible—for anything possible and proper for another person can be achieved as easily by you."

—MARCUS AURELIUS, *MEDITATIONS*, 6.19

There are two kinds of people in this world. The first looks at others who have accomplished things and thinks: *Why them? Why not me?* The other looks at those same people and thinks: *If they can do it, why can't I?*

One is zero-sum and jealous (if you win, I lose). The other is non-zero-sum (there's plenty to go around) and sees the success of others as an *inspiration*. Which attitude will propel you onward and upward? Which will drive you to bitterness and despair?

Who will you be?

June 11th
JUST DON'T MAKE THINGS WORSE

"How much more harmful are the consequences of anger and grief
than the circumstances that aroused them in us!"
—MARCUS AURELIUS, *MEDITATIONS*, 11.18.8

The first rule of holes, goes the adage, is that "if you find yourself in a hole, stop digging." This might be the most violated piece of commonsense wisdom in the world. Because what most of us do when something happens, goes wrong, or is inflicted on us is make it worse—first, by getting angry or feeling aggrieved, and next, by flailing around before we have much in the way of a plan.

Today, give yourself the most simple and doable of tasks: just don't make stuff worse. Whatever happens, don't add angry or negative emotions to the equation. Don't react for the sake of reacting. Leave it as it is. Stop digging. Then plan your way out.

June 12th
A TRAINED MIND IS BETTER THAN ANY SCRIPT

"In this way you must understand how laughable it is to say, 'Tell me what to do!' What advice could I possibly give? No, a far better request is, 'Train my mind to adapt to any circumstance.' . . . In this way, if circumstances take you off script . . . you won't be desperate for a new prompting."

—EPICTETUS, *DISCOURSES*, 2.2.20b–1; 24b–25a

It would be nice if someone could show us exactly what to do in every situation. Indeed, this is what we spend a good portion of our lives doing: preparing for this, studying for that. Saving for or anticipating some arbitrary point in the future. But plans, as the boxer Mike Tyson pointed out, last only until you're punched in the face.

Stoics do not seek to have the answer for every question or a plan for every contingency. Yet they're also not worried. Why? Because they have confidence that they'll be able to adapt and change with the circumstances. Instead of looking for instruction, they cultivate skills like creativity, independence, self-confidence, ingenuity, and the ability to problem solve. In this way, they are resilient instead of rigid. We can practice the same.

Today, we will focus on the strategic rather than the tactical. We'll remind ourselves that it's better to be taught than simply *given*, and better to be flexible than stick to a script.

June 13th
LIFE IS A BATTLEFIELD

"Don't you know life is like a military campaign? One must serve
on watch, another in reconnaissance, another on the front line. . . .
So it is for us—each person's life is a kind of battle, and a long
and varied one too. You must keep watch like a soldier and do
everything commanded. . . . You have been stationed in a key post,
not some lowly place, and not for a short time but for life."

—EPICTETUS, *DISCOURSES*, 3.24.31–36

The writer Robert Greene often uses the phrase "As in war, so in life."
It's an aphorism worth keeping close, because our life is a battle both
literally and figuratively. As a species, we fight to survive on a planet indifferent to our survival. As individuals, we fight to survive among a species
whose population numbers in the billions. Even inside our own bodies,
diverse bacteria battle it out. *Vivere est militare.* (To live is to fight.)

Today, you'll be fighting for your goal, fighting against impulses,
fighting to be the person you want to be. So what are the attributes necessary to win these many wars?

Discipline
Fortitude
Courage
Clearheadedness
Selflessness
Sacrifice

And which attributes lose wars?

Cowardice
Rashness
Disorganization
Overconfidence
Weakness
Selfishness

As in war, so these attributes matter in daily life.

June 14th
TRY THE OTHER HANDLE

"Every event has two handles—one by which it can be carried, and one by which it can't. If your brother does you wrong, don't grab it by his wronging, because this is the handle incapable of lifting it. Instead, use the other—that he is your brother, that you were raised together, and then you will have hold of the handle that carries."

—EPICTETUS, *ENCHIRIDION*, 43

The famous journalist William Seabrook suffered from such debilitating alcoholism that in 1933 he committed himself to an insane asylum, which was then the only place to get treatment for addiction. In his memoir, *Asylum*, he tells the story of the struggle to turn his life around inside the facility. At first, he stuck to his addict way of thinking—and as a result, he was an outsider, constantly getting in trouble and rebelling against the staff. He made almost no progress and was on the verge of being asked to leave.

Then one day this very quote from Epictetus—about everything having two handles—occurred to him. "I took hold now by the other handle," he related later, "and carried on." He actually began to have a good time there. He focused on his recovery with real enthusiasm. "I suddenly found it wonderful, strange, and beautiful, to be sober. . . . It was as if a veil, or scum, or film had been stripped from all things visual and auditory." It's an experience shared by many addicts when they finally stop doing things their way and actually open themselves to the perspectives and wisdom and lessons of those who have gone before them.

There is no promise that trying things this way—of grabbing the different handle—will have such momentous results for you. But why continue to lift by the handle that hasn't worked?

June 15th
LISTENING ACCOMPLISHES MORE THAN SPEAKING

"To the youngster talking nonsense Zeno said, 'The reason why we have two ears and only one mouth is so we might listen more and talk less.'"

—DIOGENES LAERTIUS, *LIVES OF EMINENT PHILOSOPHERS*, 7.1.23

Hesiod, the poet, said that "the best treasure is a sparing tongue." Robert Greene considers it a law of power: Always Say Less Than Necessary.

We talk because we think it's helping, whereas in reality it's making things hard for us. If our spouse is venting, we want to tell them what they should do. In fact, all they actually want us to do is *hear* them. In other situations, the world is trying to give us feedback or input, but we try to talk ourselves out of the problem—only to make it worse.

So today, will you be part of the problem or part of the solution? Will you hear the wisdom of the world or drown it out with more noise?

June 16th
NO SHAME IN NEEDING HELP

"Don't be ashamed of needing help. You have a duty to fulfill just like a soldier on the wall of battle. So what if you are injured and can't climb up without another soldier's help?"

—MARCUS AURELIUS, *MEDITATIONS*, 7.7

No one ever said you were born with all the tools you'd need to solve every problem you'd face in life. In fact, as a newborn you were practically helpless. Someone helped you then, and you came to understand that you could ask for that help. It was how you knew you were loved.

Well, you are still loved. You can ask anyone for help. You don't have to face everything on your own.

If you need help, comrade, just ask.

June 17th
OFFENSE OR DEFENSE?

"Fortune doesn't have the long reach we suppose, she can only lay siege to those who hold her tight. So, let's step back from her as much as possible."

—SENECA, *MORAL LETTERS*, 82.5b–6

Machiavelli, who supposedly admired Seneca, says in *The Prince* that "fortune is a woman, and it is necessary, in order to keep her down, to beat her and struggle with her." Even for the sixteenth century, it's pretty horrifying imagery. But for a ruthless and endlessly ambitious ruler, it was par for the course. Is that the nasty lifestyle you're after?

Now compare that view with Seneca's. Not only is he saying that the more you struggle with fortune, the more vulnerable you are to it, but he's also saying that the better path to security is in the "impregnable wall" of philosophy. "Philosophy," he says, helps us tame the "mad frenzy of our greed and tamps down the fury of our fears."

In sports or war, the metaphor here would be the choice between a strategy of endless, exhausting offense and a strategy of resilient, flexible defense. Which will you play? What kind of person are you?

Only you can answer that question. But you would be remiss not to consider the ultimate end of most of the princes in Machiavelli's book—and how few of them died happily in bed, surrounded by their loved ones.

June 18th
PREPARED AND ACTIVE

"Let Fate find us prepared and active. Here is the great soul—the one who surrenders to Fate. The opposite is the weak and degenerate one, who struggles with and has a poor regard for the order of the world, and seeks to correct the faults of the gods rather than their own."

—SENECA, *MORAL LETTERS*, 107.12

Whatever happens today, let it find us prepared and active: ready for problems, ready for difficulties, ready for people to behave in disappointing or confusing ways, ready to accept and make it work for us. Let's not wish we could turn back time or remake the universe according to our preference. Not when it would be far better and far easier to remake ourselves.

June 19th
STAY FOCUSED ON THE PRESENT

"Don't let your reflection on the whole sweep of life crush you.
Don't fill your mind with all the bad things that might still happen. Stay focused on the present situation and ask yourself why
it's so unbearable and can't be survived."

—MARCUS AURELIUS, *MEDITATIONS*, 8.36

When you look back at some of the most impressive, even scary,
things that you've done or endured, how were they possible?
How were you able to see past the danger or the poor odds? As Marcus
described, you were too busy with the details to let the whole sweep of
the situation crush you. In fact, you probably didn't even think about
it at the time.

A character in Chuck Palahniuk's novel *Lullaby* says, "The trick to
forgetting the big picture is to look at everything close up." Sometimes
grasping the big picture is important, and the Stoics have helped us
with that before. A lot of times, though, it's counterproductive and
overwhelming to be thinking of everything that lies ahead. So by focusing exclusively on the present, we're able to avoid or remove those intimidating or negative thoughts from our frame of view.

A man walking a tightrope tries not to think about how high up he
is. An undefeated team tries not to think about their perfect winning
streak. Like us, they're better off putting one foot in front of the other
and considering everything else to be extraneous.

June 20th
CALM IS CONTAGIOUS

"If then it's not that the things you pursue or avoid are coming at you, but rather that you in a sense are seeking them out, at least try to keep your judgment of them steady, and they too will remain calm and you won't be seen chasing after or fleeing from them."

—MARCUS AURELIUS, *MEDITATIONS*, 11.11

There is a maxim that Navy SEALs pass from officer to officer, man to man. In the midst of chaos, even in the fog of war, their battle-tested advice is this: "Calm is contagious."

Especially when that calm is coming from the man or woman in charge. If the men begin to lose their wits, if the group is unsure of what to do next, it's the leader's job to do one thing: instill calm—not by force but by example.

That's who you want to be, whatever your line of work: the casual, relaxed person in every situation who tells everyone else to take a breath and not to worry. Because you've got this. Don't be the agitator, the paranoid, the worrier, or the irrational. Be the calm, not the liability.

It will catch on.

June 21st
TAKE A WALK

"We should take wandering outdoor walks, so that the mind might
be nourished and refreshed by the open air and deep breathing."
—SENECA, *ON TRANQUILITY OF MIND*, 17.8

In a notoriously loud city like Rome, it was impossible to get much
peace and quiet. The noises of wagons, the shouting of vendors, the
hammering of a blacksmith—all filled the streets with piercing violence (to say nothing of the putrid smells of a city with poor sewage and
sanitation). So philosophers went on a lot of walks—to get where they
needed to go, to clear their heads, to get fresh air.

Throughout the ages, philosophers, writers, poets, and thinkers
have found that walking offers an additional benefit—time and space
for better work. As Nietzsche would later say: "It is only ideas gained
from walking that have any worth."

Today, make sure you take a walk. And in the future, when you get
stressed or overwhelmed, take a walk. When you have a tough problem
to solve or a decision to make, take a walk. When you want to be creative, take a walk. When you need to get some air, take a walk. When
you have a phone call to make, take a walk. When you need some exercise, take a long walk. When you have a meeting or a friend over, take
a walk together.

Nourish yourself and your mind and solve your problems along
the way.

June 22nd
THE DEFINITION OF INSANITY

> "If you are defeated once and tell yourself you will overcome, but carry on as before, know in the end you'll be so ill and weakened that eventually you won't even notice your mistake and will begin to rationalize your behavior."
>
> —EPICTETUS, *DISCOURSES*, 2.18.31

It's been said that the definition of insanity is trying the same thing over and over again but expecting a different result. Yet that's exactly what most people do. They tell themselves: *Today, I won't get angry. Today, I won't gorge myself.* But they don't actually *do* anything differently. They try the same routine and hope it will work this time. Hope is not a strategy!

Failure is a part of life we have little choice over. Learning from failure, on the other hand, is optional. We have to choose to learn. We must consciously opt to do things differently—to tweak and change until we actually get the result we're after. But that's hard.

Sticking with the same unsuccessful pattern is easy. It doesn't take any thought or any additional effort, which is probably why most people do it.

June 23rd
THE LONG WAY AROUND

"You could enjoy this very moment all the things you are praying to reach by taking the long way around—if you'd stop depriving yourself of them."

—MARCUS AURELIUS, *MEDITATIONS*, 12.1

Ask most people what they're working toward and you'll get an answer like: "I'm trying to become a [insert profession]." Or they'll tell you they're trying to get appointed to some impressive committee or position, become a millionaire, get discovered, become famous, whatever. Now you ask a couple more questions, such as "Why are you doing that?" or "What are you hoping it will be like when you get it?" and you find at the very core of it, people want freedom, they want happiness, and they want the respect of their peers.

A Stoic looks at all this and shakes his head at the immense effort and expense we put into chasing things that are simple and straightforward to acquire. It's as if we prefer to spend years building a complicated Rube Goldberg machine instead of just reaching out and picking up what we want. It's like looking all over for your sunglasses and then realizing they were on your head the whole time.

Freedom? That's easy. It's in your choices.

Happiness? That's easy. It's in your choices.

Respect of your peers? That too is in the choices you make.

And all of that is right in front of you. No need to take the long way to get there.

June 24th
THE TRULY EDUCATED AREN'T QUARRELSOME

"The beautiful and good person neither fights with anyone nor, as much as they are able, permits others to fight . . . this is the meaning of getting an education—learning what is your own affair and what is not. If a person carries themselves so, where is there any room for fighting?"

—EPICTETUS, *DISCOURSES*, 4.5.1; 7b–8a

Socrates famously traveled around Athens, approaching the people he disagreed with most, and engaging them in long discussions. In these discussions—or what record we have of them—there are many examples of his conversation mates getting exasperated, upset, or aggravated by his many questions. Indeed, the people of Athens eventually got so upset, they sentenced Socrates to death.

But Socrates never seemed to get upset himself. Even when talking about matters of life and death, he always kept his cool. He was much more interested in hearing what the other person had to say than making sure he was heard or—as most of us insist upon—winning the argument.

The next time you face a political dispute or a personal disagreement, ask yourself: *Is there any reason to fight about this? Is arguing going to help solve anything?* Would an educated or wise person really be as quarrelsome as you might initially be inclined to be? Or would they take a breath, relax, and resist the temptation for conflict? Just think of what you could accomplish—and how much better you would feel—if you could conquer the need to fight and win every tiny little thing.

June 25th
THE WISE DON'T HAVE "PROBLEMS"

"This is why we say that nothing happens to the wise person contrary to their expectations."

—Seneca, *On Tranquility of Mind*, 13.3b

Why do the wise have so few problems compared with the rest of us? There are a few simple reasons.

First, the wise seem to manage expectations as much as possible. They rarely expect what isn't possible in the first place.

Second, the wise always consider both the best and worst case scenarios. They don't just think about what they *wish* to happen, but also what very realistically *can* happen if things were to suddenly turn.

Third, the wise act with a reverse clause—meaning that they not only consider what might go wrong, but they are prepared for that to be exactly what they *want* to happen—it is an opportunity for excellence and virtue.

And if you follow it today, you too will find that nothing surprises you or happens contrary to your expectations.

June 26th
TRY THE OPPOSITE

"What assistance can we find in the fight against habit? Try the opposite!"

—EPICTETUS, *DISCOURSES*, 1.27.4

Viktor Frankl, the brilliant psychologist and Holocaust survivor, cured patients suffering from phobias or neurotic habits using a method he called "paradoxical intention." Let's say a patient couldn't sleep. The standard therapy would have been something obvious, like relaxation techniques. Frankl instead encouraged the patient to try *not* to fall asleep. He found that shifting focus off the problem deflected the patient's obsessive attention away from it and allowed them to eventually sleep normally.

Fans of the TV show *Seinfeld* might remember an episode called "The Opposite" where George Costanza magically improves his life by doing the *opposite* of whatever he'd normally do. "If every instinct you have is wrong," Jerry says to him, "then the opposite would have to be right." The larger point is that sometimes our instincts or habits get stuck in a bad pattern that pushes us further from our natural, healthy selves.

Now you shouldn't immediately toss out everything in your life— *some* stuff is working (you're reading this book!). But what if you explored opposites today? What if you broke the pattern?

June 27th
ADVERSITY REVEALS

"How does it help, my husband, to make misfortune heavier by complaining about it? This is more fit for a king—to seize your adversities head on. The more precarious his situation, the more imminent his fall from power, the more firmly he should be resolved to stand and fight. It isn't manly to retreat from fortune."

—SENECA, *OEDIPUS*, 80

As the CEO of Charles Schwab, Walt Bettinger hires hundreds of people each year and interviews hundreds more. Over his lifetime, we can safely assume he's had his share of hits, misses, and surprises when it comes to bringing people on board. But consider one technique he's used as he's gotten older: he takes a candidate to breakfast and asks the restaurant's manager to purposely mess up the candidate's breakfast order.

He's testing to see how they react. Do they get upset? Do they act rudely? Do they let this little event spoil the meeting? Do they handle the inconvenience with grace and kindness?

How you handle even minor adversity might seem like nothing, but, in fact, it reveals everything.

June 28th
NO SELF-FLAGELLATION NEEDED

"Philosophy calls for simple living, but not for penance—it's quite possible to be simple without being crude."

—SENECA, *MORAL LETTERS*, 5.5

Marcus's meditations are filled with self-criticism and so are the writings of other Stoics. It's important to remember, however, that that's as far as it goes. There was no self-flagellation, no paying penance, no self-esteem issues from guilt or self-loathing. You never hear them call themselves worthless pieces of crap, nor do they ever starve or cut themselves as punishment. Their self-criticism is *constructive*.

Laying into yourself, unduly depriving yourself, punishing yourself—that's self-flagellation, not self-improvement.

No need to be too hard on yourself. Hold yourself to a higher standard but not an impossible one. And forgive yourself if and when you slip up.

June 29th
NO EXCUSES

"It is possible to curb your arrogance, to overcome pleasure and pain, to rise above your ambition, and to not be angry with stupid and ungrateful people—yes, even to care for them."

—MARCUS AURELIUS, *MEDITATIONS*, 8.8

"I was just born this way." "I never learned anything different." "My parents set a terrible example." "Everyone else does it." What are these? Excuses that people use to justify staying as they are instead of striving to become better.

Of course it's possible to curb our arrogance, control our anger, and be a caring person. How do you think others do it? Certainly their parents weren't perfect; they didn't come out of the womb incapable of ego or immune to temptation. They worked on it. They made it a priority. They solved it like they would solve any other problem: by dedicating themselves to finding a solution, making incremental progress until they did.

They *became* who they are. Just like you can.

June 30th
THE OBSTACLE IS THE WAY

"While it's true that someone can impede our actions, they can't impede our intentions and our attitudes, which have the power of being conditional and adaptable. For the mind adapts and converts any obstacle to its action into a means of achieving it. That which is an impediment to action is turned to advance action. The obstacle on the path becomes the way."

—MARCUS AURELIUS, *MEDITATIONS*, 5.20

Today, things will happen that will be contrary to your plans. If not today, then certainly tomorrow. As a result of these obstacles, you will not be able to do what you planned. This is not as bad as it seems, because your mind is infinitely elastic and adaptable. You have the power to use the Stoic exercise of turning obstacles upside down, which takes one negative circumstance and uses it as an opportunity to practice an unintended virtue or form of excellence.

If something prevents you from getting to your destination on time, then this is a chance to practice patience.

If an employee makes an expensive mistake, this is a chance to teach a valuable lesson.

If a computer glitch erases your work, it's a chance to start over with a clean slate.

If someone hurts you, it's a chance to practice forgiveness.

If something is hard, it is a chance to get stronger.

Try this line of thinking and see whether there is a situation in which one could *not* find some virtue to practice or derive some benefit. There isn't one. Every impediment can advance action in some form or another.

JULY

DUTY

July 1st
DO YOUR JOB

"Whatever anyone does or says, for my part I'm bound to the good. In the same way an emerald or gold or purple might always proclaim: 'whatever anyone does or says, I must be what I am and show my true colors.'"

—MARCUS AURELIUS, *MEDITATIONS*, 7.15

The Stoics believed that every person, animal, and thing has a purpose or a place in nature. Even in ancient Greek and Roman times, they vaguely understood that the world was composed of millions of tiny atoms. It was this idea—this sense of an interconnected cosmos—that underpinned their sense that every person and every action was part of a larger system. Everyone had a job—a specific duty. Even people who did bad things—they were doing their job of being evil because evil is a part of life.

The most critical part of this system was the belief that you, the student who has sought out Stoicism, have the most important job: to be good! To be wise. "To remain the person that philosophy wished to make us."

Do your job today. Whatever happens, whatever other people's jobs happen to be, do yours. *Be good.*

July 2nd
ON DUTY AND CIRCUMSTANCE

"Never shirk the proper dispatch of your duty, no matter if you are freezing or hot, groggy or well-rested, vilified or praised, not even if dying or pressed by other demands. Even dying is one of the important assignments of life and, in this as in all else, make the most of your resources to do well the duty at hand."

—MARCUS AURELIUS, *MEDITATIONS*, 6.2

Will this make me rich? Will people be impressed? How hard do I need to try? How long will this take? What's in it for me? Should I do this other thing instead? These are the questions we ask ourselves amid the day's opportunities and obligations.

Marcus Aurelius had many responsibilities, as those who hold executive power do. He judged cases, heard appeals, sent troops into battle, appointed administrators, approved budgets. A lot rode on his choices and actions. Should he do this or that? What about this concern or that concern? When would he get to enjoy himself? The simple reminder above was a way to cut through the Gordian knot of incentives, complaints, fears, and competing interests.

It's what we must use to decide what to do in each and every phase of life. Morality can be complicated—but the *right thing* is usually clear and intuitive enough to feel in our gut. Our duty is rarely easy, but it is important. It's also usually the harder choice. But we must do it.

July 3rd
TURN *HAVE TO* INTO *GET TO*

> "The task of a philosopher: we should bring our will into harmony with whatever happens, so that nothing happens against our will and nothing that we wish for fails to happen."
> —EPICTETUS, *DISCOURSES*, 2.14.7

A long To-Do list seems intimidating and burdensome—all these things we *have* to do in the course of a day or a week. But a *Get To Do* list sounds like a privilege—all the things we're excited about the opportunity to experience. This isn't just semantic playing. It is a central facet of the philosopher's worldview.

Today, don't try to impose your will on the world. Instead see yourself as fortunate to receive and respond to the will *in* the world.

Stuck in traffic? A few wonderful minutes to relax and sit. Your car broke down after idling for so long? Ah, what a nice nudge to take a long walk the rest of the way. A swerving car driven by a distracted, cell-phone-wielding idiot nearly hit you as you were walking and soaked you head to toe with muddy water? What a reminder about how precarious our existence is and how silly it is to get upset about something as trivial as being late or having trouble with your commute!

Kidding aside, it might not seem like it makes a big difference to see life as something you *have* to do versus *get* to do, but there is. A huge, magnificent difference.

July 4th
PROTECT THE FLAME

"Protect your own good in all that you do, and as concerns every-thing else take what is given as far as you can make reasoned use of it. If you don't, you'll be unlucky, prone to failure, hindered and stymied."

—EPICTETUS, *DISCOURSES*, 4.3.11

The goodness inside you is like a small flame, and you are its keeper. It's your job, today and every day, to make sure that it has enough fuel, that it doesn't get obstructed or snuffed out.

Every person has their own version of the flame and is responsible for it, just as you are. If they all fail, the world will be much darker—that is something you don't control. But so long as your flame flickers, there will be some light in the world.

July 5th
NO ONE SAID IT'D BE EASY

"Good people will do what they find honorable to do, even if it requires hard work; they'll do it even if it causes them injury; they'll do it even if it will bring danger. Again, they won't do what they find base, even if it brings wealth, pleasure, or power. Nothing will deter them from what is honorable, and nothing will lure them into what is base."

—SENECA, *MORAL LETTERS*, 76.18

If doing good was easy, everyone would do it. (And if doing bad wasn't tempting or attractive, nobody would do it.) The same goes for your duty. If *anyone* could do it, it would have been assigned to someone else. But instead it was assigned to you.

Thankfully, you're not like everyone. You're not afraid of doing what is hard. You can resist superficially attractive rewards. Can't you?

July 6th
RISE AND SHINE

"On those mornings you struggle with getting up, keep this thought in mind—I am awakening to the work of a human being. Why then am I annoyed that I am going to do what I'm made for, the very things for which I was put into this world? Or was I made for this, to snuggle under the covers and keep warm? It's so pleasurable. Were you then made for pleasure? In short, to be coddled or to exert yourself?"

—MARCUS AURELIUS, *MEDITATIONS*, 5.1

It's comforting to think that even two thousand years ago the emperor of Rome (who was reportedly a bit of an insomniac) was giving himself a pep talk in order to summon up the willpower to throw the blankets off each morning and get out of bed. From the time we're first sent off to school until we retire, we're faced with that same struggle. It'd be nicer to shut our eyes and hit the snooze button a few more times. But we can't.

Because we have a job to do. Not only do we have the calling we've dedicated ourselves to, but we have the larger cause that the Stoics speak about: the greater good. We cannot be of service to ourselves, to other people, or to the world unless we get up and get working—the earlier the better. So c'mon. Get in the shower, have your coffee, and get going.

July 7th
OUR DUTY TO LEARN

"This is what you should teach me, how to be like Odysseus—how to love my country, wife and father, and how, even after suffering shipwreck, I might keep sailing on course to those honorable ends."

—SENECA, *MORAL LETTERS*, 88.7b

Many schoolteachers teach *The Odyssey* all wrong. They teach the dates, they debate whether Homer was really the author or not, whether he was blind, they explain the oral tradition, they tell students what a Cyclops is or how the Trojan Horse worked.

Seneca's advice to someone studying the classics is to forget all that. The dates, the names, the places—they hardly matter. What matters is the *moral*. If you got everything else wrong from *The Odyssey*, but you left understanding the importance of perseverance, the dangers of hubris, the risks of temptation and distraction? Then you really learned something.

We're not trying to ace tests or impress teachers. We are reading and studying to live, to be good human beings—always and forever.

July 8th
STOP MONKEYING AROUND

"Enough of this miserable, whining life. Stop monkeying around! Why are you troubled? What's new here? What's so confounding? The one responsible? Take a good look. Or just the matter itself? Then look at that. There's nothing else to look at. And as far as the gods go, by now you could try being more straightforward and kind. It's the same, whether you've examined these things for a hundred years, or only three."

—MARCUS AURELIUS, *MEDITATIONS*, 9.37

"Character," Joan Didion would write in one of her best essays, "the willingness to accept responsibility for one's own life—is the source from which self-respect springs."

Marcus is urging us not to waste time complaining about what we haven't got or how things have worked out. We have to quit monkeying around and be the owners of our own lives. Character can be developed, and when it is, self-respect will ensue. But that means starting and getting serious about it. Not later, not after certain questions have been answered or distractions dealt with, but now. Right now. Taking responsibility is the first step.

To be without this character is the worst of all fates. As Didion put it in "On Self-Respect," "To live without self-respect is to lie awake some night, beyond the reach of warm milk, the phenobarbital, and the sleeping hand on the coverlet, counting up the sins of commission and omission, the trusts betrayed, the promises subtly broken, the gifts irrevocably wasted through sloth or cowardice or carelessness."

You're so much better than that.

July 9th
THE PHILOSOPHER KING

> "For I believe a good king is from the outset and by necessity a philosopher, and the philosopher is from the outset a kingly person."
> —MUSONIUS RUFUS, *LECTURES*, 8.33.32–34

The Israeli general Herzl Halevi believes that philosophy is essential in his role as a leader and warrior. "People used to tell me that business administration is for the practical life and philosophy is for the spirit," he said. "Through the years I found it is exactly the opposite— I used philosophy much more practically." War and leadership offer an unending series of ethical decisions that require priorities, balance, and clarity. That's what philosophy helps with.

Plato knew this when he imagined a utopia ruled by a philosopher king. "Either philosophers should become kings," he said in *The Republic*, "or those now called kings should truly and sufficiently undertake philosophy." Marcus Aurelius was quite literally that philosopher king.

What does that have to do with you? There are fewer kings these days, but we're all leaders in one way or another—of families, of companies, of a team, of an audience, of a group of friends, of ourselves. It's the study of philosophy that cultivates our reason and ethics so that we can do our job well. We can't just wing it—too many people are counting on us to do it right.

July 10th
LOVE THE HUMBLE ART

"Love the humble art you have learned, and take rest in it. Pass
through the remainder of your days as one who whole-heartedly
entrusts all possessions to the gods, making yourself neither a
tyrant nor a slave to any person."

—MARCUS AURELIUS, *MEDITATIONS*, 4.31

Stop by a comedy club any weekend night in New York or Los Ange-
les and you're likely to find some of the world's biggest and most
commercially successful comedians in there, workshopping their craft
for just a handful of people. Though they make a fortune in movies or
on the road, there they are, practicing the most basic form of their art.

If you ask any of them: "Why are you doing this? Why do you still
perform?" The answer is usually: "Because I'm good at it. Because I love
it. Because I want to get better. Because I thrive on connecting with an
audience. Because I just can't *not* do it."

It's not work for them to get up on stage at Carolines or the Comedy
Cellar at 1 a.m. It's invigorating. They don't *have* to do it. They're free,
and they *choose* this.

Whatever humble art you practice: Are you sure you're making time
for it? Are you loving what you do enough to make the time? Can you
trust that if you put in the effort, the rest will take care of itself? Because
it will. Love the craft, be a craftsman.

July 11th
THE START-UP OF YOU

"But what does Socrates say? 'Just as one person delights in improving his farm, and another his horse, so I delight in attending to my own improvement day by day.'"

—EPICTETUS, *DISCOURSES*, 3.5.14

The rage these days is to start your own company—to be an *entrepreneur*. There is no question, building a business from scratch can be an immensely rewarding pursuit. It's why people put their whole lives into doing it, working countless hours and taking countless risks.

But shouldn't we be just as invested in building *ourselves* as we would be to any company?

Like a start-up, we begin as just an idea: we're incubated, put out into the world where we develop slowly, and then, over time, we accumulate partners, employees, customers, investors, and wealth. Is it really so strange to treat your own life as seriously as you might treat an idea for a business? Which one *really* is the matter of life and death?

July 12th
SOME SIMPLE RULES

"In your actions, don't procrastinate. In your conversations, don't confuse. In your thoughts, don't wander. In your soul, don't be passive or aggressive. In your life, don't be all about business."

—MARCUS AURELIUS, *MEDITATIONS*, 8.51

Simple is rarely easy. But now that you have these rules, make it your duty to put them into practice—with the first item on your to-do list, with the first conversation you have, with your soul, and, of course, with the life you make for yourself. Not just today, but every day.

Write that on the blackboard and don't forget it.

July 13th
A LEADER LEADS

"One person, on doing well by others, immediately accounts the expected favor in return. Another is not so quick, but still considers the person a debtor and knows the favor. A third kind of person acts as if not conscious of the deed, rather like a vine producing a cluster of grapes without making further demands, like a horse after its race, or a dog after its walk, or a bee after making its honey. Such a person, having done a good deed, won't go shouting from rooftops but simply moves on to the next deed just like the vine produces another bunch of grapes in the right season."

—MARCUS AURELIUS, *MEDITATIONS*, 5.6

Have you ever heard someone else repeat one of your ideas as though it were their own? Did you ever notice a younger sibling or relative mimic your behavior, perhaps the way you dress or the music you listen to? Maybe you moved to a new neighborhood and a bunch of hipsters followed. When we are young and inexperienced, we can react negatively to these situations. *Stop copying me! I was here first!*

As we mature, we start to see them in a different light. We understand that stepping up and helping is a service that leaders provide to the world. It's our duty to do this—in big situations and small ones. If we expect to be leaders, we must see that thankless service comes with the job. We must do what leaders do, because it's what leaders do—not for the credit, not for the thanks, not for the recognition. It's our duty.

July 14th
A LITTLE KNOWLEDGE IS DANGEROUS

"Every great power is dangerous for the beginner. You must therefore wield them as you are able, but in harmony with nature."

—EPICTETUS, *DISCOURSES*, 3.13.20

Great teachers are usually hardest on their most promising students. When teachers see potential, they want it to be fully realized. But great teachers are also aware that natural ability and quick comprehension can be quite dangerous to the student if left alone. Early promise can lead to overconfidence and create bad habits. Those who pick things up quickly are notorious for skipping the basic lessons and ignoring the fundamentals.

Don't get carried away. Take it slow. Train with humility.

July 15th
DOING THE RIGHT THING IS ENOUGH

"When you've done well and another has benefited by it, why like a fool do you look for a third thing on top—credit for the good deed or a favor in return?"

—MARCUS AURELIUS, *MEDITATIONS*, 7.73

The answer to the question "Why did you do the right thing?" should always be "Because it was the right thing to do." After all, when you hear or see another person do that—especially when they might have endured some hardship or difficulty as a consequence for doing that right thing—do you not think, *There, that is a human being at their finest*?

So why on earth do you need thanks or recognition for having done the right thing? It's your job.

July 16th
PROGRESS OF THE SOUL

"To what service is my soul committed? Constantly ask yourself this and thoroughly examine yourself by seeing how you relate to that part called the ruling principle. Whose soul do I have now? Do I have that of a child, a youth . . . a tyrant, a pet, or a wild animal?"

—MARCUS AURELIUS, *MEDITATIONS*, 5.11

To what are you committed? What cause, what mission, what purpose? What are you doing? And more important, why are you doing it? How does what you do every day reflect, in some way, the values you claim to care about? Are you acting in a way that's consistent with something you value, or are you wandering, unmoored to anything other than your own ambition?

When you examine these questions, you might be uncomfortable with the answers. That's good. That means you've taken the first step to correcting your behavior—to being better than those wild creatures Marcus mentions. It also means you're closer to discovering what your duty calls you to do in life. And once you discover it, you've moved a little bit closer to fulfilling it.

July 17th
DON'T ABANDON OTHERS . . . OR YOURSELF

"As you move forward along the path of reason, people will stand in your way. They will never be able to keep you from doing what's sound, so don't let them knock out your goodwill for them. Keep a steady watch on both fronts, not only for well-based judgments and actions, but also for gentleness with those who would obstruct our path or create other difficulties. For getting angry is also a weakness, just as much as abandoning the task or surrendering under panic. For doing either is an equal desertion— the one by shrinking back and the other by estrangement from family and friend."

—MARCUS AURELIUS, *MEDITATIONS*, 11.9

As we begin to make progress in our lives, we'll encounter the limitations of the people around us. It's like a diet. When everyone is eating unhealthy, there is a kind of natural alignment. But if one person starts eating healthy, suddenly there are opposing agendas. Now there's an argument about where to go for dinner.

Just as you must not abandon your new path simply because other people may have a problem with it, you must not abandon those other folks either. Don't simply write them off or leave them in the dust. Don't get mad or fight with them. After all, they're at the same place you were not long ago.

July 18th
EACH THE MASTER OF THEIR OWN DOMAIN

"My reasoned choice is as indifferent to the reasoned choice of my neighbor, as to his breath and body. However much we've been made for cooperation, the ruling reason in each of us is master of its own affairs. If this weren't the case, the evil in someone else could become my harm, and God didn't mean for someone else to control my misfortune."

—MARCUS AURELIUS, *MEDITATIONS*, 8.56

The foundation of a free country is that your freedom to swing your fist ends where someone else's nose begins. That is, someone else is free to do what they like until it interferes with your physical body and space. This saying can work as a great personal philosophy as well.

But living that way will require two important assumptions. First, you ought to live your own life in such a way that it doesn't negatively impose on others. Second, you have to be open-minded and accepting enough to let others do the same.

Can you do that? Even when you really, really disagree with the choices they're making? Can you understand that their life is their business and yours is your own? And that you've got plenty to wrestle with yourself without bothering anyone else?

July 19th
FORGIVE THEM BECAUSE THEY DON'T KNOW

"As Plato said, every soul is deprived of truth against its will. The same holds true for justice, self-control, goodwill to others, and every similar virtue. It's essential to constantly keep this in your mind, for it will make you more gentle to all."

—MARCUS AURELIUS, *MEDITATIONS*, 7.63

As he wound his way up Via Dolorosa to the top of Calvary Hill, Jesus (or *Christus* as he would have been known to Seneca and other Roman contemporaries) had suffered immensely. He'd been beaten, flogged, stabbed, forced to bear his own cross, and was set to be crucified on it next to two common criminals. There he watched the soldiers roll dice to see who would get to keep his clothes, listened as the people sneered and taunted him.

Whatever your religious inclinations, the words that Jesus spoke next—considering they came as he was subjected to unimaginable human suffering—send chills down your spine. Jesus looked upward and said simply, "Father, forgive them, for they know not what they do."

That is the same truth that Plato spoke centuries earlier and that Marcus spoke almost two centuries after Jesus; other Christians must have spoken this truth as they were cruelly executed by the Romans under Marcus's reign: Forgive them; they are deprived of truth. They wouldn't do this if they weren't.

Use this knowledge to be gentle and gracious.

July 20th
MADE FOR JUSTICE

"The unjust person acts against the gods. For insofar as the nature
of the universe made rational creatures for the sake of each other,
with an eye toward mutual benefit based on true value and never
for harm, anyone breaking nature's will obviously acts against
the oldest of gods."

—MARCUS AURELIUS, *MEDITATIONS*, 9.1.1

We say of the most heinous acts that they are crimes against nature.
We consider certain things to be an affront against humanity,
saying, "This violates everything we hold dear." However much we
differ in religion, upbringing, politics, class, or gender, we can come
together in agreement there.

Why? Because our sense of justice goes marrow deep. We don't like
it when people cut in line; we don't like freeloaders; we pass laws that
protect the defenseless; and we pay our taxes, agreeing, in part, to
redistribute our wealth to those in need. At the same time, if we think
we can get away with it, we might try to cheat or bend the rules. To
paraphrase Bill Walsh, when left to our own devices, many of us individuals seek lower ground like water.

The key, then, is to support our natural inclination to justice with
strong boundaries and strong commitments—to embrace, as Lincoln
urged a divided, angry nation to do, "the better angels of our nature."

July 21st
MADE FOR WORKING TOGETHER

"Whenever you have trouble getting up in the morning, remind yourself that you've been made by nature for the purpose of working with others, whereas even unthinking animals share sleeping. And it's our own natural purpose that is more fitting and more satisfying."

—MARCUS AURELIUS, *MEDITATIONS*, 8.12

If a dog spends all day in bed—your bed, most likely—that's fine. It's just *being* a dog. It doesn't have anywhere to be, no other obligation other than being itself. According to the Stoics, we humans have a higher obligation—not to the gods but to each other. What gets us out of bed each morning—even when we fight it like Marcus did—is *praxeis koinonikas apodidonai* (to render works held in common). Civilization and country are great projects we build together and have been building together with our ancestors for millennia. We are made for cooperation (*synergia*) with each other.

So if you need an extra boost to get out of bed this morning, if you need something more than caffeine can offer, use this. People are depending on you. Your purpose is to help us render this great work together. And we're waiting and excited for you to show up.

July 22nd
NO ONE HAS A GUN TO YOUR HEAD

"Nothing is noble if it's done unwillingly or under compulsion. Every noble deed is voluntary."

—SENECA, *MORAL LETTERS*, 66.16b

You don't *have* to do the right thing. You always have the option to be selfish, rude, awful, shortsighted, pedantic, evil, or stupid. In fact, sometimes there are incentives to break bad. Certainly, not every criminal gets caught.

But how does this line of thinking usually work out for people? What's that life like?

You don't have to do the right thing, just as you don't have to do your duty. You *get* to. You *want* to.

July 23rd
RECEIVE HONORS AND SLIGHTS
EXACTLY THE SAME WAY

"Receive without pride, let go without attachment."
—Marcus Aurelius, *Meditations*, 8.33

In the midst of the breakdown of the Roman Republic, during the civil war between Pompey and Caesar, Pompey made the decision to give control of the military fleet to Cato. It was a massive honor and hugely powerful position. But then a few days later, responding to the protests of his jealous inner circle, Pompey reversed his decision and took the command away.

It could have been seen as an enormous public humiliation—to be given a promotion and then have it taken away. The record shows that Cato's reaction was basically nothing. He responded to the honor and the dishonor the same way: with indifference and acceptance. He certainly didn't let it affect his support for the cause. In fact, after the snub, he worked to rally the soldiers before battle with inspirational speeches—the very men who should have been under his command.

That's what Marcus is saying. Do not take the slights of the day personally—or the exciting rewards and recognitions either, especially when duty has assigned you an important cause. Trivial details like the rise and fall of your position say nothing about you as a person. Only your behavior—as Cato's did—will.

July 24th
SOMEWHERE SOMEONE'S DYING

"Whenever disturbing news is delivered to you, bear in mind that
no news can ever be relevant to your reasoned choice. Can anyone
break news to you that your assumptions or desires are wrong?
No way! But they can tell you someone died—even so, what is
that to you?"

—EPICTETUS, *DISCOURSES*, 3.18.1–2

A well-meaning friend might ask you today: "What do you think
about [insert tragedy from the other side of the world]?" You, in
your equally well-meaning concern, might say, "I just feel awful about it."

In this scenario, both of you have put aside your reasoned choice
without doing a single thing for the victims suffering from the actual
tragedy. It can be so easy to get distracted by, even consumed by, horrible news from all over the world. The proper response of the Stoic
to these events is not to *not* care, but mindless, meaningless sympathy
does very little either (and comes at the cost of one's own serenity, in
most cases). If there is something you can actually do to help these suffering people, then, yes, the disturbing news (and your reaction to it) has
relevance to your reasoned choice. If *emoting* is the end of your partici-
pation, then you ought to get back to your own individual duty—to yourself, to your family, to your country.

July 25th
WHAT'S ON YOUR TOMBSTONE?

"When you see someone often flashing their rank or position, or someone whose name is often bandied about in public, don't be envious; such things are bought at the expense of life. . . . Some die on the first rungs of the ladder of success, others before they can reach the top, and the few that make it to the top of their ambition through a thousand indignities realize at the end it's only for an inscription on their gravestone."

—SENECA, *ON THE BREVITY OF LIFE*, 20

Sometimes our professional commitments can become an end unto themselves. A politician might justify the neglect of his family for his office, or a writer might believe her "genius" excuses antisocial or selfish behavior. Anyone with some perspective can see that, in fact, the politician is really just in love with fame, and the writer enjoys being condescending and feeling superior. Workaholics always make excuses for their selfishness.

While these attitudes can lead to impressive accomplishments, their cost is rarely justified. The ability to work hard and long is admirable. But you are a human *being*, not a human *doing*. Seneca points out that we're not animals. "Is it really so pleasant to die in harness?" he asked. Aleksandr Solzhenitsyn put it better: "Work is what horses die of. Everybody should know that."

July 26th
WHEN GOOD MEN DO NOTHING

"Often injustice lies in what you aren't doing, not only in what you are doing."

—MARCUS AURELIUS, *MEDITATIONS*, 9.5

History abounds with evidence that humanity is capable of doing evil, not only actively but passively. In some of our most shameful moments—from slavery to the Holocaust to segregation to the murder of Kitty Genovese—guilt wasn't limited to perpetrators but to ordinary citizens who, for a multitude of reasons, declined to get involved. It's that old line: all evil needs to prevail is for good men to do nothing.

It's not enough to just *not* do evil. You must also be a force for good in the world, as best you can.

July 27th
WHERE IS ANYTHING BETTER?

"Indeed, if you find anything in human life better than justice, truth, self-control, courage—in short, anything better than the sufficiency of your own mind, which keeps you acting according to the demands of true reason and accepting what fate gives you outside of your own power of choice—I tell you, if you can see anything better than this, turn to it heart and soul and take full advantage of this greater good you've found."

—MARCUS AURELIUS, *MEDITATIONS*, 3.6.1

We've all chased things we thought would matter. At some point, we all thought that money would be the answer, that success was the highest prize, that the undying love of a beautiful person would finally make us feel warm inside. What do we find when we actually attain these sacred objects? Not that they are empty or meaningless—only those who have never had them think that—but what we find is that they are not enough.

Money creates problems. Climbing one mountain exposes another, higher peak. There is never enough love.

There is something better out there: real virtue. It is its own reward. Virtue is the one good that reveals itself to be more than we expect and something that one cannot have in degrees. We simply have it or we don't. And that is why virtue—made up as it is of justice, honesty, discipline, and courage—is the only thing worth striving for.

July 28th
CHECK YOUR PRIVILEGE

"Some people are sharp and others dull; some are raised in a better environment, others in worse, the latter, having inferior habits and nurture, will require more by way of proof and careful instruction to master these teachings and to be formed by them—in the same way that bodies in a bad state must be given a great deal of care when perfect health is sought."

—MUSONIUS RUFUS, *LECTURES*, 1.1.33–1.3.1–3.

At the end of a frustrating exchange, you might find yourself thinking, *Ugh, this person is such an idiot.* Or asking, *Why can't they just do things right?*

But not everyone has had the advantages that you've had. That's not to say that your own life has been easy—you just had a head start over some people. That's why it is our duty to understand and be patient with others.

Philosophy is spiritual formation, care of the soul. Some need more care than others, just as some have a better metabolism or were born taller than others. The more forgiving and tolerant you can be of others—the more you can be aware of your various privileges and advantages—the more helpful and patient you will be.

July 29th
A CURE FOR THE SELF

"The person who has practiced philosophy as a cure for the self becomes great of soul, filled with confidence, invincible—and greater as you draw near."

—SENECA, *MORAL LETTERS*, 111.2

What is "a cure for the self"? Perhaps Seneca means that, through nature and nurture, we develop a unique set of characteristics—some positive and some negative. When those negative characteristics begin to have consequences in our lives, some of us turn to therapy, psychoanalysis, or the help of a support group. The point? To cure certain selfish, destructive parts of ourselves.

But of all the avenues for curing our negative characteristics, philosophy has existed the longest and helped the most people. It is concerned not just with mitigating the effects of a mental illness or a neurosis, but it is designed to encourage human flourishing. It's designed to help you live the Good Life.

Don't you deserve to flourish? Wouldn't you like to be great of soul, filled with confidence, and invincible to external events? Wouldn't you like to be like the proverbial onion, packed with layers of greatness?

Then *practice* your philosophy.

July 30th
STOIC JOY

"Trust me, real joy is a serious thing. Do you think someone can, in the charming expression, blithely dismiss death with an easy disposition? Or swing open the door to poverty, keep pleasures in check, or meditate on the endurance of suffering? The one who is comfortable with turning these thoughts over is truly full of joy, but hardly cheerful. It's exactly such a joy that I would wish for you to possess, for it will never run dry once you've laid claim to its source."

—SENECA, *MORAL LETTERS*, 23.4

We throw around the word "joy" casually. "I'm overjoyed at the news." "She's a joy to be around." "It's a joyous occasion." But none of those examples really touches on true joy. They are closer to "cheer" than anything else. Cheerfulness is surface level.

Joy, to Seneca, is a deep state of being. It is what we feel inside us and has little to do with smiles or laughing. So when people say that the Stoics are dour or depressive, they're really missing the point. Who cares if someone is bubbly when times are good? What kind of accomplishment is that?

But can you be fully content with your life, can you bravely face what life has in store from one day to the next, can you bounce back from every kind of adversity without losing a step, can you be a source of strength and inspiration to others around you? That's *Stoic joy*—the joy that comes from purpose, excellence, and duty. It's a serious thing— far more serious than a smile or a chipper voice.

July 31st
YOUR CAREER IS NOT A LIFE SENTENCE

"How disgraceful is the lawyer whose dying breath passes while at court, at an advanced age, pleading for unknown litigants and still seeking the approval of ignorant spectators."

—SENECA, *ON THE BREVITY OF LIFE*, 20.2

Every few years, a sad spectacle is played out in the news. An old millionaire, still lord of his business empire, is taken to court. Shareholders and family members go to court to argue that he is no longer mentally competent to make decisions—that the patriarch is not fit to run his own company and legal affairs. Because this powerful person refused to ever relinquish control or develop a succession plan, he is subjected to one of life's worst humiliations: the public exposure of his most private vulnerabilities.

We must not get so wrapped up in our work that we think we're immune from the reality of aging and life. Who wants to be the person who can never let go? Is there so little meaning in your life that your only pursuit is work until you're eventually carted off in a coffin?

Take pride in your work. But it is not all.

AUGUST

PRAGMATISM

THE DAILY STOIC

August 1st
DON'T GO EXPECTING PERFECTION

"That cucumber is bitter, so toss it out! There are thorns on the path, then keep away! Enough said. Why ponder the existence of nuisance? Such thinking would make you a laughing-stock to the true student of Nature, just as a carpenter or cobbler would laugh if you pointed out the sawdust and chips on the floors of their shops. Yet while those shopkeepers have dustbins for disposal, Nature has no need of them."

—MARCUS AURELIUS, *MEDITATIONS*, 8.50

We want things to go perfectly, so we tell ourselves that we'll get started once the conditions are right, or once we have our bearings. When, really, it'd be better to focus on making do with how things actually are.

Marcus reminded himself: "Don't await the perfection of Plato's *Republic*." He wasn't expecting the world to be exactly the way he wanted it to be, but Marcus knew instinctively, as the Catholic philosopher Josef Pieper would later write, that "he alone can do good who knows what things are like and what their situation is."

Today, we won't let our honest understanding of the world stop us from trying to make the best of it. Nor will we let petty annoyances and minor obstacles get in the way of the important job we have to do.

230   PRAGMATISM

August 2nd
WE CAN WORK ANY WAY

"Indeed, how could exile be an obstacle to a person's own cultivation, or to attaining virtue when no one has ever been cut off from learning or practicing what is needed by exile?"
—MUSONIUS RUFUS, *LECTURES*, 9.37.30–31, 9.39.1

Late in his life, after a surgery, Theodore Roosevelt was told he might be confined to a wheelchair for the remainder of his days. With his trademark ebullience, he responded, "All right! I can work that way too!"

This is how we can respond to even the most disabling turns of fate—by working within whatever room is left. Nothing can prevent us from learning. In fact, difficult situations are often opportunities for their own kinds of learning, even if they're not the kinds of learning we'd have preferred.

Musonius Rufus, for his part, was exiled three times (twice by Nero and once by Vespasian), but being forcibly expelled from his life and his home didn't impinge on his study of philosophy. In his way, he responded by saying "All right! I can work that way too." And he did, managing to squeeze in some time between exiles with a student named Epictetus and thus helping to bring Stoicism to the world.

August 3rd
THE GOOD LIFE IS ANYWHERE

"At this moment you aren't on a journey, but wandering about, being driven from place to place, even though what you seek—to live well—is found in all places. Is there any place more full of confusion than the Forum? Yet even there you can live at peace, if needed."

—SENECA, *MORAL LETTERS*, 28.5b–6a

A well-known writer once complained that after becoming successful, wealthy friends were always inviting him to their beautiful, exotic houses. "Come to our home in the south of France," they would say. Or, "Our Swiss ski chalet is a wonderful place to write." The writer traveled the world, living in luxury, hoping to find inspiration and creativity in these inspiring manors and mansions. Yet it rarely happened. There was always the allure of another, better house. There were always distractions, always so many things to do—and the writer's block and insecurity that plagues creative types traveled with him wherever he went.

We tell ourselves that we need the right setup before we finally buckle down and get serious. Or we tell ourselves that some vacation or time alone will be good for a relationship or an ailment. This is self-deceit at its finest.

It's far better that we become pragmatic and adaptable—able to do what we need to do anywhere, anytime. The place to do your work, to live the good life, is *here*.

August 4th
NO BLAME, JUST FOCUS

"You must stop blaming God, and not blame any person. You must completely control your desire and shift your avoidance to what lies within your reasoned choice. You must no longer feel anger, resentment, envy, or regret."

—EPICTETUS, *DISCOURSES*, 3.22.13

Nelson Mandela was imprisoned for resistance to the brutal apartheid regime in South Africa for twenty-seven years. For eighteen of those years, he had a bucket for a toilet, a hard cot in a small cell, and once a year he was allowed a single visitor—for thirty minutes. It was vicious treatment meant to isolate and break down the prisoners. And yet, in spite of that, Mandela became a figure of dignity within the prison.

Though he was deprived of many things, he still found creative ways to assert his will. As one of his fellow prisoners, Neville Alexander, explained on *Frontline*, "He [Mandela] always made the point, if they say you must run, insist on walking. If they say you must walk fast, insist on walking slowly. That was the whole point. We are going to set the terms." He pretended to jump rope and shadowboxed to stay in shape. He held his head higher than other prisoners, encouraged them when times got tough, and always retained his sense of self-assurance.

That self-assurance is yours to claim as well. No matter what happens today, no matter where you find yourself, shift to what lies within your reasoned choices. Ignore, as best you can, the emotions that pop up, which would be so easy to distract yourself with. Don't get emotional—get focused.

August 5th
SILENCE IS STRENGTH

"Silence is a lesson learned from the many sufferings of life."
—SENECA, *THYESTES*, 309

Recall the last time you said a really boneheaded thing, something that came back to bite you. Why did you say it? Chances are you didn't need to, but you thought doing so would make you look smart or cool or part of the group.

"The more you say," Robert Greene has written, "the more likely you are to say something foolish." To that we add: the more you say, the more likely you are to blow past opportunities, ignore feedback, and cause yourself suffering.

The inexperienced and fearful talk to reassure themselves. The ability to listen, to deliberately keep out of a conversation and subsist without its validity is rare. Silence is a way to build strength and self-sufficiency.

August 6th
THERE IS ALWAYS MORE ROOM
TO MANEUVER THAN YOU THINK

"Apply yourself to thinking through difficulties—hard times can
be softened, tight squeezes widened, and heavy loads made lighter
for those who can apply the right pressure."
—SENECA, *ON TRANQUILITY OF MIND*, 10.4b

Have you ever been hopelessly losing a game that suddenly broke
wide open and you won? Remember that time when you thought
you were certain to fail the test, but with an all-nighter and some luck
you managed to eke out a decent score? That hunch you pursued that
others would have given up on—that turned out brilliantly?

It's that kind of energy and creativity and above all *faith* in yourself
that you need right now. Defeatism won't get you anywhere (except
defeat). But focusing your entire effort on the little bit of room, the tiny
scrap of an opportunity, is your best shot. An aide to Lyndon Johnson
once remarked that around the man "there was a feeling—if you did
everything, you would win." *Everything*. Or as Marcus Aurelius put
it, if it's humanly possible, you can do it.

August 7th
PRAGMATIC AND PRINCIPLED

"Wherever a person can live, there one can also live well; life is also
in the demands of court, there too one can live well."
—MARCUS AURELIUS, *MEDITATIONS*, 5.16

William Lee Miller, in his unique "ethical biography" of Abraham
Lincoln, makes an important point about this famous president:
our deification of the man makes a point to pretend he wasn't a politician. We focus on his humble beginnings, his self-education, his beautiful speeches. But we gloss over his job, which was politics. That misses
what was so truly impressive about him: Lincoln was all the things he
was—compassionate, deliberate, fair, open-minded, and purposeful—
while being a politician. He was what we admire in a profession we
believe to be filled exclusively with the opposite of that type of person.

Principles and pragmatism are not at odds. Whether you live in the
snake pit of Washington, D.C., work among the materialism of Wall
Street, or grew up in a closed-minded small town, you can live well.
Plenty of others have.

August 8th
START WITH WHERE THE WORLD IS

> "Do now what nature demands of you. Get right to it if that's in your power. Don't look around to see if people will know about it. Don't await the perfection of Plato's *Republic*, but be satisfied with even the smallest step forward and regard the outcome as a small thing."

—MARCUS AURELIUS, *MEDITATIONS*, 9.29.(4)

Have you ever heard the expression "Don't let perfect be the enemy of good enough"? The idea is not to settle or compromise your standards, but rather not to become trapped by idealism.

The community organizer Saul Alinsky opens his book *Rules for Radicals* with a pragmatic but inspiring articulation of that idea:

> "As an organizer I start from where the world is, as it is, not as I would like it to be. That we accept the world as it is does not in any sense weaken our desire to change it into what we believe it should be—it is necessary to begin where the world is if we are going to change it to what we think it should be."

There is plenty that you could do right now, today, that would make the world a better place. There are plenty of small steps that, were you to take them, would help move things forward. Don't excuse yourself from doing them because the conditions aren't right or because a better opportunity might come along soon. Do what you can, *now*. And when you've done it, keep it in perspective, don't overblow the results. Shun both ego and excuse, before and after.

August 9th
STICK WITH JUST THE FACTS

"Don't tell yourself anything more than what the initial impressions report. It's been reported to you that someone is speaking badly about you. This is the report—the report wasn't that you've been harmed. I see that my son is sick—but not that his life is at risk. So always stay within your first impressions, and don't add to them in your head—this way nothing can happen to you."

—MARCUS AURELIUS, *MEDITATIONS*, 8.49

At first, this can seem like the opposite of everything you've been taught. Don't we cultivate our minds and critical thinking skills precisely so we don't simply accept things at face value? Yes, most of the time. But sometimes this approach can be counterproductive.

What a philosopher also has is the ability, as Nietzsche put it, "to stop courageously, at the surface" and see things in plain, objective form. Nothing more, nothing less. Yes, Stoics were "superficial," he said, "*out of profundity.*" Today, while other people are getting carried away, that's what you're going to practice. A kind of straightforward pragmatism—seeing things as their initial impressions make them.

August 10th
PERFECTION IS THE ENEMY OF ACTION

"We don't abandon our pursuits because we despair of ever perfecting them."

—EPICTETUS, *DISCOURSES*, 1.2.37b

Psychologists speak of cognitive distortions—exaggerated thinking patterns that have a destructive impact on the life of the patient. One of the most common is known as all-or-nothing thinking (also referred to as splitting). Examples of this include thoughts like:

- If you're not with me, you're against me.
- So-and-so is all good/bad.
- Because this wasn't a complete success, it is a total failure.

This sort of extreme thinking is associated with depression and frustration. How could it not be? Perfectionism rarely begets perfection—only disappointment.

Pragmatism has no such hang-ups. It'll take what it can get. That's what Epictetus is reminding us. We're never going to be perfect—if there is even such a thing. We're human, after all. Our pursuits should be aimed at progress, however little that it's possible for us to make.

August 11th
NO TIME FOR THEORIES, JUST RESULTS

"When the problem arose for us whether habit or theory was better for getting virtue—if by theory is meant what teaches us correct conduct, and by habit we mean being accustomed to act according to this theory—Musonius thought habit to be more effective."
—MUSONIUS RUFUS, *LECTURES*, 5.17.31–32, 5.19.1–2

As Hamlet says,

"There are more things in heaven and earth, Horatio,
Than are dreamt of in your philosophy."

There is no time to chop logic over whether our theories are correct. We're dealing with the real world here. What matters is how you're going to deal with this situation right in front of you and whether you're going to be able to move past it and onto the next one. That's not saying that anything goes—but we can't forget that although theories are clean and simple, situations rarely are.

August 12th
MAKE THE WORDS YOUR OWN

"Many words have been spoken by Plato, Zeno, Chrysippus, Posidonius, and by a whole host of equally excellent Stoics. I'll tell you
how people can prove their words to be their own—by putting
into practice what they've been preaching."

—SENECA, *MORAL LETTERS*, 108.35; 38

One of the criticisms of Stoicism by modern translators and teachers is the amount of repetition. Marcus Aurelius, for example, has
been dismissed by academics as not being original because his writing
resembles that of other, earlier Stoics. This criticism misses the point.

Even before Marcus's time, Seneca was well aware that there was a
lot of borrowing and overlap among the philosophers. That's because
real philosophers weren't concerned with authorship, only what worked.
More important, they believed that what was *said* mattered less than
what was *done*.

And this is as true now as it was then. You're welcome to take all of
the words of the great philosophers and use them to your own liking
(they're dead; they don't mind). Feel free to tweak and edit and improve
as you like. Adapt them to the real conditions of the real world. The
way to prove that you truly understand what you speak and write, that
you truly are original, is to put them into practice. Speak them with
your actions more than anything else.

August 13th
TAKE CHARGE AND END YOUR TROUBLES

"You've endured countless troubles—all from not letting your ruling reason do the work it was made for—enough already!"

—MARCUS AURELIUS, *MEDITATIONS*, 9.26

How many things you fear have actually come to pass? How many times has anxiety driven you to behave in a way you later regret? How many times have you let jealousy or frustration or greed lead you down a bad road?

Letting our reason rule the day might seem like more work, but it saves us quite a bit of trouble. As Ben Franklin's proverb put it: "An ounce of prevention is worth a pound of cure."

Your brain was designed to do this work. It was meant to separate what is important from what is senseless, to keep things in perspective, to only become troubled by that which is worth becoming troubled about. You only need to put it to use.

August 14th
THIS ISN'T FOR FUN. IT'S FOR LIFE

"Philosophy isn't a parlor trick or made for show. It's not concerned with words, but with facts. It's not employed for some pleasure before the day is spent, or to relieve the uneasiness of our leisure. It shapes and builds up the soul, it gives order to life, guides action, shows what should and shouldn't be done—it sits at the rudder steering our course as we vacillate in uncertainties. Without it, no one can live without fear or free from care. Countless things happen every hour that require advice, and such advice is to be sought out in philosophy."

—SENECA, *MORAL LETTERS*, 16.3

There is a story about Cato the Elder, whose great-grandson Cato the Younger became a towering figure in Roman life. One day Cato witnessed a fine oration from Carneades, a Skeptic philosopher, who waxed poetically on the importance of justice. Yet the next day Cato found Carneades arguing passionately about the *problems* with justice—that it was merely a device invented by society to create order. Cato was aghast at this kind of "philosopher," who treated such a precious topic like a debate where one would argue both sides of an issue purely for show. What on earth was the point?

And so he lobbied the Senate to have Carneades sent back to Athens, where he could no longer corrupt the Roman youth with his rhetorical tricks. To a Stoic, the idea of idly discussing some issue—of believing or arguing two contradictory ideas—is an absurd waste of time, energy, and belief. As Seneca said, philosophy is not a fun trick. It's for use—for life.

August 15th
THE SUPREME COURT OF YOUR MIND

"This can be swiftly taught in very few words: virtue is the only good; there is no certain good without virtue; and virtue resides in our nobler part, which is the rational one. And what can this virtue be? True and steadfast judgment. For from this will arise every mental impulse, and by it every appearance that spurs our impulses will be rendered clear."

—SENECA, *MORAL LETTERS*, 71.32

Think about someone you know who has character of granite. Why are they so dependable, trustworthy, excellent? Why do they have a sterling reputation?

You might see a pattern: consistency. They are honest not only when it's convenient. They are not only there for you when it counts. The qualities that make them admirable come through in every action ("arise with every mental impulse").

Why do we revere people like Theodore Roosevelt, for example? It isn't because he was brave once, or courageous once, or tough once. It's because those qualities are shot through every one of the stories about him. When he was young and weak, he became a boxer. When he was younger and frail, he went to a gym in his home, every day, for hours on end. When he was shattered by the loss of his wife and mother on the same day, he went to The Badlands and herded cattle. And on and on.

You become the sum of your actions, and as you do, what flows from that—your impulses—reflect the actions you've taken. Choose wisely.

August 16th
ANYTHING CAN BE AN ADVANTAGE

"Just as the nature of rational things has given to each person their rational powers, so it also gives us this power—just as nature turns to its own purpose any obstacle or any opposition, sets its place in the destined order, and co-opts it, so every rational person can convert any obstacle into the raw material for their own purpose."

—MARCUS AURELIUS, *MEDITATIONS*, 8.35

At five feet three inches tall, Muggsy Bogues was the shortest player ever to play professional basketball. Throughout his career, he was snickered at, underestimated, and counted out.

But Bogues succeeded by turning his height into the very thing that made him nationally known. Some people looked at his size as a curse, but he saw it as a blessing. He found the advantages contained within it. In fact, on the court small size has many advantages: speed and quickness, the ability to steal the ball from unsuspecting (and significantly taller) players, to say nothing of the fact that players just plain underestimated him.

Could this approach not be useful in your life? What things do you think have been holding you back that, in fact, can be a hidden source of strength?

August 17th
THE BUCK STOPS HERE

"For nothing outside my reasoned choice can hinder or harm it—my reasoned choice alone can do this to itself. If we would lean this way whenever we fail, and would blame only ourselves and remember that nothing but opinion is the cause of a troubled mind and uneasiness, then by God, I swear we would be making progress."

—EPICTETUS, *DISCOURSES*, 3.19.2–3

Today, see if you can go without blaming a single person or single thing. Someone messes up your instructions—it's on you for expecting anything different. Someone says something rude—it's your sensitivity that interpreted their remark this way. Your stock portfolio takes a big loss—what did you expect making such a big bet? Why are you checking the market day to day anyway?

Whatever it is, however bad it may be, see whether you can make it a whole day laying it all on your reasoned choice. If you can't make it for a day, see if you can make it for an hour. If not for an hour, then for ten minutes.

Start where you need to. Even one minute without playing the blame game is progress in the art of living.

August 18th
ONLY FOOLS RUSH IN

"A good person is invincible, for they don't rush into contests in which they aren't the strongest. If you want their property, take it—take also their staff, profession, and body. But you will never compel what they set out for, nor trap them in what they would avoid. For the only contest the good person enters is that of their own reasoned choice. How can such a person not be invincible?"

—EPICTETUS, *DISCOURSES*, 3.6.5–7

One of the most fundamental principles of martial arts is that strength should not go against strength. That is: don't try to beat your opponent where they are strongest. But that's exactly what we do when we try to undertake some impossible task we haven't bothered to think through. Or we let someone put us on the spot. Or we say yes to everything that comes our way.

Some people think that "choosing your battles" is weak or calculating. How could reducing the amount of times we fail or minimizing the number of needless injuries inflicted upon us be weak? How is that a bad thing? As the saying goes, discretion is the better part of valor. The Stoics call it reasoned choice. That means be reasonable! Think hard before choosing, and make yourself unbeatable.

August 19th
CORRALLING THE UNNECESSARY

"It is said that if you would have peace of mind, busy yourself with little. But wouldn't a better saying be do what you must and as required of a rational being created for public life? For this brings not only the peace of mind of doing few things, but the greater peace of doing them well. Since the vast majority of our words and actions are unnecessary, corralling them will create an abundance of leisure and tranquility. As a result, we shouldn't forget at each moment to ask, is this one of the unnecessary things? But we must corral not only unnecessary actions but unnecessary thoughts, too, so needless acts don't tag along after them."

—MARCUS AURELIUS, *MEDITATIONS*, 4.24

The Stoics were not monks. They didn't retreat to the sanctuary of a monastery or a temple. They were politicians, businessmen, soldiers, artists. They practiced their philosophy amid the busyness of life—just as you are attempting to do.

The key to accomplishing that is to ruthlessly expunge the inessential from our lives. What vanity obligates us to do, what greed signs us up for, what ill discipline adds to our plate, what a lack of courage prevents us from saying no to. All of this we must cut, cut, cut.

August 20th
WHERE IT COUNTS

"Inwardly, we ought to be different in every respect, but our outward dress should blend in with the crowd."

—SENECA, *MORAL LETTERS*, 5.2

Diogenes the Cynic was a controversial philosopher who wandered the streets like a homeless person. A few thousand years later, his utterances still make us think. But if most of us had seen him at the time, we'd have thought: *Who is that crazy guy?*

It's tempting to take philosophy to extremes, but who does that serve? In fact, rejection of the basics of society alienates other people, even threatens them. More important, outward transformation—in our clothes, in our cars, in our grooming—might feel important but is superficial compared with the inward change. That's the change that only we know about.

August 21st
DON'T BE MISERABLE IN ADVANCE

"It's ruinous for the soul to be anxious about the future and miserable in advance of misery, engulfed by anxiety that the things it desires might remain its own until the very end. For such a soul will never be at rest—by longing for things to come it will lose the ability to enjoy present things."

—SENECA, *MORAL LETTERS*, 98.5b–6a

The way we nervously worry about some looming bad news is strange if you think about it. By definition, the waiting means it hasn't happened yet, so that feeling bad in advance is totally voluntary. But that's what we do: chewing our nails, feeling sick to our stomachs, rudely brushing aside the people around us. Why? Because something bad *might* occur soon.

The pragmatist, the person of action, is too busy to waste time on such silliness. The pragmatist can't worry about every possible outcome in advance. Think about it. Best case scenario—if the news turns out to be better than expected, all this time was wasted with needless fear. Worst case scenario—we were miserable for extra time, by choice.

And what better use could you make of that time? A day that could be your last—you want to spend it in worry? In what other area could you make some progress while others might be sitting on the edges of their seat, passively awaiting some fate?

Let the news come when it does. Be too busy working to care.

August 22nd
DON'T SWEAT THE SMALL STUFF

"It is essential for you to remember that the attention you give to any action should be in due proportion to its worth, for then you won't tire and give up, if you aren't busying yourself with lesser things beyond what should be allowed."

—MARCUS AURELIUS, *MEDITATIONS*, 4.32b

In 1997, a psychotherapist named Richard Carlson published a book called *Don't Sweat the Small Stuff . . . and It's All Small Stuff.* It quickly became one of the fastest-selling books of all time and spent years on the bestseller lists, ultimately selling millions of copies in many languages.

Whether you read the book or not, Carlson's pithy articulation of this timeless idea is worth remembering. Even Cornelius Fronto, Marcus Aurelius's rhetoric teacher, would have thought it a superior way of expressing the wisdom his student attempted in the quote above. They both say the same thing: don't spend your time (the most valuable and least renewable of all your resources) on the things that don't matter. What about the things that don't matter but you're absolutely obligated to do? Well, spend as little time and worry on them as possible.

If you give things more time and energy than they deserve, they're no longer lesser things. You've *made* them important by the life you've spent on them. And sadly, you've made the important things—your family, your health, your true commitments—less so as a result of what you've stolen from them.

August 23rd
IT'S IN YOUR SELF-INTEREST

"Therefore, explain why a wise person shouldn't get drunk—not with words, but by the facts of its ugliness and offensiveness. It's most easy to prove that so-called pleasures, when they go beyond proper measure, are but punishments."

—SENECA, *MORAL LETTERS*, 83.27

Is there a less effective technique to persuading people to do something than haranguing them? Is there anything that turns people off more than abstract notions? That's why the Stoics don't say, "Stop doing this, it's a sin." Instead they say, "Don't do this because it will make you miserable." They don't say, "Pleasure isn't pleasurable." They say, "Endless pleasure becomes its own form of punishment." Their methods of persuasion hew the line in *The 48 Laws of Power*: "Appeal to People's Self-Interest Never to Their Mercy or Gratitude."

If you find yourself trying to persuade someone to change or do something differently, remember what an effective lever self-interest is. It's not that this or that is *bad*, it's that it is in their best interest to do it a different way. And *show* them—don't moralize.

And what happens when you apply this way of thinking to your own behavior?

August 24th
PILLAGE FROM ALL SOURCES

"I'll never be ashamed to quote a bad writer with a good saying."
—SENECA, *ON TRANQUILITY OF MIND*, 11.8

One of the striking things about Seneca's letters and essays is how often he quotes the philosopher Epicurus. Why is that strange? Because Stoicism and Epicureanism are supposed to be diametrically opposed philosophies! (In reality the differences while significant tend to be overblown.)

But this is true to form for Seneca. He was looking for wisdom, *period*. It didn't matter where it came from. This is something that a lot of fundamentalists—in religion, philosophy, anything—seem to miss. Who cares whether some bit of wisdom is from a Stoic, who cares whether it perfectly jibes with Stoicism? What matters is whether it makes your life better, whether it makes you better.

What wisdom or help would you be able to find today if you stopped caring about affiliations and reputations? How much more could you see if you just focused on merit?

August 25th
RESPECT THE PAST, BUT BE OPEN TO THE FUTURE

"Won't you be walking in your predecessors' footsteps? I surely will use the older path, but if I find a shorter and smoother way, I'll blaze a trail there. The ones who pioneered these paths aren't our masters, but our guides. Truth stands open to everyone, it hasn't been monopolized."

—SENECA, *MORAL LETTERS*, 33.11

Traditions are often time-tested best practices for doing something. But remember that today's conservative ideas were once controversial, cutting-edge, and innovative. This is why we can't be afraid to experiment with new ideas.

In Seneca's case, he might be embracing some new philosophical insight that improves on the writing of Zeno or Cleanthes. In our case, perhaps a breakthrough in psychology improves on the writing of Seneca or Marcus Aurelius. Or perhaps we have a breakthrough of our own. If these ideas are true and better, embrace them—use them. You don't need to be a prisoner of dead old men who stopped learning two thousand years ago.

August 26th
SEEKING OUT SHIPWRECKS

"I was shipwrecked before I even boarded . . . the journey showed me this—how much of what we have is unnecessary, and how easily we can decide to rid ourselves of these things whenever it's necessary, never suffering the loss."

—SENECA, *MORAL LETTERS*, 87.1

Zeno, widely considered to be the founder of the school of Stoicism, was a merchant before he was a philosopher. On a voyage between Phoenicia and Peiraeus, his ship sank along with its cargo. Zeno ended up in Athens, and while visiting a bookstore he was introduced to the philosophy of Socrates and, later, an Athenian philosopher named Crates. These influences drastically changed the course of his life, leading him to develop the thinking and principles that we now know as Stoicism. According to the ancient biographer Diogenes Laertius, Zeno joked, "Now that I've suffered shipwreck, I'm on a good journey," or according to another account, "You've done well, Fortune, driving me thus to philosophy," he reportedly said.

The Stoics weren't being hypothetical when they said we ought to act with a reverse clause and that even the most unfortunate events can turn out to be for the best. The entire philosophy is founded on that idea!

August 27th
LAUGH, OR CRY?

"Heraclitus would shed tears whenever he went out in public—
Democritus laughed. One saw the whole as a parade of miseries,
the other of follies. And so, we should take a lighter view of things
and bear them with an easy spirit, for it is more human to laugh
at life than to lament it."

—SENECA, *ON TRANQUILITY OF MIND*, 15.2

Is this observation the origin of that famous expression about frustrating news: "I don't know whether to laugh or cry?" The Stoics saw little purpose in getting angry or sad about things that are indifferent to our feelings. Especially when those feelings end up making *us* feel worse.

It's also another bit of evidence that the Stoics were hardly some depressing, bitter group of old men. Even when things were really bad, when the world made them want to weep in despair or rage, they *chose* to laugh about it.

Like Democritus, we can make that same choice. There is more humor than hate to be found in just about every situation. And at least humor is productive—making things less heavy, not more so.

August 28th
THE OPULENT STOIC

"The founder of the universe, who assigned to us the laws of life, provided that we should live well, but not in luxury. Everything needed for our well-being is right before us, whereas what luxury requires is gathered by many miseries and anxieties. Let us use this gift of nature and count it among the greatest things."

—SENECA, *MORAL LETTERS*, 119.15b

Even in his own time, Seneca was criticized for preaching Stoic virtues while accumulating one of the largest fortunes in Rome. Seneca was so rich that some historians speculate that major loans he made to the inhabitants of what is now Britain caused what became a horrifically brutal uprising there. His critics' derisive nickname for him was "The Opulent Stoic."

Seneca's response to this criticism is pretty simple: he might have wealth, but he didn't *need* it. He wasn't dependent on it or addicted to it. Nor, despite his large bank account, was he considered to be anything close to Rome's most lavish spenders and pleasure hunters. Whether his rationalization was true or not (or whether he was a tad hypocritical), his is a decent prescription for navigating today's materialistic and wealth-driven society.

This is the pragmatic instead of the moralistic approach to wealth.

We can still live well without becoming slaves to luxury. And we don't need to make decisions that force us to continue to work and work and work and drift further from study and contemplation in order to get more money to pay for the things we don't need. There is no rule that says financial success *must* mean that you live beyond your means. Remember: humans can be happy with very little.

August 29th
WANT NOTHING = HAVE EVERYTHING

"No person has the power to have everything they want, but it is in their power not to want what they don't have, and to cheerfully put to good use what they do have."

—SENECA, *MORAL LETTERS*, 123.3

Is there a person so rich that there is literally *nothing* they can't afford? Surely there isn't. Even the richest people regularly fail in their attempts to buy elections, to purchase respect, class, love, and any number of other things that are not for sale.

If obscene wealth will never get you everything you want, is that the end of it? Or is there another way to solve for that equation? To the Stoics, there is: by changing what it is that you want. By changing how you think, you'll manage to get it. John D. Rockefeller, who was as rich as they come, believed that "a man's wealth must be determined by the relation of his desires and expenditures to his income. If he feels rich on $10 and has everything he desires, he really is rich."

Today, you could try to increase your wealth, or you could take a shortcut and just *want less*.

August 30th
WHEN YOU FEEL LAZY

> "Anything that must yet be done, virtue can do with courage and promptness. For anyone would call it a sign of foolishness for one to undertake a task with a lazy and begrudging spirit, or to push the body in one direction and the mind in another, to be torn apart by wildly divergent impulses."
>
> —SENECA, *MORAL LETTERS*, 74.31b-32

If you start something and right away feel yourself getting lazy and irritated, first ask yourself: *Why am I doing this?* If it really is a necessity, ask yourself: *What's behind my reluctance? Fear? Spite? Fatigue?*

Don't forge ahead hoping that someone will come along and relieve you of this task you don't want to do. Or that someone else will suddenly explain why what you're doing matters. Don't be the person who says yes with their mouth but no with their actions. Steve Jobs told *BusinessWeek* in 2005, only midway through Apple's stunning rise to becoming one of the world's most valuable companies: "Quality is much better than quantity. . . . One home run is much better than two doubles."

August 31st
CONSIDER YOUR FAILINGS TOO

"Whenever you take offense at someone's wrongdoing, immediately turn to your own similar failings, such as seeing money as good, or pleasure, or a little fame—whatever form it takes. By thinking on this, you'll quickly forget your anger, considering also what compels them—for what else could they do? Or, if you are able, remove their compulsion."

—MARCUS AURELIUS, *MEDITATIONS*, 10.30

Earlier we were reminded of Socrates's tolerant belief that "no one does wrong on purpose." The clearest proof of that hypothesis? All the times *we* did wrong without malice or intention. Remember them? The time you were rude because you hadn't slept in two days. The time you acted on bad information. The time you got carried away, forgot, didn't understand. The list goes on and on.

This is why it is so important not to write people off or brand them as enemies. Be as forgiving of them as you are of yourself. Cut them the same slack you would for yourself so that you can continue to work with them and make use of their talents.

PART III

The
DISCIPLINE
of **WILL**

SEPTEMBER

FORTITUDE AND RESILIENCE

September 1st
A STRONG SOUL IS BETTER THAN GOOD LUCK

"The rational soul is stronger than any kind of fortune—from its own share it guides its affairs here or there, and is itself the cause of a happy or miserable life."

—SENECA, *MORAL LETTERS*, 98.2b

Cato the Younger had enough money to dress in fine clothing. Yet he often walked around Rome barefoot, indifferent to assumptions people made about him as he passed. He could have indulged in the finest food. He chose instead to eat simple fare. Whether it was raining or intensely hot, he went bareheaded by choice.

Why not indulge in some easy relief? Because Cato was training his soul to be strong and resilient. Specifically, he was learning indifference: an attitude of "let come what may" that would serve him well in the trenches with the army, in the Forum and the Senate, and in his life as a father and statesman.

His training prepared him for any conditions, any kind of luck. If we undergo our own training and preparations, we might find ourselves similarly strengthened.

September 2nd
THE PHILOSOPHER'S SCHOOL IS A HOSPITAL

"Men, the philosopher's lecture-hall is a hospital—you shouldn't walk out of it feeling pleasure, but pain, for you aren't well when you enter it."

—EPICTETUS, *DISCOURSES*, 3.23.30

Have you ever been to physical therapy or rehab? No matter what the name implies or how many people you see lying about, getting massages, it's not a fun place to be. It turns out that healing *hurts*. The trained experts know exactly where to exert pressure and what to subject to stress so that they can strengthen where the patient is weak and help stimulate the areas that have atrophied.

Stoic philosophy is a lot like that. Some observations or exercises will touch one of your pressure points. It's nothing personal. It's *supposed* to hurt. That's how you'll develop the will to endure and persevere through life's many difficulties.

September 3rd
FIRST, A HARD WINTER TRAINING

"We must undergo a hard winter training and not rush into things
for which we haven't prepared."

—EPICTETUS, *DISCOURSES*, 1.2.32

Before the advent of modern warfare, armies typically disbanded during the winter. War was not the total war as we understand it today, but more like a series of raids punctuated by the rare decisive battle.

When Epictetus says we ought to go through "hard winter training"—the Greek word is *cheimaskêsai*—he was disputing the notion that there is such a thing as part-time soldiering (or part-time anything for that matter). In order to achieve victory, one must dedicate every second and every resource into preparation and training. LeBron James doesn't take a summer break—he uses it to work on other aspects of his game. The U.S. military trains its soldiers day and night when not at war, in preparation for when they have to go to war; when they do go to war, they fight until it's over.

The same is true for us. We can't do this life thing halfheartedly. There's no time off. There aren't even weekends. We are always preparing for what life might throw at us—and when it does, we're ready and don't stop until we've handled it.

September 4th
HOW CAN YOU KNOW IF YOU'VE NEVER BEEN TESTED?

"I judge you unfortunate because you have never lived through misfortune. You have passed through life without an opponent— no one can ever know what you are capable of, not even you."

—SENECA, *ON PROVIDENCE*, 4.3

Most people who have gone through difficult periods in their life come to later wear those experiences as badges of honor. "Those were the days," they might say, even though now they live in much better circumstances. "To be young and hungry again," another might say wistfully. "It was the best thing that ever happened to me," or "I wouldn't change a thing about it." As tough as those periods were, they were ultimately formative experiences. They made those people who they are.

There's another benefit of so-called misfortune. Having experienced and survived it, we walk away with a better understanding of our own capacity and inner strength. Passing a trial by fire is empowering because you know that in the future you can survive similar adversity. "What does not kill me makes me stronger," Nietzsche said.

So today if things look like they might take a bad turn or your luck might change, why worry? This might be one of those formative experiences you will be grateful for later.

266   FORTITUDE AND RESILIENCE

September 5th
FOCUS ON WHAT IS YOURS ALONE

"Remember, then, if you deem what is by nature slavish to be free, and what is not your own to be yours, you will be shackled and miserable, blaming both gods and other people. But if you deem as your own only what is yours, and what belongs to others as truly not yours, then no one will ever be able to coerce or to stop you, you will find no one to blame or accuse, you will do nothing against your will, you will have no enemy, no one will harm you, because no harm can affect you."

—EPICTETUS, *ENCHIRIDION*, 1.3

After Captain James Stockdale was shot down over Vietnam, he endured seven and a half years in various prison camps. He was subjected to brutal torture but always struggled to resist. Once, when his captors intended to force him to appear in a propaganda video, he purposely and severely injured himself to make that impossible.

When Stockdale's plane was hit, he told himself that he was "entering the world of Epictetus." He didn't mean that he was attending a philosophy seminar. He knew what he was to face when he crash-landed. He knew it wouldn't be easy to survive.

Interviewed by Jim Collins for the business classic *Good to Great*, Stockdale explained there was one group that had the most trouble in the prison. "It was the optimists," he said, ". . . the ones who said, 'We're going to be out by Christmas.' And Christmas would come, and Christmas would go. Then they'd say, 'We're going to be out by Easter.' And Easter would come, and Easter would go. And then Thanksgiving, and then it would be Christmas again. And they died of a broken heart."

But Stockdale persevered and did make it out. He quenched his desires and focused exclusively on what he did control: himself.

September 6th
THEY CAN THROW YOU IN CHAINS, BUT . . .

"You can bind up my leg, but not even Zeus has the power to break my freedom of choice."

—EPICTETUS, *DISCOURSES*, 1.1.23

It was said that Epictetus walked with a permanent limp as a result of being chained up as a slave. Two thousand years later, James Stockdale also had his legs chained in irons (and his arms bound behind his back and pulled from the ceiling, repeatedly wrenching them from their sockets). Future senator John McCain was in that same prison, subjected to much of the same abuse. Because his father was famous, McCain was repeatedly offered by his captors a chance to abandon his men and be sent home early. He too held tightly to his freedom of choice, declining to submit to that temptation even though it meant a loss of the physical freedom he must have ached for.

None of these men broke. No one could make them sacrifice their principles. That's the thing—someone can throw you in chains, but they don't have the power to change who you are. Even under the worst torture and cruelties that humans can inflict on one another, our power over our own mind and our power to make our own decisions can't be broken—only relinquished.

September 7th
OUR HIDDEN POWER

"Consider who you are. Above all, a human being, carrying no
greater power than your own reasoned choice, which oversees all
other things, and is free from any other master."

—EPICTETUS, *DISCOURSES*, 2.10.1

The psychologist Viktor Frankl spent three years imprisoned in various concentration camps, including Auschwitz. His family and his wife had been killed, his life's work destroyed, his freedom taken from him. He quite literally had nothing left. Yet, as he discovered after much thought, he still retained one thing: the ability to determine *what this suffering meant*. Not even the Nazis could take that from him.

Further, Frankl realized that he could actually find positives in his situation. Here was an opportunity to continue testing and exploring his psychological theories (and perhaps revise them). He could still be of service to others. He even took some solace in the fact that his loved ones were spared the pain and misery that he faced daily in that camp.

Your hidden power is your ability to use reason and make choices, however limited or small. Think about the areas of your life where you are under duress or weighed down by obligation. What are the choices available to you, day after day? You might be surprised at how many there actually are. Are you taking advantage? Are you finding the positives?

September 8th
DO NOT BE DECEIVED BY FORTUNE

"No one is crushed by Fortune, unless they are first deceived by her . . . those who aren't pompous in good times, don't have their bubbles burst with change. Against either circumstance, the stable person keeps their rational soul invincible, for it's precisely in the good times they prove their strength against adversity."

—SENECA, *ON CONSOLATION TO HELVIA*, 5.4b, 5b–6

In 41 AD, Seneca was exiled from Rome to Corsica—for what exactly, we are not sure, but the rumors were that he had an affair with the sister of the emperor. Shortly afterward, he sent a letter to his mother seeking to reassure her and comfort her in her grief. But in many ways, he must have been speaking to himself as well—scolding himself a little for this unexpected twist he was taking pretty hard.

He'd managed to achieve some measure of political and social success. He might have chased some pleasures of the flesh. Now he and his family were dealing with the consequences—as we all must bear for our behavior and for the risks we take.

How would he respond? How would he deal with it? Well, at the very least, his instincts were to comfort his mother instead of simply bemoaning his own suffering. Though some other letters show that Seneca begged and lobbied for his return to Rome and power (a request eventually granted), he seems to have borne the pain and disgrace of exile fairly well. The philosophy that he'd long studied prepared him for this kind of adversity and gave him the determination and patience he needed to wait it out. When he found his fortune restored as he returned to power, philosophy prevented him from taking it for granted or becoming dependent on it. This was good because fortune had another turn in store for him. When the new emperor turned his wrath on Seneca, philosophy found him ready and prepared once again.

September 9th
NOTHING TO FEAR BUT FEAR ITSELF

"But there is no reason to live and no limit to our miseries if we let
our fears predominate."

—SENECA, *MORAL LETTERS*, 13.12b

In the early days of what would become known as the Great Depression, a new president named Franklin Delano Roosevelt was sworn in and gave his first inaugural address. As the last president to hold office before the Twentieth Amendment was ratified, FDR wasn't able to take office until March—meaning that the country had been without strong leadership for months. Panic was in the air, banks were failing, and people were scared.

You've probably heard the "nothing to fear but fear itself" sound bite that FDR gave in that famous speech, but the full line is worth reading because it applies to many difficult things we face in life:

"Let me assert my firm belief that the only thing we have to fear is
fear itself—nameless, unreasoning, unjustified terror which par-
alyzes needed efforts to convert retreat into advance."

The Stoics knew that fear was to be feared because of the miseries it creates. The things we fear pale in comparison to the damage we do to ourselves and others when we unthinkingly scramble to avoid them. An economic depression is bad; a panic is worse. A tough situation isn't helped by terror—it only makes things harder. And that's why we must resist it and reject it if we wish to turn this situation around.

September 10th
PREPARING ON THE SUNNY DAY

"Here's a lesson to test your mind's mettle: take part of a week in which you have only the most meager and cheap food, dress scantly in shabby clothes, and ask yourself if this is really the worst that you feared. It is when times are good that you should gird yourself for tougher times ahead, for when Fortune is kind the soul can build defenses against her ravages. So it is that soldiers practice maneuvers in peacetime, erecting bunkers with no enemies in sight and exhausting themselves under no attack so that when it comes they won't grow tired."

—SENECA, *MORAL LETTERS*, 18.5–6

What if you spent one day a month experiencing the effects of poverty, hunger, complete isolation, or any other thing you might fear? After the initial culture shock, it would start to feel normal and no longer quite so scary.

There are plenty of misfortunes one can practice, plenty of problems one can solve in advance. Pretend your hot water has been turned off. Pretend your wallet has been stolen. Pretend your cushy mattress was far away and that you have to sleep on the floor, or that your car was repossessed and you have to walk everywhere. Pretend you lost your job and need to find a new one. Again, don't just *think* about these things, but *live them*. And do it now, while things are good. As Seneca reminds us: "It is precisely in times of immunity from care that the soul should toughen itself beforehand for occasions of greater stress. . . . If you would not have a man flinch when the crisis comes, train him before it comes."

September 11th
WHAT WOULD LESS LOOK LIKE?

"Let us get used to dining out without the crowds, to being a slave to fewer slaves, to getting clothes only for their real purpose, and to living in more modest quarters."

—SENECA, *ON TRANQUILITY OF MIND*, 9.3b

The writer Stefan Zweig—known for his Stoic-esque wisdom—was at one point one of the bestselling authors in the world, only to have his life destroyed by the rise of Hitler. It's a sad yet timeless rhythm of history: politicians are run out of office for taking a stand we later recognize as courageous. Countless hardworking and prosperous couples have their money stolen by financial crooks. Someone is accused of a crime but not vindicated until years later.

At any moment we may be toppled from our perch and made to do with *less*—less money, less recognition, less access, less resources. Even the "less-es" that come with age: less mobility, less energy, less freedom. But we can prepare for that, in some way, by familiarizing ourselves with what that might feel like.

One way to protect yourself from the swings of fate—and from the emotional vertigo that can result—is by living within your means *now*. So today, we can try to get used to having and surviving on less so that if we are ever forced to have less, it would not be so bad.

September 12th
BE DOWN TO EARTH, OR BE BROUGHT DOWN

"Zeno always said that nothing was more unbecoming than putting on airs, especially with the young."

—DIOGENES LAERTIUS,
LIVES OF THE EMINENT PHILOSOPHERS, 7.1.22

Isocrates's famous letter to Demonicus (which later became the inspiration for Polonius's "To thine own self be true" speech) holds a similar warning to Zeno. Writing to the young man, Isocrates advises: "Be affable in your relations with those who approach you, and never haughty; for the pride of the arrogant even slaves can hardly endure."

One of the most common tropes in art—from ancient literature to popular movies—is the brash and overconfident young man who has to be taken down a peg by an older, wiser man. It's a cliché because it's a fact of life: people tend to get ahead of themselves, thinking they've got it all figured out and are better than those that don't. It becomes so unpleasant to put up with that someone has to drop some knowledge on them.

But this is an entirely avoidable confrontation. If the bubble is never inflated, it won't need to be popped. Overconfidence is a great weakness and a liability. But if you are already humble, no one will need to humble you—and the world is much less likely to have nasty surprises in store for you. If you stay down to earth, no one will need to bring you—oftentimes crushingly so—back down.

September 13th
PROTECTING OUR INNER FORTRESS FROM FEAR

"No, it is events that give rise to fear—when another has power over them or can prevent them, that person becomes able to inspire fear. How is the fortress destroyed? Not by iron or fire, but by judgments . . . here is where we must begin, and it is from this front that we must seize the fortress and throw out the tyrants."

—EPICTETUS, *DISCOURSES*, 4.1.85–86; 87a

The Stoics give us a marvelous concept: the Inner Citadel. It is this fortress, they believed, that protects our soul. Though we might be physically vulnerable, though we might be at the mercy of fate in many ways, our inner domain is impenetrable. As Marcus Aurelius put it (repeatedly, in fact), "stuff cannot touch the soul."

But history teaches us that impenetrable fortresses can still be breached, if betrayed from the inside. The citizens inside the walls—if they fall prey to fear or greed or avarice—can open the gates and let the enemy in. This is what many of us do when we lose our nerve and give in to fear.

You've been granted a strong fortress. Don't betray it.

September 14th
A DIFFERENT WAY TO PRAY

"Try praying differently, and see what happens: Instead of asking for 'a way to sleep with her,' try asking for 'a way to stop desiring to sleep with her.' Instead of 'a way to get rid of him,' try asking for 'a way to not crave his demise.' Instead of 'a way to not lose my child,' try asking for 'a way to lose my fear of it.'"

—MARCUS AURELIUS, *MEDITATIONS*, 9.40.(6)

Prayer has a religious connotation, but in life we all find ourselves hoping and asking for things. In a tough situation, we might silently ask for help; or, after a tough break, for a second chance from above; during a sports game, we might sit on the edge of our seat wishing for some outcome. "C'mon, c'mon, c'mon," we say. "*Please . . .*" Even if it is to no one in particular, we're still praying. Yet it's so revealing in these moments, when we're privately, powerfully yearning for something, just how nakedly selfish our requests usually are.

We want divine intervention so that our lives will magically be easier. But what about asking for fortitude and strength so you can do what you need to do? What if you sought clarity on what you do control, what is already within your power? You might find your prayers have already been answered.

September 15th
A GARDEN IS NOT FOR SHOW

"First practice not letting people know who you are—keep your philosophy to yourself for a bit. In just the manner that fruit is produced—the seed buried for a season, hidden, growing gradually so it may come to full maturity. But if the grain sprouts before the stalk is fully developed, it will never ripen. . . . That is the kind of plant you are, displaying fruit too soon, and the winter will kill you."

—EPICTETUS, *DISCOURSES*, 4.8.35b–37

After all you've read, it might be tempting to think: *This stuff is great. I get it. I'm a Stoic.* But it's not that easy. Just because you agree with the philosophy doesn't mean the roots have fully taken hold in your mind.

Fooling with books so you can sound smart or have an intimidating library is like tending a garden to impress your neighbors. Growing one to feed a family? That's a pure and profitable use of your time. The seeds of Stoicism are long underground. Do the work required to nurture and tend to them. So that they—and you—are prepared and sturdy for the hard winters of life.

September 16th
ANYONE CAN GET LUCKY,
NOT EVERYONE CAN PERSEVERE

"Success comes to the lowly and to the poorly talented, but the special characteristic of a great person is to triumph over the disasters and panics of human life."

—SENECA, *ON PROVIDENCE*, 4.1

Perhaps you know people who've been extraordinarily lucky in life. Maybe they hit the genetic lottery or have skated through classes and careers with ease. Despite never planning, making reckless decisions, jumping from one thing to the next, they've somehow survived without a scratch. There's a saying: "God favors fools."

It's natural to be a bit envious of these folks. We want the easy life too—or so we think. But is the easy life really that admirable?

Anyone can get lucky. There's no skill in being oblivious, and no one would consider that greatness.

On the other hand, the person who perseveres through difficulties, who keeps going when others quit, who makes it to their destination through hard work and honesty? That's admirable, because their survival was the result of fortitude and resilience, not birthright or circumstance. A person who overcame not just the external obstacles to success but mastered themselves and their emotions along the way? That's much more impressive. The person who has been dealt a harder hand, understood it, but still triumphed? That's greatness.

September 17th
DEALING WITH HATERS

"What if someone despises me? Let them see to it. But I will see to it that I won't be found doing or saying anything contemptible. What if someone hates me? Let them see to that. But I will see to it that I'm kind and good-natured to all, and prepared to show even the hater where they went wrong. Not in a critical way, or to show off my patience, but genuinely and usefully."

—MARCUS AURELIUS, *MEDITATIONS*, 11.13

When someone has a strong opinion about something, it usually says more about *them* than whatever or whomever the opinion happens to be about. This is especially true when it comes to resentment and hatred of other people. (It is a sad irony that the prejudiced often harbor secret attractions to those they so publicly hate.)

For this reason, the Stoic does two things when encountering hatred or ill opinion in others. They ask: *Is this opinion inside my control?* If there is a chance for influence or change, they take it. But if there isn't, they accept this person as they are (and never hate a hater). Our job is tough enough already. We don't have time to think about what other people are thinking, even if it's about us.

September 18th
DEALING WITH PAIN

"Whenever you suffer pain, keep in mind that it's nothing to be ashamed of and that it can't degrade your guiding intelligence, nor keep it from acting rationally and for the common good. And in most cases you should be helped by the saying of Epicurus, that pain is never unbearable or unending, so you can remember these limits and not add to them in your imagination. Remember too that many common annoyances are pain in disguise, such as sleepiness, fever and loss of appetite. When they start to get you down, tell yourself you are giving in to pain."

—MARCUS AURELIUS, *MEDITATIONS*, 7.64

In 1931, on a trip to New York City, Winston Churchill was struck crossing the street by a car going more than thirty miles an hour. A witness at the scene was sure that he had been killed. He would spend some eight days in the hospital, with cracked ribs and a severe head wound.

Churchill somehow retained consciousness. When he spoke to the police, he went to great lengths to insist that he was completely to blame and wanted no harm to come to the driver. Later, the driver came to visit Churchill at the hospital. When Churchill heard that the driver was out of work, he tried to offer *him*—the man who had nearly killed him—some money. More than his own pain, he was worried that the publicity from the accident would hurt the man's job prospects and sought to help how he could.

"Nature is merciful," he later wrote in a newspaper article about the experience, "and does not try her children, man or beast, beyond their compass. It is only where the cruelty of man intervenes that hellish torments appear. For the rest—live dangerously; take things as they come; dread naught, all will be well."

In the years to come, Churchill and the world would witness some of the most hellish torments that man could invent. Yet he—along with many of our ancestors—endured that pain as well. As horrible as it was, eventually all would be well again. Because like Epicurus says, nothing is unending. You just need to be strong and gracious enough to get through it.

September 19th
FLEXIBILITY OF THE WILL

"Remember that to change your mind and to follow someone's correction are consistent with a free will. For the action is yours alone—to fulfill its purpose in keeping with your impulse and judgment, and yes, with your intelligence."

—MARCUS AURELIUS, *MEDITATIONS*, 8.16

When you set your mind to a task, do you always follow through? It's an impressive feat if you do. But don't let yourself become a prisoner of that kind of determination. That asset might become a liability someday.

Conditions change. New facts come in. Circumstances arise. If you can't adapt to them—if you simply proceed onward, unable to adjust according to this additional information—you are no better than a robot. The point is not to have an iron will, but an *adaptable* will—a will that makes full use of reason to clarify perception, impulse, and judgment to act effectively for the right purpose.

It's not weak to change and adapt. Flexibility is its own kind of strength. In fact, this flexibility *combined* with strength is what will make us resilient and unstoppable.

September 20th
LIFE ISN'T A DANCE

"The art of living is more like wrestling than dancing, because an artful life requires being prepared to meet and withstand sudden and unexpected attacks."

—MARCUS AURELIUS, *MEDITATIONS*, 7.61

Dancing is a popular metaphor for life. One must be limber and agile and go along with the music. One must feel and follow and flow with their partner. But anyone who has tried to do something difficult, where there is competition or an adversary, knows that the dancing metaphor is insufficient. Nobody ever gets up on stage and tries to tackle a dancer. The dancer never gets choked out by a rival.

For a wrestler, on the other hand, adversity and the unexpected are part and parcel of what they do. Their sport is a battle, just like life. They are fighting an opponent as well as their own limitations, emotions, and training.

Life, like wrestling, requires more than graceful movement. We have to undergo hard training and cultivate an indomitable will to prevail. Philosophy is the steel against which we sharpen that will and strengthen that resolve.

September 21st
MAINTAIN COMPOSURE, MAINTAIN CONTROL

"When forced, as it seems, by circumstances into utter confusion,
get a hold of yourself quickly. Don't be locked out of the rhythm
any longer than necessary. You'll be able to keep the beat if you
are constantly returning to it."

—MARCUS AURELIUS, *MEDITATIONS*, 6.11

We're going to get caught off guard from time to time. Not just
by "black swan" type events—a terrorist attack or a financial
panic—but also by minor, unexpected occurrences. Your car battery
dies, your friend cancels at the last minute, you suddenly don't feel well.
These situations have a way of throwing us into confusion and disar-
ray. We've made an assumption about the world and built plans on top
of that assumption. Now that the assumption has collapsed, so too
might our organization or understanding.

That's perfectly OK! It happens. A line of infantrymen will face
withering attacks—what's key is that they don't allow chaos to reign.
Musicians will experience technical difficulties and lose their place
from time to time. In both cases, it just matters that they get back into
position as quickly as possible.

The same is true for you today. The order and the peace might be
interrupted by a new circumstance. OK. Get a hold of yourself and find
your way back.

September 22nd
NO PAIN, NO GAIN

"Difficulties show a person's character. So when a challenge confronts you, remember that God is matching you with a younger sparring partner, as would a physical trainer. Why? Becoming an Olympian takes sweat! I think no one has a better challenge than yours, if only you would use it like an athlete would that younger sparring partner."

—EPICTETUS, *DISCOURSES*, 1.24.1–2

The Stoics loved to use metaphors from the Olympics, especially wrestling. Like us, they saw sports as both a fun pastime as well as a training ground to practice for the challenges one will inevitably face in the course of living. As General Douglas MacArthur once said, in words later engraved at the gymnasium at West Point:

UPON THE FIELDS OF FRIENDLY STRIFE

ARE SOWN THE SEEDS

THAT, UPON OTHER FIELDS, ON OTHER DAYS

WILL BEAR THE FRUITS OF VICTORY.

Everyone has found themselves outmatched by an opponent, frustrated by some skill or attribute they have that we don't—height, speed, vision, whatever. How we choose to respond to that struggle tells us about who we are as athletes and who we'll be as people. Do we see it as a chance to learn and get stronger? Do we get frustrated and complain? Or worse, do we call it off and find an easier game to play, one that makes us feel good instead of challenged?

The greats don't avoid these tests of their abilities. They seek them out because they are not just the measure of greatness, they are the pathway to it.

September 23rd
THE MOST SECURE FORTRESS

"Remember that your ruling reason becomes unconquerable when it rallies and relies on itself, so that it won't do anything contrary to its own will, even if its position is irrational. How much more unconquerable if its judgments are careful and made rationally? Therefore, the mind freed from passions is an impenetrable fortress—a person has no more secure place of refuge for all time."

—MARCUS AURELIUS, *MEDITATIONS*, 8.48

Bruce Lee once made an interesting claim: "I fear not the man who has practiced ten thousand kicks once," he said, "but I fear the man who has practiced one kick ten thousand times." When we repeat an action so often it becomes unconscious behavior, we can default to it without thinking.

Training in the martial arts or combat is a deeply thoughtful study of movement. We sometimes think of soldiers as automatons, but what they've actually built is a steady pattern of unconscious behaviors. Any of us can build these.

When Marcus says that a mind can get to a place where "it won't do anything contrary to its own will, even if its position is irrational," what he means is that proper training can change your default habits. Train yourself to give up anger, and you won't be angry at every fresh slight. Train yourself to avoid gossip, and you won't get pulled into it. Train yourself on any habit, and you'll be able to unconsciously go to that habit in trying times.

Think about which behaviors you'd like to be able to default to if you could. How many of them have you practiced only once? Let today be twice.

September 24th
IT COULD HAPPEN TO YOU

"Being unexpected adds to the weight of a disaster, and being a surprise has never failed to increase a person's pain. For that reason, nothing should ever be unexpected by us. Our minds should be sent out in advance to all things and we shouldn't just consider the normal course of things, but what could actually happen. For is there anything in life that Fortune won't knock off its high horse if it pleases her?"

—SENECA, *MORAL LETTERS*, 91.3a–4

In the year 64, during the reign of Nero, a fire tore through the city of Rome. The French city of Lyons sent a large sum of money to aid the victims. The next year the citizens of Lyons were suddenly struck by a tragic fire of their own, prompting Nero to send an equal sum to its victims. As Seneca wrote about the event to a friend in one of his letters, he must have been struck by the poetry—one city helping another, only to be struck by similar disaster not long after.

How often does that happen to us? We comfort a friend during a breakup, only to be surprised when our own relationship ends. We must prepare in our minds for the possibility of extreme reversals of fate. The next time you make a donation to charity, don't just think about the good turn you're doing, but take a moment to consider that one day you may need to receive charity yourself.

As far as we know, Seneca truly *lived* these words. Just a year or so after writing this letter, he was falsely accused of plotting against Nero. The price? Seneca was sentenced to commit suicide. As the historian Tacitus relates the scene, Seneca's closest friends wept and protested the verdict. "Where," Seneca asked them repeatedly, "are your maxims of philosophy, or the preparations of so many years' study against evils to come? Who knew not Nero's cruelty?" That is: he knew it could happen to him too, and so he was prepared for it.

September 25th
THE VULNERABILITY OF DEPENDENCE

"Show me someone who isn't a slave! One is a slave to lust, another
to greed, another to power, and all are slaves to fear. I could name
a former Consul who is a slave to a little old woman, a millionaire
who is the slave of the cleaning woman. . . . No servitude is more
abject than the self-imposed."

—SENECA, *MORAL LETTERS*, 47.17

We're *all* addicts in one way or another. We're addicted to our
routines, to our coffee, to our comfort, to someone else's approval.
These dependencies mean we're not in control of our own lives—the
dependency is.

"Anyone who truly wants to be free," Epictetus said, "won't desire
something that is actually in someone else's control, unless they want
to be a slave." The subjects of our affection can be removed from us
at a moment's notice. Our routines can be disrupted, the doctor can
forbid us from drinking coffee, we can be thrust into uncomfortable
situations.

This is why we must strengthen ourselves by testing these dependencies before they become too great. Can you try going without this
or that for a day? Can you put yourself on a diet for a month? Can you
resist the urge to pick up the phone to make that call? Have you ever
taken a cold shower? It's not so bad after the first couple of times. Have
you ever driven a friend's car while the nicer one you own was in the
shop? Was it really that bad? Make yourself invulnerable to your
dependency on comfort and convenience, or one day your vulnerability
might bring you to your knees.

September 26th
WHAT TIME OFF IS FOR

"Leisure without study is death—a tomb for the living person."
—SENECA, *MORAL LETTERS*, 82.4

You deserve a vacation. You work hard. You sacrifice. You push yourself. It's time for a break. Hop a plane, check into your hotel, and head to the beach—but tuck a book under your arm (and not a trashy beach read). Make sure you enjoy your relaxation like a poet—not idly but *actively*, observing the world around you, taking it all in, better understanding your place in the universe. Take a day off from work every now and then, but not a day off from learning.

Maybe your goal is to make enough money so that you can retire early. Good for you! But the purpose of retirement is not to live a life of indolence or to run out the clock, as easy as that might be to do. Rather, it's to allow for the pursuit of your real calling now that a big distraction is out of the way. To sit around all day and do nothing? To watch endless amounts of television or simply travel from place to place so that you might cross locations off a checklist? That is not life. It's not freedom either.

September 27th
WHAT WILL PROSPERITY REVEAL?

"For even peace itself will supply more reason for worry. Not even safe circumstances will bring you confidence once your mind has been shocked—once it gets in the habit of blind panic, it can't provide for its own safety. For it doesn't really avoid danger, it just runs away. Yet we are exposed to greater danger with our backs turned."

—SENECA, *MORAL LETTERS*, 104.10b

There's an old proverb that money doesn't change people, it just makes them more of who they are. Robert Caro has written that "power doesn't corrupt, it *reveals*." In some ways, prosperity—financial and personal—is the same way.

If your mind has developed a certain cast—the habit of panicking, in Seneca's example—then it won't matter how good things get for you. You're still primed for panic. Your mind will still find things to worry about, and you'll still be miserable. Perhaps more so even, because now you have more to lose.

This is why it's foolish to hope for good fortune. If you were to hope for one thing, you could hope for the strength of character that's able to thrive in good fortune. Or better, *work* for that kind of character and confidence. Consider every action and every thought—think of them as building blocks of your indestructible character. Then work to make each one strong and significant in its own right.

September 28th
YOU HOLD THE TRUMP CARD

"How appropriate that the gods put under our control only the most powerful ability that governs all the rest—the ability to make the right use of external appearances—and that they didn't put anything else under our control. Was this simply because they weren't willing to give us more? I think if it had been possible they would have given us more, but it was impossible.

—EPICTETUS, *DISCOURSES*, 1.1.7–8

We could look at the upcoming day and despair at all the things we don't control: other people, our health, the temperature, the outcome of a project once it leaves our hands.

Or we could look out at that very same day and rejoice at the one thing we do control: the ability to decide what any event means.

This second option offers the ultimate power—a true and fair form of control. If you had control over other people, wouldn't other people have control over you? Instead, what you've been granted is the fairest and most usable of trump cards. While you don't control external events, you retain the ability to decide how you *respond* to those events. You control what every external event means to you personally.

This includes the difficult one in front of you right now. You'll find, if you approach it right, that this trump card is plenty.

September 29th
YOUR ACTUAL NEEDS ARE SMALL

"Nothing can satisfy greed, but even a small measure satisfies nature. So it is that the poverty of an exile brings no misfortune, for no place of exile is so barren as not to produce ample support for a person."

—SENECA, *ON CONSOLATION TO HELVIA*, 10.11b

It can be beneficial to reflect on what you used to accept as normal. Consider your first paycheck—how *big* it seemed then. Or your first apartment, with its own bedroom and bathroom and the ramen you gladly scarfed down in the kitchen. Today, as you've become more successful, these conditions would hardly feel sufficient. In fact, you probably want even more than what you have right now. Yet just a few years ago those paltry conditions were not only enough, they felt great!

When we become successful, we forget how strong we used to be. We are so used to what we have, we half believe we'd die without it. Of course, this is just the comfort talking. In the days of the world wars, our parents and grandparents made do with rationed gas, butter, and electricity. They were fine, just as you have been fine when you had less.

Remember today that you'd be OK if things suddenly went wrong. Your actual needs are small. There is very little that could happen that would truly threaten your survival. Think about that—and adjust your worries and fears accordingly.

September 30th
YOU CAN'T TOUCH ME

"If you lay violent hands on me, you'll have my body, but my mind will remain with Stilpo."

—Zeno, quoted in Diogenes Laertius, *Lives of the Eminent Philosophers*, 7.1.24

Zeno is not claiming magic powers but simply that while his body can be victimized, philosophy protects his mind—cultivated under his teacher, Stilpo—with an inner fortress whose gates can never be broken from the outside, only surrendered.

Look at Rubin "Hurricane" Carter, the boxer wrongly convicted of homicide who spent nearly twenty years in prison. He would say, "I don't acknowledge the existence of the prison. It doesn't exist for me." Of course, the prison literally existed, and he was physically inside it. But he refused to let his mind be contained by it.

That's a power that you have too. Hopefully you'll never have to use this power in a situation of violence or grave injustice; however, in the midst of any and every kind of adversity, it is there. No matter what's happening to your body, no matter what the outside world inflicts on you, your mind can remain philosophical. It's still yours. It's untouchable—and in a way, then, so are you.

OCTOBER

VIRTUE AND KINDNESS

October 1st
LET VIRTUE SHINE BRIGHT

"Does the light of a lamp shine and keep its glow until its fuel is spent? Why shouldn't your truth, justice, and self-control shine until you are extinguished?"

—MARCUS AURELIUS, *MEDITATIONS*, 12.15

Seneca, repeating Heraclitus, writes that "we mortals are lighted and extinguished." The light of reason suffuses the universe. Whether the wick of your lamp is being lit for the first time, after a long period of darkness, or even right before the proverbial big sleep, it makes no difference.

Here is where you are right now, and it's as good a place as any to let virtue shine and continue to shine for as long as you exist.

October 2nd
THE MOST VALUABLE ASSET

"But the wise person can lose nothing. Such a person has everything stored up for themselves, leaving nothing to Fortune, their own goods are held firm, bound in virtue, which requires nothing from chance, and therefore can't be either increased or diminished."

—SENECA, *ON THE FIRMNESS OF THE WISE*, 5.4

Some people put their money in assets—stocks, bonds, property. Others invest in relationships or accomplishments, knowing that they can draw on these things just as easily as others can draw funds from a bank account. But a third type, Seneca says, invests in themselves—in being a good and wise person.

Which of these assets is most immune to market fluctuations and disasters? Which is most resilient in the face of trials and tribulations? Which will never abandon you? Seneca's own life is an interesting example. He became quite wealthy as a friend of the emperor, but as Nero became more and more deranged, Seneca realized he needed to get out. He offered Nero a deal: he would give Nero all his money and return all of Nero's gifts in exchange for complete and total freedom.

Ultimately, Nero rejected this offer, but Seneca left anyway, retiring in relative peace. But one day, the executioners came with their mortal decree. In that moment, what did Seneca rely on? It wasn't his money. It wasn't his friends, who, although they meant well, were a considerable source of grief and mourning. It was his virtue and inner strength.

It was Seneca's most trying moment—his last and his finest.

October 3rd
A MANTRA OF MUTUAL INTERDEPENDENCE

"Meditate often on the interconnectedness and mutual interdependence of all things in the universe. For in a sense, all things are mutually woven together and therefore have an affinity for each other—for one thing follows after another according to their tension of movement, their sympathetic stirrings, and the unity of all substance."

—MARCUS AURELIUS, *MEDITATIONS*, 6.38

Anne Lamott once observed that all writers "are little rivers running into one lake," all contributing to the same big project. The same is true in many industries—though sadly, even inside the same company, people selfishly forget they're working together. As human beings we all breathe the atoms that made up our ancestors and flow into the same earth when we die.

Over and over again, the Stoics reminded themselves of the interconnectedness of life. Perhaps that was because life in Greece and Rome was particularly harsh. Animals and people were slaughtered senselessly to amuse the masses in the Colosseum (events lamented in the Stoic writings). Countries were conquered and its citizens sold into slavery to expand the empire (the futility of which the Stoics also lamented). This kind of cruelty is possible only when we forget how we're related to our fellow human beings and the environment.

Today, take a moment to remember that we are woven together and that each of us plays a role (good, bad, or ugly) in this world.

October 4th
ALL FOR ONE, ONE FOR ALL

"That which isn't good for the hive, isn't good for the bee."
—MARCUS AURELIUS, *MEDITATIONS*, 6.54

Inherent in the Stoic concept of *sympatheia* is the notion of an inter-connected cosmos in which everything in the universe is part of a larger whole. Marcus Aurelius was one of the first writers to articulate the notion of cosmopolitanism—saying that he was a citizen of the world, not just of Rome.

The idea that you're a bee in the hive is a reminder of this perspective. Marcus even states the reverse of that idea later in his *Meditations*, just so he doesn't forget: "That which doesn't harm the community can't harm the individual."

Just because something is bad for you doesn't mean it's bad for everyone. Just because something is good for you definitely doesn't mean it's good for everyone. Think of the hedge fund managers who bet massively against the economy—they profited by rooting for essentially everyone and everything else to fail. Is that who you want to be? A good Stoic understands that proper impulses, and the right actions that arise from them, naturally carry the good of the whole, which is the wise person's only good. Conversely, good and wise actions by the whole are what's good for the individual.

October 5th
WORDS CAN'T BE UNSAID

"Better to trip with the feet than with the tongue."

—ZENO, QUOTED IN DIOGENES LAERTIUS,
LIVES OF THE EMINENT PHILOSOPHERS, 7.1.26

You can always get up after you fall, but remember, what has been said can never be unsaid. Especially cruel and hurtful things.

October 6th
LOOKING OUT FOR EACH OTHER

"It's in keeping with Nature to show our friends affection and to celebrate their advancement, as if it were our very own. For if we don't do this, virtue, which is strengthened only by exercising our perceptions, will no longer endure in us."

—SENECA, *MORAL LETTERS*, 109.15

Watching other people succeed is one of the toughest things to do—especially if we are not doing well ourselves. In our hunter-gatherer minds, we suspect that life is a zero-sum game—that for someone to have more means that we might end up with less.

But like all parts of philosophy, empathy and selflessness are a matter of practice. As Seneca observed, it's possible to learn to "rejoice in all their successes and be moved by their every failure." This is what a virtuous person does.

They teach themselves to actively cheer for other people—even in cases where that might come at their own expense—and to put aside jealousy and possessiveness. You can do that too.

October 7th
A SELFISH REASON TO BE GOOD

"The person who does wrong, does wrong to themselves. The unjust person is unjust to themselves—making themselves evil."

—Marcus Aurelius, *Meditations*, 9.4

The next time you do something wrong, try to remember how it made you feel. Rarely does one say, "I felt great!"

There is a reason there's often vomit at crime scenes. Instead of the catharsis the person thought they'd feel when they let themselves get out of control or when they got their revenge, they ended up making themselves sick. We feel a version of this when we lie, when we cheat, when we screw someone over.

So in that split second before your ill-gotten gains kick in, ask: *How do I feel about myself?* Is that moment when fear rises in your throat because you suspect you may get caught really worth it?

Self-awareness and wrongdoing rarely go together. If you need a selfish reason to not do wrong—put yourself in touch with these feelings. They're a powerful disincentive.

October 8th
A HIGHER PLEASURE

"Yes, getting your wish would have been so nice. But isn't that exactly why pleasure trips us up? Instead, see if these things might be even nicer—a great soul, freedom, honesty, kindness, saintliness. For there is nothing so pleasing as wisdom itself, when you consider how sure-footed and effortless the works of understanding and knowledge are."

—MARCUS AURELIUS, *MEDITATIONS*, 5.9

Nobody can argue that pleasure doesn't *feel* good. That's pretty much what it does by definition.

But today Marcus Aurelius is reminding you—just as he reminded himself—that those pleasures hardly stand up to virtue. The dopamine rush that comes from sex is momentary. So is the pride of an accomplishment or the hearty applause of a crowd. These pleasures are powerful, but they wear off and leave us wanting more. What lasts longer (and remains more within our circle of control)? Wisdom, good character, sobriety, and kindness.

October 9th
SET THE STANDARDS AND USE THEM

"When the standards have been set, things are tested and weighed. And the work of philosophy is just this, to examine and uphold the standards, but the work of a truly good person is in using those standards when they know them."

—EPICTETUS, *DISCOURSES*, 2.11.23–25

We go through our days responding and reacting, but it's rare to really pause and ask: *Is this thing I'm about to do consistent with what I believe?* Or, better: *Is this the kind of thing the person I would like to be should do?*

The work of living is to set standards and then *not* compromise them. When you're brushing your teeth, choosing your friends, losing your temper, falling in love, instructing your child, or walking your dog—all of these are opportunities.

Not, *I want to do good*—that's an excuse. But, *I will do good in this particular instance, right now.* Set a standard; hold fast to it. That's all there is.

October 10th
REVERENCE AND JUSTICE

"Leave the past behind, let the grand design take care of the future, and instead only rightly guide the present to reverence and justice. Reverence so that you'll love what you've been allotted, for nature brought you both to each other. Justice so that you'll speak the truth freely and without evasion, and so that you'll act only as the law and value of things require."

—MARCUS AURELIUS, *MEDITATIONS*, 12.1

Aulus Gellius relates that Epictetus once said, "If anyone would take two words to heart and take pains to govern and watch over themselves by them, they will live an impeccable and immensely tranquil life. The two words are: persist and resist." That's great advice. But what principles should determine what we persist in and what we ought to resist?

Marcus supplies that answer: reverence and justice. In other words, virtue.

October 11th
HONESTY AS OUR DEFAULT

"How rotten and fraudulent when people say they intend to 'give it to you straight.' What are you up to, dear friend? It shouldn't need your announcement, but be readily seen, as if written on your forehead, heard in the ring of your voice, a flash in your eyes—just as the beloved sees it all in the lover's glance. In short, the straight-forward and good person should be like a smelly goat—you know when they are in the room with you."

—MARCUS AURELIUS, *MEDITATIONS*, 11.15

All of us have used phrases like that before. "I'm going to be straight-forward with you here . . ." "I'll be honest . . ." "No disrespect but . . ." Empty expressions or not, they prompt the question: If you have to preface your remarks with indicators of honesty or directness, what does that say about everything else you say? If you say you're being honest *now*, does that mean you usually aren't?

What if, instead, you cultivated a life and a reputation in which honesty was as bankable as a note from the U.S. Treasury, as emphatic and explicit as a contract, as permanent as a tattoo? Not only would it save you from needing to use the reassurances that other, less scrupulous people must engage in, it will make you a better person.

October 12th
ALWAYS LOVE

"Hecato says, 'I can teach you a love potion made without any drugs, herbs, or special spell—if you would be loved, love.'"

—SENECA, *MORAL LETTERS*, 9.6

In 1992, Barbara Jordan addressed the Democratic National Convention and railed against the greed and selfishness and divisiveness of the previous decade. People were ready for a change. "Change it to what?" she asked. "Change that environment of the 80s to an environment which is characterized by a devotion to the public interest, public service, tolerance, and love. Love. Love. Love."

Love. Love. Love. Love. Why? Because, as the Beatles put it, "In the end, the love you take is equal to the love you make." Not just in politics, not just in tolerance, but in our personal lives. There is almost no situation in which hatred helps. Yet almost every situation is made better by love—or empathy, understanding, appreciation—even situations in which you are in opposition to someone.

And who knows, you might just get some of that love back.

October 13th
REVENGE IS A DISH BEST NOT SERVED

"The best way to avenge yourself is to not be like that."

—MARCUS AURELIUS, *MEDITATIONS*, 6.6

"How much better to heal than seek revenge from injury. Vengeance wastes a lot of time and exposes you to many more injuries than the first that sparked it. Anger always outlasts hurt. Best to take the opposite course. Would anyone think it normal to return a kick to a mule or a bite to a dog?"

—SENECA, *ON ANGER*, 3.27.2

Let's say that someone has treated you rudely. Let's say someone got promoted ahead of you because they took credit for your work or did something dishonest. It's natural to think: *Oh, that's how the world works,* or *One day it will be my turn to be like that.* Or most common: *I'll get them for this.* Except these are the worst possible responses to bad behavior.

As Marcus and Seneca both wrote, the proper response—indeed the best revenge—is to exact no revenge at all. If someone treats you rudely and you respond with rudeness, you have not done anything but prove to them that they were justified in their actions. If you meet other people's dishonesty with dishonesty of your own, guess what? You're proving them right—now everyone *is* a liar.

Instead, today, let's seek to be better than the things that disappoint or hurt us. Let's try to be the example we'd like others to follow. It's awful to be a cheat, to be selfish, to feel the need to inflict pain on our fellow human beings. Meanwhile, living morally and well is quite nice.

October 14th
DON'T GET MAD. HELP

"Are you angry when someone's armpits stink or when their breath is bad? What would be the point? Having such a mouth and such armpits, there's going to be a smell emanating. You say, they must have sense, can't they tell how they are offending others? Well, you have sense too, congratulations! So, use your natural reason to awaken theirs, show them, call it out. If the person will listen, you will have cured them without useless anger. No drama nor unseemly show required."

—MARCUS AURELIUS, *MEDITATIONS*, 5.28

The person sitting next to you on the plane, the one who is loudly chattering and knocking around in your space? The one you're grinding your teeth about, hating from the depth of your soul because they're rude, ignorant, obnoxious? In these situations, you might feel it takes everything you have to restrain yourself from murdering them.

It's funny how *that* thought comes into our heads before, you know, politely asking them to stop, or making the minor scene of asking for a different seat. We'd rather be pissed off, bitter, raging inside than risk an awkward conversation that might actually help this person and make the world a better place. We don't just want people to be better, we expect it to magically happen—that we can simply will other people to change, burning holes into their skull with our angry stare.

Although when you think about it that way, it makes you wonder who the rude one actually is.

October 15th
GIVE PEOPLE THE BENEFIT OF THE DOUBT

"Everything turns on your assumptions about it, and that's on you. You can pluck out the hasty judgment at will, and like steering a ship around the point, you will find calm seas, fair weather and a safe port."

—MARCUS AURELIUS, *MEDITATIONS*, 12.22

"Even a dog," Supreme Court Justice Oliver Wendell Holmes once said, "distinguishes between being stumbled over and being kicked." Yet if you've ever accidentally stepped on your dog, you know that the first reaction is usually a bark or a yelp or a quick snap of the jaws. In the instant, there is no distinction—just pain. Then it sees who it was, hears your soothing voice, and goes right back to wagging its tail.

A virtuous person does not jump to hasty judgments about other people. A virtuous person is generous with assumptions: that something was an accident, that someone didn't know, that it won't happen again. This makes life easier to bear and makes us more tolerant. Meanwhile, assuming malice—the most hasty of judgments—makes everything harder to bear.

Be deliberate and accommodating with your assumptions about other people and you'll find, as Marcus says, calmer seas and fairer weather.

October 16th
SPREAD THE WORD

"Some people with exceptional minds quickly grasp virtue, or produce it within themselves. But other dim and lazy types, hindered
by bad habits, must have their rusty souls constantly scrubbed
down. . . . The weaker sorts will be helped and lifted from their
bad opinions if we put them in the care of philosophy's principles."

—SENECA, *MORAL LETTERS*, 95.36–37

Stoicism is not an evangelical religion. You're not obligated to save
anyone—there's no risk of hell if a soul remains in ignorance of the
teachings of Epictetus or Marcus Aurelius.

But now that you've learned and studied a better path, you can be
of service to others. You can share your wisdom or insight with a friend
or stranger—remembering that behavior is always a better example
than a lecture.

Everyone deserves to benefit from "philosophy's principles" as Seneca put it. If you see someone who is in need of help, or has asked for
guidance, provide it. You owe them that much.

October 17th
THE BENEFIT OF KINDNESS

"A benefit should be kept like a buried treasure, only to be dug up
in necessity. . . . Nature bids us to do well by all. . . . Wherever there
is a human being, we have an opportunity for kindness."

—SENECA, *ON THE HAPPY LIFE*, 24.2–3

The first person you meet today—passing acquaintance or friend—
no matter the context—positive or negative—is an opportunity
for kindness. Or as different translators have taken this line from Seneca to mean, it is an opportunity for *benefit*. For both of you. You can
seek to understand where they are coming from. You can seek to understand who they are, what they need, and what forces or impulses might
be acting on them. And you can treat them well and be better off for it.

The same is true with the second person you encounter, and the
third. Of course, there is no guarantee that they will return the favor,
but that's not our concern. As always, we're going to focus on what we
control: in this case, the ability to choose to respond with kindness.

October 18th
FRENEMIES

> "There's nothing worse than a wolf befriending sheep. Avoid false friendship at all costs. If you are good, straightforward, and well meaning it should show in your eyes and not escape notice."
>
> —MARCUS AURELIUS, *MEDITATIONS*, 11.15

It's pretty obvious that one should keep away from the wicked and two-faced as much as possible—the jealous friend, the narcissistic parent, the untrustworthy partner. At first glance, Marcus Aurelius is reminding us to avoid false friends.

But what if we turn it around? What if, instead, we ask about the times that we have been false to *our* friends? Ultimately that's what Stoicism is about—not judging other people's behavior, but judging our own.

We've all been a frenemy at one point or another. We've been nice to their face—usually because there was something in it for us—but later, in different company, we said how we really felt. Or we've strung someone along, cared only when things were going well, or declined to help even though someone really needed us.

This behavior is beneath us—and worth remembering the next time we accuse someone else of being a bad friend.

October 19th
GOOD HABITS DRIVE OUT BAD HABITS

> "Since habit is such a powerful influence, and we're used to pursuing our impulses to gain and avoid outside our own choice, we should set a contrary habit against that, and where appearances are really slippery, use the counterforce of our training."
>
> —EPICTETUS, *DISCOURSES*, 3.12.6

When a dog is barking loudly because someone is at the door, the worst thing you can do is yell. To the dog, it's like you're barking too! When a dog is running away, it's not helpful to chase it—again, now it's like you're both running. A better option in both scenarios is to give the dog something else to do. Tell it to sit. Tell it to go to its bed or kennel. Run in the other direction. Break the pattern, interrupt the negative impulse.

The same goes for us. When a bad habit reveals itself, counteract it with a commitment to a contrary virtue. For instance, let's say you find yourself procrastinating today—don't dig in and fight it. Get up and take a walk to clear your head and reset instead. If you find yourself saying something negative or nasty, don't kick yourself. Add something positive and nice to qualify the remark.

Oppose established habits, and use the counterforce of training to get traction and make progress. If you find yourself cutting corners during a workout or on a project, say to yourself: "OK, now I am going to go even further or do even better."

Good habits have the power to drive out bad habits. And habits are easy to pick up—as we all know.

VIRTUE AND KINDNESS

October 20th
MARKS OF THE GOOD LIFE

"You have proof in the extent of your wanderings that you never found the art of living anywhere—not in logic, nor in wealth, fame, or in any indulgence. Nowhere. Where is it then? In doing what human nature demands. How is a person to do this? By having principles be the source of desire and action. What principles? Those to do with good and evil, indeed in the belief that there is no good for a human being except what creates justice, self-control, courage and freedom, and nothing evil except what destroys these things."

—MARCUS AURELIUS, *MEDITATIONS*, 8.1.(5)

What's the meaning of life? Why was I born? Most of us struggle with these questions—sometimes when we're young, sometimes not until we're older. Rarely do we find much in the way of direction. But that's simply because we miss the point. As Viktor Frankl points out in *Man's Search for Meaning*, it is not our question to ask. Instead, it is *we* who are being asked the question. It's our lives that are the answer.

No amount of travel or reading or clever sages can tell you what you want to know. Instead, it is *you* who must find the answer in your actions, in living the good life—by embodying the self-evident principles of justice, self-control, courage, freedom, and abstaining from evil.

October 21st
HEROES, HERE AND NOW

"Such behavior! People don't want to praise their contemporaries whose lives they actually share, but hold great expectations for the praise of future generations—people they haven't met or ever will! This is akin to being upset that past generations didn't praise you."

—MARCUS AURELIUS, *MEDITATIONS*, 6.18

Alexandria, the city in Egypt, still bears the name of its founder, Alexander the Great, some 2,300 years after he set foot there. How cool would it feel to have a city named after you for so many centuries? To know that people are still saying your name?

Here's a thought: it wouldn't be cool. Because, like Alexander, you'll be dead. You'll have no idea whether your name lasted down through the centuries. No one gets to enjoy their own legacy—by definition.

Worse, think of all the horrible things Alexander did to achieve what he did. He fought pointless wars. He had a terrible temper—even killing his best friend in a drunken fight. He was ruthless and a slave to his ambition. Is he really so admirable?

Instead of wasting even a second considering the opinions of future people—people who are not even born yet—focus every bit of yourself on being the best person you can be in the present moment. On doing the right thing, right now. The distant future is irrelevant. Be good and noble and impressive now—while it still matters.

October 22nd
IT'S EASY TO GET BETTER. BUT BETTER AT WHAT?

"So someone's good at taking down an opponent, but that doesn't
make them more community-minded, or modest, or well-prepared
for any circumstance, or more tolerant of the faults of others."
—MARCUS AURELIUS, *MEDITATIONS*, 7.52

Self-improvement is a noble pursuit. Most people don't even bother.
But among those who do, it's possible for vanity and superficiality
to corrupt this process. Do you want six-pack abs because you are
challenging yourself and committing to a difficult goal? Or is it because
you want to impress people with your shirt off? Are you running that
marathon because you want to test your limits or because you're running away from your problems at home?

Our will shouldn't be directed at becoming the person who is in
perfect shape or who can speak multiple languages but who doesn't
have a second for other people. What's the point of winning at sports
but losing in the effort to be a good husband, wife, father, mother, son,
or daughter? Let's not confuse getting better at *stuff* with being a better *person*. One is a much bigger priority than the other.

October 23rd
SHOW THE QUALITIES YOU WERE MADE FOR

"People aren't in awe of your sharp mind? So be it. But you have many other qualities you can't claim to have been deprived of at birth. Display then those qualities in your own power: honesty, dignity, endurance, chastity, contentment, frugality, kindness, freedom, persistence, avoiding gossip, and magnanimity."

—MARCUS AURELIUS, *MEDITATIONS*, 5.5

It's easy to blame our circumstances. One person curses that they weren't born taller, another that they're not smarter, with a different complexion, or born in a different country. It'd be hard to find a single person on this planet—from supermodels on down—who doesn't think they're deficient in at least some way. But whatever your perceived deficits are, remember that there are positive qualities that you can develop that don't depend on genetic accidents.

You have the *choice* to be truthful. You have the *choice* to be dignified. You can *choose* to endure. You can *choose* to be happy. You can choose to be chaste. You can choose to be thrifty. You can choose to be kind to others. You can choose to be free. You can persist under difficult odds. You can avoid trafficking in gossip. You can choose to be gracious.

And honestly, aren't the traits that are the result of effort and skill more impressive anyway?

October 24th
THE FOUNTAIN OF GOODNESS

"Dig deep within yourself, for there is a fountain of goodness ever
ready to flow if you will keep digging."

—MARCUS AURELIUS, *MEDITATIONS*, 7.59

Today, we could hope that goodness comes our way—good news,
good weather, good luck. Or we could *find* it ourselves, *in* ourselves. Goodness isn't something that's going to be delivered by mail.
You have to dig it up inside your own soul. You find it within your own
thoughts, and you make it with your own actions.

October 25th
TWO TASKS

"What, then, makes a person free from hindrance and self-determining? For wealth doesn't, neither does high-office, state or kingdom—rather, something else must be found . . . in the case of living, it is the knowledge of how to live."

—EPICTETUS, *DISCOURSES*, 4.1.62–64

You have two essential tasks in life: to be a good person and to pursue the occupation that you love. Everything else is a waste of energy and a squandering of your potential.

How does one do that? OK, that's a tougher question. But the philosophy we see from the Stoics makes it simple enough: say no to distractions, to destructive emotions, to outside pressure. Ask yourself: *What is it that only I can do? What is the best use of my limited time on this planet?* Try to do the right thing when the situation calls for it. Treat other people the way you would hope to be treated. And understand that every small choice and tiny matter is an opportunity to practice these larger principles.

That's it. That's what goes into the most important skill of all: how to live.

October 26th
THREE PARTS, ONE AIM

"The best and the greatest number of authors have asserted that philosophy consists of three parts: the moral, the natural, and the rational. The first puts the soul in order. The second thoroughly examines the natural order of things. The third inquires into the proper meaning of words, and their arrangements and proofs which keep falsehoods from creeping in to displace truth."

—SENECA, *MORAL LETTERS*, 89.9

These three parts—the moral, the natural, and the rational—have one aim. As different as they are, they have the same purpose: to help you live a good life ruled by reason.

Not in the future, but right now.

October 27th
WE REAP WHAT WE SOW

"Crimes often return to their teacher."

—SENECA, *THYESTES*, 311

It's ironic that Seneca would have one of his characters utter this line. As we know, for many years Seneca served as the tutor and mentor to the emperor Nero. There is a lot of evidence that Seneca was, in fact, a positive moral influence on the deranged young man, but even at the time, Seneca's contemporaries found it strange that a philosopher would serve as the right hand to such an evil person. They even used the Greek word *tyrannodidaskalos*—tyrant teacher—to describe him. And just as Shakespeare observed in *Macbeth*, "Bloody instructions, which, being taught, return / To plague th'inventor," Seneca's collaboration with Nero ultimately ended with the student murdering the teacher.

It's something to think about when you consider whom to work with and whom to do business with in life. If you show a client how to do something unethical or illegal, might they return the favor to an unsuspecting you later on? If you provide a bad example to your employees, to your associates, to your children, might they betray you or hurt you down the road? What goes around comes around, is the saying. Karma is a notion we have imported from the East, along similar lines.

Seneca paid a price for his instructions to Nero. As has been true throughout the ages, his hypocrisy—avoidable or not—was costly. So too will be yours.

October 28th
WE WERE MADE FOR EACH OTHER

"You'll more quickly find an earthly thing kept from the earth than you will a person cut off from other human beings."

—MARCUS AURELIUS, *MEDITATIONS*, 9.9.3

Naturally, Marcus Aurelius and the rest of the Stoics were not familiar with Newtonian physics. But they knew that what went up must come down. That's the analogy he's using here: our mutual interdependence with our fellow human beings is stronger than the law of gravity.

Philosophy attracts introverts. The study of human nature can make you aware of other people's faults and can breed contempt for others. So do struggle and difficulty—they isolate us from the world.

But none of that changes that we are, as Aristotle put it, social animals. We need each other. We must be there for each other. We must take care of each other (and to allow others to care for us in return). To pretend otherwise is to violate our nature, to be more or less than what it means to be a human being.

October 29th
CHARACTER IS FATE

> "Each person acquires their own character, but their official roles are designated by chance. You should invite some to your table because they are deserving, others because they may come to deserve it."
>
> —SENECA, *MORAL LETTERS*, 47.15b

In the hiring process, most employers look at where someone went to school, what jobs they've held in the past. This is because past success can be an indicator of future successes. But is it always? There are plenty of people who were successful because of luck. Maybe they got into Oxford or Harvard because of their parents. And what about a young person who hasn't had time to build a track record? Are they worthless?

Of course not. This is why *character* is a far better measure of a man or woman. Not just for jobs, but for friendships, relationships, for everything. Heraclitus put it as a maxim: "Character is fate."

When you seek to advance your own position in life, character is the best lever—perhaps not in the short term, but certainly over the long term. And the same goes for the people you invite into your life.

October 30th
WHO GETS THE LION'S SHARE?

"Aren't you ashamed to reserve for yourself only the remnants of your life and to dedicate to wisdom only that time can't be directed to business?"

—SENECA, *ON THE BREVITY OF LIFE*, 3.5b

In one of his letters, Seneca tells a story about Alexander the Great. Apparently as Alexander was conquering the world, certain countries would offer him pieces of their territory in hopes that he'd leave them alone in exchange. Alexander would tell them, writes Seneca, that he hadn't come all the way to Asia to accept whatever they would give him, but instead they were going to have to accept whatever he chose to leave them.

According to Seneca, we should treat philosophy the same way in our lives. Philosophy shouldn't have to accept what time or energy is left over from other occupations but instead we should graciously make time for those other pursuits only once our study is finished.

If real self-improvement is what we're after, why do we leave our reading until those few minutes before we shut off the lights and go to bed? Why do we block off eight to ten hours in the middle of the day to be at the office or to go to meetings but block out no time for thinking about the big questions? The average person somehow manages to squeeze in twenty-eight hours of television per week—but ask them if they had time to study philosophy, and they will probably tell you they're too busy.

October 31st
YOU WERE BORN GOOD

"The human being is born with an inclination toward virtue."

—MUSONIUS RUFUS, *LECTURES*, 2.7.1–2

The notion of original sin has weighed down humankind for centuries. In reality, we're made to help each other and be good to each other. We wouldn't have survived as a species otherwise.

There is hardly an idea in Stoic philosophy that wouldn't be immediately agreeable to a child or that doesn't jibe with common sense. The ideas within it go to the core of who we are and what we know to be true. The only things they conflict with are the various inventions of society—which usually serve some selfish interest more than they benefit the common good.

You were born good. "All of us have been made by nature," Rufus said, "so that we can live free from error and nobly—not that one can and another can't, but all." You were born with an attraction to virtue and self-mastery. If you've gotten far from that, it's not out of some inborn corruption but from a nurturing of the wrong things and the wrong ideas. As Seneca has pointed out, philosophy is a tool to strip it all away—to get back to our true nature.

NOVEMBER

ACCEPTANCE / *AMOR FATI*

November 1st
ACCEPTING WHAT IS

"Don't seek for everything to happen as you wish it would, but rather wish that everything happens as it actually will—then your life will flow well."

—EPICTETUS, *ENCHIRIDION*, 8

"It is easy to praise providence for anything that may happen if you have two qualities: a complete view of what has actually happened in each instance and a sense of gratitude. Without gratitude what is the point of seeing, and without seeing what is the object of gratitude?"

—EPICTETUS, *DISCOURSES*, 1.6.1–2

Something happened that we wish had not. Which of these is easiest to change: our opinion or the event that is past?

The answer is obvious. Accept what happened and change your wish that it had not happened. Stoicism calls this the "art of acquiescence"—to accept rather than fight every little thing.

And the most practiced Stoics take it a step further. Instead of simply *accepting* what happens, they urge us to actually *enjoy* what has happened—whatever it is. Nietzsche, many centuries later, coined the perfect expression to capture this idea: *amor fati* (a love of fate). It's not just accepting, it's *loving* everything that happens.

To wish for what has happened to happen is a clever way to avoid disappointment because nothing is contrary to your desires. But to actually feel gratitude for what happens? To love it? That's a recipe for happiness and joy.

November 2nd
BINDING OUR WISHES TO WHAT WILL BE

"But I haven't at any time been hindered in my will, nor forced against it. And how is this possible? I have bound up my choice to act with the will of God. God wills that I be sick, such is my will. He wills that I should choose something, so do I. He wills that I reach for something, or something be given to me—I wish for the same. What God doesn't will, I do not wish for."

—EPICTETUS, *DISCOURSES*, 4.1.89

When General Dwight D. Eisenhower wrote to his wife on the eve of the invasion of Normandy, he told her, "Everything we could think of has been done, the troops are fit, everybody is doing his best. The answer is in the lap of the gods." He'd done everything he could—and now, what would happen would happen and as Epictetus might say, he was ready to bear whatever that was. In fact, Eisenhower had written another letter that night and prepared it for release in case the invasion failed. If failure was what God—or fate or luck or whatever you want to call it—willed, he was ready.

There is a wonderful lesson there. The man in charge of perhaps the most powerful army the world had ever assembled, on the eve of the most expertly organized and planned invasion the world will hopefully ever know, was humble enough to know that the outcome ultimately belonged to someone or something bigger than him.

And so it goes with all our ventures. No matter how much preparation, no matter how skilled or smart we are, the ultimate outcome is in the lap of the gods. The sooner we know that, the better we will be.

November 3rd
FOLLOWING THE DOCTOR'S ORDERS

"Just as we commonly hear people say the doctor prescribed someone particular riding exercises, or ice baths, or walking without
shoes, we should in the same way say that nature prescribed someone to be diseased, or disabled, or to suffer any kind of impairment. In the case of the doctor, prescribed means something
ordered to help aid someone's healing. But in the case of nature,
it means that what happens to each of us is ordered to help aid
our destiny."

—MARCUS AURELIUS, *MEDITATIONS*, 5.8.

The Stoics were masters at analogies and used them as a tool to help
strengthen their reasoning.

Here, Marcus observes how willingly we will put up with unpleas-
antness if commanded to by the magic words "doctor's orders." The
doctor says you've got to take this nasty medicine, and you'll do it. The
doctor tells you you have to start sleeping hanging upside down like a
bat. You'll feel silly, but soon enough you'll get to dangling because you
think it will make you better.

On the other hand, when it comes to external events, we fight like
hell if anything happens contrary to our plans. But what if, Marcus
asks, a doctor had prescribed this exact thing as a part of our treatment? What if this was as good for us as medicine?

Well, what if?

November 4th
NOT GOOD, NOR BAD

"There is no evil in things changing, just as there is no good in persisting in a new state."

—MARCUS AURELIUS, *MEDITATIONS*, 4.42

When people say change is good, they're usually trying to reassure someone (or themselves). Because instinctively we view change as bad—or at least we're suspicious of it.

The Stoics want you to do away with those labels altogether. Change isn't good. The status quo isn't bad. They just *are*.

Remember, events are objective. It's only our opinion that says something is good or bad (and thus worth fighting against or fighting for). A better attitude? To decide to make the most of everything. But to do that you must first cease fighting.

November 5th
A HIGHER POWER

> "This is the very thing which makes up the virtue of the happy person and a well-flowing life—when the affairs of life are in every way tuned to the harmony between the individual divine spirit and the will of the director of the universe."
>
> —CHRYSIPPUS, QUOTED IN DIOGENES LAERTIUS,
> *LIVES OF THE EMINENT PHILOSOPHERS*, 7.1.88

In undergoing a twelve-step program, many addicts struggle most with step 2: acknowledging a higher power. Addicts often fight this one. At first they claim it's because they're atheists or because they don't like religion or because they don't understand why it matters.

But they later realize that this is just the addiction talking—it's another form of selfishness and self-absorption. The actual language of the step is pretty easy to swallow: "[We] came to believe that a Power greater than ourselves could restore us to sanity." Subsequent steps ask the addict to submit and let go. The second step really has less to do with "god" than those other steps—the letting go. It's about attuning to the universe and discarding the toxic idea that we're at the center of it.

It's no wonder that the Stoics are popular with those in twelve-step programs. It's also clear that this wisdom is beneficial to us all. You don't have to believe there is a god directing the universe, you just need to stop believing that *you're* that director. As soon as you can attune your spirit to that idea, the easier and happier your life will be, because you will have given up the most potent addiction of all: control.

November 6th
SOMEONE ELSE IS SPINNING THE THREAD

"If the breaking day sees someone proud,
The ending day sees them brought low.
No one should put too much trust in triumph,
No one should give up hope of trials improving.
Clotho mixes one with the other and stops
Fortune from resting, spinning every fate around.
No one has had so much divine favor
That they could guarantee themselves tomorrow.
God keeps our lives hurtling on,
Spinning in a whirlwind."

—SENECA, *THYESTES*, 613

The novelist Cormac McCarthy was living in a motel room when he heard a knock at the door. It was a messenger—he'd been awarded the MacArthur "genius" grant and $250,000. Unexpected events can be good as well as bad.

Who could dream of such an unexpected twist? Who but Clotho, one of the three Greek goddesses of fate, who "spins" the thread of human life? To the ancients, she was the one who decided the course of the events of our lives—some good, some bad. As the playwright Aeschylus wrote, "When the gods send evil, one cannot escape it." The same was true for great destiny and good fortune.

Their resigned attitude might seem strange to us today, but they understood who was really in control (not them, not us!). No amount of prosperity, no amount of difficulty, is certain or forever. A triumph becomes a trial, a trial becomes a triumph. Life can change in an instant. Remember, today, how often it does.

November 7th
HOW TO BE POWERFUL

"Don't trust in your reputation, money, or position, but in the strength that is yours—namely, your judgments about the things that you control and don't control. For this alone is what makes us free and unfettered, that picks us up by the neck from the depths and lifts us eye to eye with the rich and powerful."

—EPICTETUS, *DISCOURSES*, 3.26.34–35

In a scene in Steven Pressfield's classic novel about Alexander the Great, *The Virtues of War*, Alexander reaches a river crossing only to be confronted by a philosopher who refuses to move. "This man has conquered the world!" one of Alexander's men shouts. "What have you done?" The philosopher responds, with complete confidence, "I have conquered the need to conquer the world."

We do know that Alexander did clash with Diogenes the Cynic, a philosopher known for his rejection of what society prizes and, by extension, Alexander's self-image. Just as in Pressfield's fictional encounter, in Diogenes's real confrontation with Alexander, the philosopher was more powerful than the most powerful man in the world—because, unlike him, Diogenes had fewer wants. They were able to look each other in the eye and see who really had control over himself, who had achieved the self-mastery required for real and lasting power.

You can have that too. It just means focusing inward on acquiring power rather than outward. As Publilius Syrus, himself a former slave, put it: "Would you have a great empire? Rule over yourself!"

November 8th
ACTORS IN A PLAY

"Remember that you are an actor in a play, playing a character according to the will of the playwright—if a short play, then it's short; if long, long. If he wishes you to play the beggar, play even that role well, just as you would if it were a cripple, a honcho, or an everyday person. For this is your duty, to perform well the character assigned you. That selection belongs to another."

—EPICTETUS, *ENCHIRIDION*, 17

Marcus Aurelius didn't want to be emperor. He wasn't a politician who sought office, and he wasn't a true heir to the throne. As far as we can tell from his letters and from history, what he really wanted was to be a philosopher. But the powerful elite in Rome, including the emperor Hadrian, saw something in him. Groomed for power, Marcus was adopted and put in line for the throne because they knew he could handle it. Meanwhile, Epictetus lived much of his life as a slave and was persecuted for his philosophical teachings. Both did quite a lot with the roles they were assigned.

Our station in life can be as random as a roll of the dice. Some of us are born into privilege, others into adversity. Sometimes we're given exactly the opportunities we want. At other times we're given a lucky break, but to us it feels like a burden.

The Stoics remind us that whatever happens to us today or over the course of our lives, wherever we fall on the intellectual, social, or physical spectra, our job is not to complain or bemoan our plight but to do the best we can to accept it and fulfill it. Is there still room for flexibility or ambition? Of course! The history of the stage is littered with stories of bit parts that turned into starring roles and indelible characters that were expanded in future adaptations. But even this begins with acceptance and understanding—and a desire to excel at what we have been assigned.

November 9th
ALL IS FLUID

"The universe is change. Life is opinion."

—MARCUS AURELIUS, *MEDITATIONS*, 4.3.4b

In Plutarch's *Life of Theseus*, he describes how the ship of Theseus, an Athenian hero, was preserved by the people of Athens in battle-ready condition for many centuries. Each time a board decayed, it would be replaced until eventually every stick of wood in it had been replaced. Plutarch asks: Is it still the ship of Theseus, or is it a new one?

In Japan, a famous Shinto shrine is rebuilt every twenty-three years. It's gone through more than sixty of those cycles. Is it one shrine, 1,400 years old? Or sixty consecutive shrines? Even the U.S. Senate, given its staggered elections, could be said to have never been fully turned over. Is it the same body formed in the days of George Washington?

Our understanding of what something *is* is just a snapshot—an ephemeral opinion. The universe is in a constant state of change. Our nails grow and are cut and keep growing. New skin replaces dead skin. Old memories are replaced by new memories. Are we still the same people? Are the people around us the same? Nothing is exempt from this fluidity, not even the things we hold most sacred.

November 10th
ALWAYS THE SAME

"Think by way of example on the times of Vespasian, and you'll
see all these things: marrying, raising children, falling ill, dying,
wars, holiday feasts, commerce, farming, flattering, pretending,
suspecting, scheming, praying that others die, grumbling over one's
lot, falling in love, amassing fortunes, lusting after office and power.
Now that life of theirs is dead and gone . . . the times of Trajan,
again the same . . ."

—MARCUS AURELIUS, *MEDITATIONS*, 4.32

Ernest Hemingway opens his book *The Sun Also Rises* with a Bible
verse: "One generation passeth, and another generation cometh; but
the earth abideth forever. The sun also riseth, and the sun goeth down,
and resteth to the place where he arose." It was this passage, his editor
would say, that "contained all the wisdom of the ancient world."

And what wisdom is that? One of the most striking things about
history is just how long human beings have been doing what they do.
Though certain attitudes and practices have come and gone, what's left
are people—living, dying, loving, fighting, crying, laughing.

Breathless media reports or popular books often perpetuate the
belief that we've reached the apex of humanity, or that this time, things
really are different. The irony is that people have believed that for centuries.

Strong people resist this notion. They know that with a few excep-
tions, things are the same as they've always been and always will be.
You're just like the people who came before you, and you're but a brief
stopover until the people just like you who will come after. The earth
abides forever, but we will come and go.

November 11th
IT'S NOT THE THING, IT'S WHAT WE MAKE OF IT

"When you are distressed by an external thing, it's not the thing itself that troubles you, but only your judgment of it. And you can wipe this out at a moment's notice."

—MARCUS AURELIUS, *MEDITATIONS*, 8.47

Imagine you've dreamed of a life in politics. You're young, you're vigorous, and you've held increasingly powerful positions over the course of your career. Then at thirty-nine, you start to feel run down. Your doctors tell you that you have polio and your life will never be the same. Your career is over—right?

This is the story of Franklin Delano Roosevelt, now widely regarded as one of America's greatest political leaders. He was, at middle age, diagnosed with polio after spending years preparing for and dreaming about the presidency.

It's impossible to understand FDR without understanding this disability. The "external thing" was that he was crippled—this was a literal fact—but his judgment of it was that it did not cripple his career or his personhood. Though he was certainly the victim of a then incurable disease, he wiped away—almost immediately—the victim's mentality.

Let's not confuse acceptance with passivity.

November 12th
THE STRONG ACCEPT RESPONSIBILITY

"If we judge as good and evil only the things in the power of our own choice, then there is no room left for blaming gods or being hostile to others."

—MARCUS AURELIUS, *MEDITATIONS*, 6.41

A sign on President Harry Truman's desk read, THE BUCK STOPS HERE. As president, with more power and control than pretty much anyone else, he knew that, good or bad, there wasn't anyone he could blame for stuff other than himself. There was no one to pass the buck to. The chain ended there, in the Oval Office.

As the president of our own lives—and knowing that our powers begin and end with our reasoned choice—we would do well to internalize this same attitude. We don't control things outside that sphere, but we do control our attitudes and our responses to those events—and that's plenty. It's enough that we go into each and every day knowing that there is no one to pass the buck to. It ends with us.

November 13th
NEVER COMPLAIN, NEVER EXPLAIN

"Don't allow yourself to be heard any longer griping about public life, not even with your own ears!"

—MARCUS AURELIUS, *MEDITATIONS*, 8.9

Not only do even the most fortunate of us complain, it often seems like the more fortunate we are, the more time we have to do so. Marcus Aurelius was a reluctant chief executive—just as you might be a reluctant accountant, kid's soccer coach, or lawyer. Or perhaps you generally like your job, but you could do without a few of its attendant responsibilities. Where does that thinking get you? Nowhere, other than in a negative state of mind.

It calls to mind a motto of British prime minister Benjamin Disraeli: "Never complain, never explain." He said this because, like Marcus, he knew that the burdens of responsibility were immense. It's so easy to complain about this or that, or to try to make excuses and justifications for the things you've done. But that doesn't accomplish anything—and it never lightens the load.

November 14th
YOU CHOOSE THE OUTCOME

"He was sent to prison. But the observation 'he has suffered evil,' is an addition coming from you."

—EPICTETUS, *DISCOURSES*, 3.8.5b–6a

This is classic Stoic thinking, as you've gathered by now. An event itself is objective. How we describe it—that it was unfair, or it's a great calamity, or that they did it on purpose—is on us.

Malcolm X (then Malcolm Little) went into prison a criminal, but he left as an educated, religious, and motivated man who would help in the struggle for civil rights. Did he suffer an evil? Or did he choose to make his experience a positive one?

Acceptance isn't passive. It's the first step in an active process toward self-improvement.

November 15th
EVERYTHING IS CHANGE

"Meditate often on the swiftness with which all that exists and is coming into being is swept by us and carried away. For substance is like a river's unending flow, its activities continually changing and causes infinitely shifting so that almost nothing at all stands still."

—MARCUS AURELIUS, *MEDITATIONS*, 5.23

Marcus borrows this wonderful metaphor from Heraclitus, who said, "No man steps in the same river twice." Because the river has changed, and so has the man.

Life is in a constant state of change. And so are we. To get upset by things is to wrongly assume that they will last. To kick ourselves or blame others is grabbing at the wind. To resent change is to wrongly assume that you have a choice in the matter.

Everything is change. Embrace that. Flow with it.

November 16th
HOPE AND FEAR ARE THE SAME

"Hecato says, 'cease to hope and you will cease to fear.' . . . The primary cause of both these ills is that instead of adapting ourselves to present circumstances we send out thoughts too far ahead."

—SENECA, *MORAL LETTERS*, 5.7b–8

Hope is generally regarded as good. Fear is generally regarded as bad. To a Stoic like Hecato (known as Hecato of Rhodes), they are the same—both are projections into the future about things we do not control. Both are the enemy of this present moment that you are actually in. Both mean you're living a life in opposition to *amor fati*.

It's not about overcoming our fears but understanding that both hope and fear contain a dangerous amount of *want* and *worry* in them. And, sadly, the want is what causes the worry.

November 17th
JUDGE NOT, LEST . . .

"When philosophy is wielded with arrogance and stubbornly, it is the cause for the ruin of many. Let philosophy scrape off your own faults, rather than be a way to rail against the faults of others."

—SENECA, *MORAL LETTERS*, 103.4b–5a

Remember, the proper direction of philosophy—of all the things we're doing here—is focused inward. To make *ourselves* better and to leave other people to that task for themselves and their own journey. Our faults are in our control, and so we turn to philosophy to help scrape them off like barnacles from the hull of a ship. Other people's faults? Not so much. That's for them to do.

Leave other people to their faults. Nothing in Stoic philosophy empowers you to judge them—only to accept them. Especially when we have so many of our own.

November 18th
FOUR HABITS OF THE STOIC MIND

"Our rational nature moves freely forward in its impressions when it:
1) accepts nothing false or uncertain;
2) directs its impulses only to acts for the common good;
3) limits its desires and aversions only to what's in its own power;
4) embraces everything nature assigns it."

—MARCUS AURELIUS, *MEDITATIONS*, 8.7

If you notice, Marcus repeatedly reminds himself what Stoicism is. These bullet points are helpful to those of us reading thousands of years later, but really they were intended to be helpful to him. Maybe that day he had accepted a bad impression or had acted selfishly. Maybe he had pinned his hopes on something outside his control or complained and fought against something that had happened. Or maybe it had just been awhile since he'd thought about these things and wanted a reminder.

Whatever his case was, or whatever ours is today, let's align our minds along these four critical habits:

1. Accept only what is true.
2. Work for the common good.
3. Match our needs and wants with what is in our control.
4. Embrace what nature has in store for us.

November 19th
MAXIMS FROM THREE WISE MEN

"For any challenge we should hold three thoughts at our command:
'Lead on God and Destiny,
To that Goal fixed for me long ago.
I will follow and not stumble; even if my will
is weak I will soldier on.'"
—CLEANTHES

"Whoever embraces necessity count as wise,
skilled in divine matters."
—EURIPIDES

"If it pleases the gods, so be it. They may well kill me, but they can't
hurt me."
—PLATO'S *CRITO* AND *APOLOGY*

—EPICTETUS, *ENCHIRIDION*, 53

These three quotes compiled by Epictetus show us—in wisdom across history—the themes of tolerance, flexibility, and, ultimately, acceptance. Cleanthes and Euripides evoke destiny and fate as concepts that help ease acceptance. When one has a belief in a greater or higher power (be it God or gods), then there is no such thing as an event going contrary to plan.

Even if you don't believe in a deity, you can take some comfort in the various laws of the universe or even the circle of life. What happens to us as individuals can seem random or upsetting or cruel or inexplicable, when in fact these events make perfect sense when our perspective is zoomed out, even just slightly.

Let's practice this perspective today. Pretend that each event—whether desired or unexpected—was willed to happen, willed specifically for you. You wouldn't fight that, would you?

November 20th
BEHOLD, NOW AS EVER

"If you've seen the present, you've seen all things, from time imme-
morial into all of eternity. For everything that happens is related
and the same."

—MARCUS AURELIUS, *MEDITATIONS*, 6.37

The events that will transpire today are the same as the things that
have always occurred. People living and dying, animals living and
dying, clouds rolling in and rolling out, air sucked in and sucked out,
as it has for aeons. This moment right now, to paraphrase Emerson, is
a quotation of the moments that have come before and will come ever
after.

This idea is expressed nowhere more beautifully than in the Christianity hymn *Gloria Patri*. "As it was in the beginning, and now, and
always, and to the ages of ages." This thought is not supposed to be
depressing or uplifting. It's just a fact. However, it can have a calming,
centering effect. No need to get excited, no need to wait on pins and
needles. If you haven't seen this before, someone else has. That can be
a relief.

November 21st
ONCE IS ENOUGH, ONCE IS FOREVER

"A good isn't increased by the addition of time, but if one is wise
for even a moment, they will be no less happy than the person who
exercises virtue for all time and happily passes their life in it."

—Chrysippus quoted by Plutarch in *Moralia*: "Against the
Stoics on Common Conceptions," 1062 (Loeb, p. 682)

Perhaps wisdom and happiness are like winning a medal in the
Olympics. It doesn't matter whether you won a hundred years ago
or ten minutes ago, or whether you won just once or in multiple events.
It doesn't matter whether someone beats your time or score down the
road, and it doesn't matter whether you never compete again. You'll
always be a medalist, and you'll always know what it feels like. No one
can take that away—and it would be impossible to feel *more* of that
feeling.

The Juilliard-trained actor Evan Handler, who not only survived
acute myeloid leukemia but also severe depression, has talked about his
decision to take antidepressants, which he did for a deliberately brief
time. He took them because he wanted to know what true, normal happiness felt like. Once he did, he knew he would stop. He could go back
to the struggle like everyone else. He had the ideal for a moment and
that was enough.

Perhaps today will be the day when we experience happiness or
wisdom. Don't try to grab that moment and hold on to it with all your
might. It's not under your control how long it lasts. Enjoy it, recognize
it, remember it. Having it for a moment is the same as having it forever.

November 22nd
THE GLASS IS ALREADY BROKEN

"Fortune falls heavily on those for whom she's unexpected. The one always on the lookout easily endures."

—SENECA, *ON CONSOLATION TO HELVIA*, 5.3

There is a story of a Zen master who had a beautiful prized cup. The master would repeat to himself, "The glass is already broken." He enjoyed the cup. He used it. He showed it off to visitors. But in his mind, it was already broken. And so one day, when it actually did break, he simply said, "Of course."

This is how the Stoics think too. There is supposedly a true story about Epictetus and a lamp. He never locked his house, and so his expensive lamp was stolen. When Epictetus replaced it, he replaced it with a cheaper one so he could be less attached to it if it were stolen again.

Devastation—that feeling that we're absolutely crushed and shocked by an event—is a factor of how unlikely we considered that event in the first place. No one is *wrecked* by the fact that it's snowing in the winter, because we've accepted (and even anticipated) this turn of events. What about the occurrences that surprise us? We might not be so shocked if we took the time to consider their possibility.

November 23rd
ATTACHMENTS ARE THE ENEMY

"In short, you must remember this—that if you hold anything dear outside of your own reasoned choice, you will have destroyed your capacity for choice."

—EPICTETUS, *DISCOURSES*, 4.4.23

According to Anthony de Mello, "there is one thing and only one thing that causes unhappiness. The name of that thing is Attachment." Attachments to an image you have of a person, attachments to wealth and status, attachments to a certain place or time, attachments to a job or to a lifestyle. All of those things are dangerous for one reason: they are outside of our reasoned choice. How long we keep them is not in our control.

As Epictetus realized some two thousand years before de Mello, our attachments are what make it so hard to accept change. Once we have them, we don't want to let go. We become slaves to maintaining the status quo. We are like the Red Queen in *Alice in Wonderland*—running faster and faster to stay in the same place.

But everything is in a constant state of change. We have certain things for a while and then lose them. The only permanent thing is *prohairesis*, our capacity for reasoned choice. The things we are attached to can come and go, our choice is resilient and adaptable. The sooner we become aware of this the better. The easier it will be to accept and adapt to what does happen.

November 24th
TRAIN TO LET GO OF WHAT'S NOT YOURS

"Whenever you experience the pangs of losing something, don't treat it like a part of yourself but as a breakable glass, so when it falls you will remember that and won't be troubled. So too, whenever you kiss your child, sibling, or friend, don't layer on top of the experience all the things you might wish, but hold them back and stop them, just as those who ride behind triumphant generals remind them they are mortal. In the same way, remind yourself that your precious one isn't one of your possessions, but something given for now, not forever . . ."

—EPICTETUS, *DISCOURSES*, 3.24.84–86a

At a Roman triumph, the majority of the public would have their eyes glued to the victorious general at the front—one of the most coveted spots during Roman times. Only a few would notice the aide in the back, right behind the commander, whispering into his ear, "Remember, thou art mortal." What a reminder to hear at the peak of glory and victory!

In our own lives, we can train to be that whisper. When there is something we prize—or someone that we love—we can whisper to ourselves that it is fragile, mortal, and not truly ours. No matter how strong or invincible something feels, it never is. We must remind ourselves that it can break, can die, can leave us.

Loss is one of our deepest fears. Ignorance and pretending don't make things any better. They just mean the loss will be all the more jarring when it occurs.

November 25th
FUNNY HOW THAT WORKS OUT

"As for me, I would choose being sick over living in luxury, for being sick only harms the body, whereas luxury destroys both the body and the soul, causing weakness and incapacity in the body, and lack of control and cowardice in the soul. What's more, luxury breeds injustice because it also breeds greediness."

—MUSONIUS RUFUS, *LECTURES*, 20.95.14–17

Stories about lottery winners tend to share one lesson: suddenly coming into a great deal of money is a curse, not a blessing. Just a few years after they get their big check, many lottery winners are actually in worse financial shape. They've lost friends, they've gotten divorced. Their whole lives have been turned into a nightmare as a result of their obscenely good fortune.

It's like that Metallica lyric (fittingly from a song called "No Leaf Clover"): "Then it comes to be that the soothing light at the end of your tunnel / Is just a freight train coming your way."

And yet the most common response from a cancer survivor, the person who went through the thing we all dread and fear? "It was the best thing that ever happened to me."

Funny how that works out, isn't it?

November 26th
THE ALTAR OF NO DIFFERENCE

"We are like many pellets of incense falling on the same altar. Some collapse sooner, others later, but it makes no difference."

—MARCUS AURELIUS, *MEDITATIONS*, 4.15

What's the difference between you and the richest person in the world? One has a little more money than the other. What's the difference between you and the oldest person in the world? One has been around a little longer than the other. Same goes for the tallest, smartest, fastest, and on down the line.

Measuring ourselves against other people makes acceptance difficult, because we want what *they* have, or we want how things *could* have gone, not what we happen to have. But that makes no difference.

Some might see this line from Marcus as pessimistic, whereas others see it as optimistic. It's really just *truth*. We're all here and we're all going to leave this earth eventually, so let's not concern ourselves with petty differences in the meantime. We have too much to do.

November 27th
THE PLEASURE OF TUNING OUT THE NEGATIVE

"How satisfying it is to dismiss and block out any upsetting or foreign impression, and immediately to have peace in all things."

—MARCUS AURELIUS, *MEDITATIONS*, 5.2

The Stoics were mercifully spared the information overload endemic to today's society. They had no social media, no newspapers, no television chatter to rile them up. But even back then, an undisciplined person would have found plenty to be distracted and upset by.

Part of the Stoic mindset then was a sort of a cultivated ignorance. Publilius Syrus's epigram expresses it well: "Always shun that which makes you angry." Meaning: turn your mind away from the things that provoke it. If you find that discussing politics at the dinner table leads to fighting, why do you keep bringing it up? If your sibling's life choices bother you, why don't you stop picking at them and making them your concern? The same goes for so many other sources of aggravation.

It's not a sign of weakness to shut them out. Instead, it's a sign of strong will. Try saying: "I know the reaction I typically take in these situations, and I'm not going to do it this time." And then follow it with: "I'm also going to remove this stimulus from my life in the future as well."

Because what follows is peace and serenity.

November 28th
IT'S NOT ON THEM, IT'S ON YOU

"If someone is slipping up, kindly correct them and point out what
they missed. But if you can't, blame yourself—or no one."
—MARCUS AURELIUS, *MEDITATIONS*, 10.4

A good teacher knows that when a student is failing, the blame falls
on the instructor, not the pupil. How much more generous and
tolerant would we be if we could extend this understanding to other
spheres in our life? To be able to see that if a friend is unreliable, maybe
it's because they don't know what's wrong or because we haven't tried
to help them fix their flaw. If an employee is underperforming, just talk
to them or figure out if they're lacking in support. If someone is being
annoying, try talking to them about the problem with their behavior,
or ask yourself: *Why am I being so sensitive?*

And if this doesn't work, try letting it go. It might be an isolated
incident anyway.

November 29th
YOU'RE GOING TO BE OK

"Don't lament this and don't get agitated."

—MARCUS AURELIUS, *MEDITATIONS*, 7.43

There's that feeling we get when something happens: *It's all over now. All is lost.* What follows are complaints and pity and misery—the impotent struggle against something that's already occurred.

Why bother? We have no idea what the future holds. We have no idea what's coming up around the bend. It could be more problems, or this could be the darkness before the dawn.

If we're Stoic, there is one thing we can be sure of: whatever happens, we're going to be OK.

November 30th
FOLLOW THE *LOGOS*

"The person who follows reason in all things will have both leisure and a readiness to act—they are at once both cheerful and self-composed."

—MARCUS AURELIUS, *MEDITATIONS*, 10.12b

The guiding reason of the world—the Stoics called this the *logos*—works in mysterious ways. Sometimes, the *logos* gives us what we want, other times it gives us precisely what we do not want. In either case, they believed that the *logos* was an all-powerful force that governed the universe.

There is a helpful analogy to explain the *logos*: We are like a dog leashed to a moving cart. The direction of the cart will determine where we go. Depending on the length of the leash, we also have a fair amount of room to explore and determine the pace, but ultimately what each of us must choose is whether we will go willingly or be painfully dragged. Which will it be?

Cheerful acceptance? Or ignorant refusal? In the end, they amount to the same.

DECEMBER

MEDITATION ON MORTALITY

December 1st
PRETEND TODAY IS THE END

"Let us prepare our minds as if we'd come to the very end of life. Let us postpone nothing. Let us balance life's books each day. . . . The one who puts the finishing touches on their life each day is never short of time."

—SENECA, *MORAL LETTERS*, 101.7b–8a

"Live each day as if it were your last" is a cliché. Plenty say it, few actually do it. How reasonable would that be anyway? Surely Seneca isn't saying to forsake laws and considerations—to find some orgy to join because the world is ending.

A better analogy would be a soldier about to leave on deployment. Not knowing whether they'll return or not, what do they do?

They get their affairs in order. They handle their business. They tell their children or their family that they love them. They don't have time for quarreling or petty matters. And then in the morning they are ready to go—hoping to come back in one piece but prepared for the possibility that they might not.

Let us live today that same way.

December 2nd
DON'T MIND ME, I'M ONLY DYING SLOW

"Let each thing you would do, say or intend be like that of a dying person."

—MARCUS AURELIUS, *MEDITATIONS*, 2.11.1

Have you ever heard some ask: "What would you do if you found out tomorrow that you had cancer?" The question is designed to make you consider how different life might be if you were suddenly given just a few months or weeks to live. There's nothing like a terminal illness to wake people up.

But here's the thing: you already have a terminal diagnosis. We all do! As the writer Edmund Wilson put it, "Death is one prophecy that never fails." Every person is born with a death sentence. Each second that passes by is one you'll never get back.

Once you realize this, it will have a profound impact on what you do, say, and think. Don't let another day tick away in ignorance of the reality that you're a dying person. We all are. Can today be the day we stop pretending otherwise?

December 3rd
THE PHILOSOPHER AS AN ARTISAN OF LIFE AND DEATH

"Philosophy does not claim to get a person any external possession. To do so would be beyond its field. As wood is to the carpenter, bronze to the sculptor, so our own lives are the proper
material in the art of living."

—EPICTETUS, *DISCOURSES*, 1.15.2

Philosophy is not some idle pursuit appropriate only for academics
or the rich. Instead, it is one of the most essential activities that a
human being can engage in. Its purpose, as Henry David Thoreau said
a few thousand years after Epictetus, is to help us "solve the problems
of life, not only theoretically but practically." This aligns nicely with
Cicero's famous line: "*To philosophize is to learn how to die.*"

You're not reading these quotes and doing these thought exercises
for fun. Though they may be enjoyable and help you lighten up, their
aim is to help you sculpt and improve your life. And because all of us
have but one life and one death, we should treat each experience like a
sculptor with his chisels, carving until, to paraphrase Michelangelo,
we set free the angel in the marble.

We are trying to do this difficult thing—living and dying—as well
as we can. And to do that, we must remember what we've learned and
the wise words we've been given.

December 4th
YOU DON'T OWN THAT

"Anything that can be prevented, taken away, or coerced is not a person's own—but those things that can't be blocked are their own."

—EPICTETUS, *DISCOURSES*, 3.24.3

The conservationist Daniel O'Brien has said that he doesn't "own" his several-thousand-acre buffalo ranch in South Dakota, he just lives there while the bank lets him make mortgage payments on it. It's a joke about the economic realities of ranching, but it also hints at the idea that land doesn't belong to one individual, that it will far outlast us and our descendants. Marcus Aurelius used to say that we don't own anything and that even our lives are held in trust.

We may claw and fight and work to own things, but those things can be taken away in a second. The same goes for other things we like to think are "ours" but are equally precarious: our status, our physical health or strength, our relationships. How can these really be ours if something other than us—fate, bad luck, death, and so on—can dispossess us of them without notice?

So what do we own? Just our lives—and not for long.

December 5th
THE BENEFITS OF SOBERING THOUGHTS

"Keep death and exile before your eyes each day, along with everything that seems terrible—by doing so, you'll never have a base
thought nor will you have excessive desire."

—EPICTETUS, *ENCHIRIDION*, 21

Political winds could change in an instant, depriving you of the most
basic freedoms you take for granted. Or, no matter who you are or
how safely you've lived your life, there's someone out there who would
rob and kill you for a couple dollars.

As it's written in the timeless *Epic of Gilgamesh*:

"Man is snapped off like a reed in the canebrake!
The comely young man, the pretty young woman—
All too soon in their prime Death abducts them!"

Death is not the only unexpected interruption we might face—our
plans can be dashed to pieces by a million things. Today might be a bit
more pleasant if you ignore those possibilities, but at what cost?

December 6th
THE SWORD DANGLES OVER YOU

"Don't behave as if you are destined to live forever. What's fated hangs over you. As long as you live and while you can, become good now."

—MARCUS AURELIUS, *MEDITATIONS*, 4.17

There is an ancient story of a courtier who had made light of the responsibilities of his king. To prove he was mistaken, the king arranged to switch places with the courtier so he could experience what it was like to be a king. The king made one other adjustment: he hung a sword by a hair over the throne to illustrate the peril and burden of kingship as well as the constant fear of assassination. We call that dangling reminder of death and difficulty the Sword of Damocles.

The reality is that a similar sword hangs over all of us—life can be taken from us at any moment. And that threat can send us in one of two directions: we can fear and dread it, or we can use it to motivate us. To do good, to be good. Because the sword is dangling, and there's nothing else to be concerned with. Would you rather it catch you in the middle of some shameful, selfish act? Would you rather it catch you *waiting* to be good in the future?

December 7th
THE CARDS WE'RE DEALT

"Think of the life you have lived until now as over and, as a dead man, see what's left as a bonus and live it according to Nature. Love the hand that fate deals you and play it as your own, for what could be more fitting?"

—MARCUS AURELIUS, *MEDITATIONS*, 7.56–57

We have an irrational fear of acknowledging our own mortality. We avoid thinking about it because we think it will be depressing. In fact, reflecting on mortality often has the opposite effect—invigorating us more than saddening us. Why? Because it gives us clarity.

If you were suddenly told you had but a week to live, what changes would you make? If you died but were resuscitated, how different would your perspective be?

When, as Shakespeare's Prospero puts it, "every third thought shall be my grave," there's no risk of getting caught up in petty matters or distractions. Instead of denying our fear of death, let's let it make us the best people we can be.

Today.

December 8th
DON'T HIDE FROM YOUR FEELINGS

"It's better to conquer grief than to deceive it."

—SENECA, *ON CONSOLATION TO HELVIA*, 17.1b

W e've all lost people we were close to—a friend, a colleague, a parent, a grandparent. While we were suffering from our grief, some well-meaning person did their best to take our mind off it or make us think about something else for a couple hours. However kind, these gestures are misguided.

The Stoics are stereotyped as suppressing their emotions, but their philosophy was actually intended to teach us to face, process, and deal with emotions *immediately* instead of running from them. Tempting as it is to deceive yourself or hide from a powerful emotion like grief— by telling yourself and other people that you're fine—awareness and understanding are better. Distraction might be pleasant in the short term—by going to gladiatorial games, as a Roman might have done, for example. Focusing is better in the long term.

That means facing it now. Process and parse what you are feeling. Remove your expectations, your entitlements, your sense of having been wronged. Find the positive in the situation, but also sit with your pain and accept it, remembering that it is a part of life. That's how one conquers grief.

December 9th
SPENDTHRIFTS OF TIME

"Were all the geniuses of history to focus on this single theme, they could never fully express their bafflement at the darkness of the human mind. No person would give up even an inch of their estate, and the slightest dispute with a neighbor can mean hell to pay; yet we easily let others encroach on our lives—worse, we often pave the way for those who will take it over. No person hands out their money to passersby, but to how many do each of us hand out our lives! We're tight-fisted with property and money, yet think too little of wasting time, the one thing about which we should all be the toughest misers."

—SENECA, *ON THE BREVITY OF LIFE*, 3.1–2

Today there will be endless interruptions: phone calls, emails, visitors, unexpected events. Booker T. Washington observed that "the number of people who stand ready to consume one's time, to no purpose, is almost countless."

A philosopher, on the other hand, knows that their default state should be one of reflection and inner awareness. This is why they so diligently protect their personal space and thoughts from the intrusions of the world. They know that a few minutes of contemplation are worth more than any meeting or report. They also know how little time we're actually given in life—and how quickly our stores can be depleted.

Seneca reminds us that while we might be good at protecting our physical property, we are far too lax at enforcing our mental boundaries. Property can be regained; there is quite a bit of it out there—some of it still untouched by man. But time? Time is our most irreplaceable asset—we cannot buy more of it. We can only strive to waste as little as possible.

December 10th
DON'T SELL YOURSELF TOO CHEAPLY

"I say, let no one rob me of a single day who isn't going to make a full return on the loss."

—SENECA, *ON TRANQUILITY OF MIND*, 1.11b

People spend a lot more money when they use credit cards than when they have to pull out actual cash. If you ever wondered why credit card companies and banks push cards so aggressively, this is why. The more credit cards you have, the more you'll spend.

Do we treat the days of our lives like we treat our money? Because we don't exactly know how many days we'll be alive, and because we try our hardest *not* to think about the fact that someday we'll die, we're pretty liberal with how freely we spend our time. We let people and obligations impose on that time, only rarely asking: *What am I getting in return here?*

Seneca's maxim is the equivalent of cutting up your credit cards and switching to cash. He says to put real thought into every transaction: *Am I getting my money's worth here? Is this a fair trade?*

December 11th
DIGNITY AND BRAVERY

"As Cicero says, we hate gladiators if they are quick to save their
lives by any means; we favor them if they show contempt for their
lives."

—SENECA, *ON TRANQUILITY OF MIND*, 11.4b

Lyndon Johnson's college classmates used to tell an embarrassing
story about him. Johnson apparently had a big mouth and felt he had
to constantly dominate and intimidate others. Yet his biographer, Robert Caro, makes it clear that when someone stood up to young Lyndon,
he proved himself to be a complete coward. In one instance, during an
argument over a poker game, instead of fighting, Johnson threw himself on a bed and "began kicking his feet in the air with a frantic,
windmilling motion . . . like a girl." He shouted, "If you hit me, I'll kick
you! If you hit me, I'll kick you!"

Later in his life, Johnson also worked extremely hard to avoid serving in World War II and lived it up in California while other soldiers
fought and died abroad. He later claimed to be a war hero. It was one
of his most shameful lies.

We do not need to disregard our physical safety or engage in wanton
acts of violence to be brave. But nobody respects a coward. Nobody
likes a shirker of duty. Nobody admires a person who puts too high a
price on their own comfort and needs.

That's the irony of cowardice. It's aimed at self-protection, but it
creates shameful secrets. Self-preservation is hardly worth it because
of everything it costs in return.

Be brave. Be dignified.

December 12th
THE BEAT GOES ON

> "Walk the long gallery of the past, of empires and kingdoms suc-
> ceeding each other without number. And you can also see the
> future, for surely it will be exactly the same, unable to deviate
> from the present rhythm. It's all one whether we've experienced
> forty years or an aeon. What more is there to see?"
>
> —MARCUS AURELIUS, *MEDITATIONS*, 7.49

All things die. Not just people but companies, kingdoms, religions, and ideas—eventually. The Roman Republic lasted 450 years. The Roman Empire, of which Marcus Aurelius was considered to be one of the "five good emperors," lasted 500 years. The longest recorded life of a human being is 122 years. The average life expectancy in the United States is a little over seventy-eight years. In other countries, in other eras, it has been more and it has been less. But in the end, we all succumb, as Marcus said, to the rhythm of events—of which there is always a final, determined beat. There is no need to dwell on this fact, but there is no point in ignoring it either.

December 13th
IT'S JUST A NUMBER

"You aren't bothered, are you, because you weigh a certain amount and not twice as much? So why get worked up that you've been given a certain lifespan and not more? Just as you are satisfied with your normal weight, so you should be with the time you've been given."

—MARCUS AURELIUS, *MEDITATIONS*, 6.49

They say age is just a number, but to some people it's a very important one—otherwise, women wouldn't lie about being younger, and ambitious young men wouldn't lie about being older. Rich people and health nuts spend billions of dollars in an effort to move the expiration date from around seventy-eight years to hopefully *forever*.

The number of years we manage to eke out doesn't matter, only what those years are composed of. Seneca put it best when he said, "Life is long if you know how to use it." Sadly, most people don't—they waste the life they've been given. Only when it is too late do they try to compensate for that waste by vainly hoping to put more time on the clock.

Use today. Use every day. Make yourself satisfied with what you have been given.

December 14th
WHAT WE SHOULD KNOW BY THE END

"Soon you will die, and still you aren't sincere, undisturbed, or free from suspicion that external things can harm you, nor are you gracious to all, knowing that wisdom and acting justly are one and the same."

—MARCUS AURELIUS, *MEDITATIONS*, 4.37

From what we understand, Marcus wrote many of his meditations later in life, when he was suffering from serious illnesses. So when he says, "Soon you will die," he was speaking frankly to himself about his own mortality. How scary that must have been. He was staring at the real possibility of death and not liking what he saw in these last minutes.

Sure, he'd accomplished many things in his life, but his emotions were still the cause of discomfort, pain, and frustration. He knew that with his limited time left, better choices would provide relief.

Hopefully, you have a lot more time left—but that makes it even more important to make headway while you still can. We are unfinished products up until the end, as Marcus knew very well. But the earlier we learn it, the more we can enjoy the fruits of the labor on our character—and the sooner we can be free (or *freer*) of insincerity, anxiety, ungraciousness, and un-Stoic-ness.

December 15th
A SIMPLE WAY TO MEASURE OUR DAYS

"This is the mark of perfection of character—to spend each day as if it were your last, without frenzy, laziness, or any pretending."

—MARCUS AURELIUS, *MEDITATIONS*, 7.69

The Stoics didn't think that anyone could be perfect. The idea of becoming a sage—the highest aspiration of a philosopher—wasn't realistic. This was just their Platonic ideal.

Still, they started every day hoping to get a little closer to that mark. There was much to gain in the trying. Can you actually live today like it is your last day? Is it even possible to embody completeness or perfection in our *ethos* (character), effortlessly doing the right thing for a full twenty-four hours? Is it possible for more than a minute?

Maybe not. But if trying was enough for the Stoics, it should be enough for us too.

December 16th
EVERLASTING GOOD HEALTH

"I tell you, you only have to learn to live like the healthy person does . . . living with complete confidence. What confidence? The only one worth holding, in what is trustworthy, unhindered, and can't be taken away—your own reasoned choice."

—EPICTETUS, *DISCOURSES*, 3.26.23b–24

As the Stoics say repeatedly, it's dangerous to have faith in what you do not control. But your own reasoned choice? Well, for now that *is* in your control. Therefore it is one of the few things you can have confidence in. It's the one area of health that can't suddenly be given a terminal diagnosis (except for the one we all get the day we're born). It's the only one that remains pristine and never wears down—it's only the user who quits it; never will it quit the user.

In this passage, Epictetus points out that slaves and workers and philosophers alike can live this way. Socrates, Diogenes, and Cleanthes lived this way—even while they had families and while they were struggling students.

And so can you.

December 17th
KNOW THYSELF—BEFORE IT'S TOO LATE

"Death lies heavy upon one
who, known exceedingly well by all,
dies unknown to himself."

—SENECA, *THYESTES*, 400

S ome of the most powerful and important people in the world seem
to have almost no self-awareness. Although total strangers know
endless amounts of trivia about them, celebrities—because they are too
busy or because it hurts too much—appear to know very little about
themselves.

We can be guilty of the same sin. We ignore Socrates's dictum to
"know thyself"—often realizing we have done so at our peril, years
later, when we wake up one day and realize how rarely we have asked
ourselves questions like: *Who am I? What's important to me? What do
I like? What do I need?*

Now—right now—you have the time to explore yourself, to understand your own mind and body. Don't wait. Know yourself. Before it's
impossibly late.

December 18th
WHAT COMES TO US ALL

"Both Alexander the Great and his mule-keeper were brought to the same place by death—they were either received into the all-generative reason, or scattered among the atoms."

—MARCUS AURELIUS, *MEDITATIONS*, 6.24

In a world that is in many ways becoming more and more unequal, there aren't many truly equalitarian experiences left. When Benjamin Franklin observed that "in this world nothing can be said to be certain, except death and taxes," he couldn't have known how good some people would get at avoiding their taxes. But death? That's still the one thing that everyone experiences.

We all face the same end. Whether you conquer the known world or shine the shoes of the people who do, at the end death will be a radical equalizer—a lesson in abject humility. Shakespeare had Hamlet trace out the logic in stark terms for both Alexander and Julius Caesar:

"Imperious Caesar, dead and turn'd to clay,
   Might stop a hole to keep the wind away:
   O, that that earth, which kept the world in awe,
   Should patch a wall to expel the winter flaw!"

The next time you feel yourself getting high and mighty—or conversely, feeling low and inferior—just remember, we all end up the same way. In death, no one is better, no one is worse. All our stories have the same finale.

December 19th
HUMAN SCALE

"Think of the whole universe of matter and how small your share. Think about the expanse of time and how brief—almost momentary—the part marked for you. Think of the workings of fate and how infinitesimal your role."

—MARCUS AURELIUS, *MEDITATIONS*, 5.24

The amount of matter in the universe is immense—on the order of trillions of atoms. What percentage of that matter does one human body constitute?

The earth, as far as science tells us, is some 4.5 billion years old and shows no sign of ending soon. Our time on the earth, on the other hand, will be what? Several decades, maybe?

Sometimes we need to have the facts and figures spelled out in front of us to fully realize the scale at which humans happen to exist in the big scheme of things.

Consider this the next time you feel self-important, or like everything rises and falls on what you do next. It doesn't. You're just one person among many, doing your best among many. That's all you need to do.

December 20th
FEAR THE FEAR OF DEATH

"Do you then ponder how the supreme of human evils, the surest
mark of the base and cowardly, is not death, but the fear of death?
I urge you to discipline yourself against such fear, direct all your
thinking, exercises, and reading this way—and you will know the
only path to human freedom."

—EPICTETUS, *DISCOURSES*, 3.26.38–39

To steel himself before he committed suicide rather than submit to
Julius Caesar's destruction of the Roman Republic, the great Stoic
philosopher Cato read a bit of Plato's *Phaedo*. In it, Plato writes, "It is the
child within us that trembles before death." Death is scary because it is
such an unknown. No one can come back and tell us what it is like. We
are in the dark about it.

As childlike and ultimately ignorant as we are about death, there
are plenty of wise men and women who can at least provide some
guidance. There's a reason that the world's oldest people never seem to
be afraid of death: they've had more time to think about it than we have
(and they realized how pointless worrying was). There are other wonderful resources: Florida Scott-Maxwell's Stoic diary during her terminal illness, *The Measure of My Days*, is one. Seneca's famous words to
his family and friends, who had broken down and begged with his
executioners, is another. "Where," Seneca gently chided them, "are
your maxims of philosophy, or the preparation of so many years' study
against evils to come?" Throughout philosophy there are inspiring,
brave words from brave men and women who can help us face this fear.

There is another helpful consideration about death from the Stoics.
If death is truly the end, then what is there exactly to fear? For everything from your fears to your pain receptors to your worries and your
remaining wishes, they will perish with you. As frightening as death
might seem, remember: it contains within it the end of fear.

December 21st
WHAT DO YOU HAVE TO SHOW FOR YOUR YEARS?

"Many times an old man has no other evidence besides his age to prove he has lived a long time."

—SENECA, *ON TRANQUILITY OF MIND*, 3.8b

How long have you been alive? Take the years, multiply them by 365, and then by 24. How many hours have you lived? What do you have to show for all of them?

The answer for many people is: not enough. We had so many hours that we took them for granted. All we have to show for our time on this planet are rounds of golf, years spent at the office, time spent watching mediocre movies, a stack of mindless books we hardly remember reading, and maybe a garage full of toys. We're like the character in Raymond Chandler's *The Long Goodbye*: "Mostly, I just kill time," he says, "and it dies hard."

One day, our hours will begin to run out. It would be nice to be able to say: "Hey, I really made the most of it." Not in the form of achievements, not money, not status—you know what the Stoics think of all that—but in wisdom, insight, and real progress in the things that all humans struggle against.

What if you could say that you really made something of this time that you had? What if you could prove that you really did live [insert number] years? And not just lived them, but lived them *fully*?

December 22nd
STAKE YOUR OWN CLAIM

"For it's disgraceful for an old person, or one in sight of old age, to have only the knowledge carried in their notebooks. Zeno said this . . . what do you say? Cleanthes said that . . . what do you say? How long will you be compelled by the claims of another? Take charge and stake your own claim—something posterity will carry in its notebook."

—SENECA, *MORAL LETTERS*, 33.7

Musing in his notebook about the topic of immortality, Ralph Waldo Emerson complained how writers dance around a difficult topic by relying on quotes. "I hate quotation," he wrote. "Tell me what you know."

Seneca was throwing down the same gauntlet some twenty centuries before. It's easier to quote, to rely on the wise words of others. Especially when the people you're deferring to are such towering figures!

It's harder (and more intimidating) to venture out on your own and express your own thoughts. But how do you think those wise and true quotes from those towering figures were created in the first place?

Your own experiences have value. You have accumulated your own wisdom too. Stake your claim. Put something down for the ages—in words and also in example.

December 23rd
WHAT ARE YOU SO AFRAID OF LOSING?

"You are afraid of dying. But, come now, how is this life of yours anything but death?"

—SENECA, *MORAL LETTERS*, 77.18

Seneca tells an amazing story about an obscenely wealthy Roman who was carried around by slaves on a litter. On one occasion, after being lifted out of a bath, the Roman asked, "Am I sitting down yet?" Seneca's point was essentially: What kind of sad pathetic life is it if you're so disconnected from the world that you don't even know whether you're on the ground? How did the man know whether he was even *alive* at all?

Most of us are afraid of dying. But sometimes this fear begs the question: To protect what exactly? For a lot of people the answer is: hours of television, gossiping, gorging, wasting potential, reporting to a boring job, and on and on and on. Except, in the strictest sense, is this actually a life? Is this worth gripping so tightly and being afraid of losing?

It doesn't sound like it.

THE DAILY STOIC

December 24th
MEANINGLESS . . . LIKE A FINE WINE

"You know what wine and liqueur tastes like. It makes no difference whether a hundred or a thousand bottles pass through your bladder—you are nothing more than a filter."

—SENECA, *MORAL LETTERS*, 77.16

Here we have another contemptuous expression, this time from Seneca, who, given his reputation for opulence, probably enjoyed a nice drink from time to time. His point will probably rattle anyone for whom success and adulthood has turned them into a wine snob (though the logic can be applied just as easily to foodies, techies, audiophiles, and the like).

As fun and exciting and pleasurable as these pleasures are, it's worth putting them in their place. You don't get a prize at the end of your life for having consumed more, worked more, spent more, collected more, or learned more about the various vintages than everyone else. You are just a conduit, a vessel that temporarily held or interacted with these fancy items.

If you find yourself lusting over them, this meditation might help reduce their luster just a smidge.

MEDITATION ON MORTALITY

December 25th
DON'T BURN THE CANDLE AT BOTH ENDS

"The mind must be given relaxation—it will rise improved and sharper after a good break. Just as rich fields must not be forced—for they will quickly lose their fertility if never given a break—so constant work on the anvil will fracture the force of the mind. But it regains its powers if it is set free and relaxed for a while. Constant work gives rise to a certain kind of dullness and feebleness in the rational soul."

—SENECA, *ON TRANQUILITY OF MIND*, 17.5

One can't read Marcus Aurelius and Seneca and not be struck by the difference between these two radically different personalities. Each had his own strengths and weaknesses. Which would you rather have entrusted with the immense responsibility of an empire? Probably Marcus. But who would you rather be as a person? Probably Seneca.

One of the reasons is that Seneca seems to have had what we would now refer to as work/life balance. Whereas Marcus can read as though he's worn down and tired, Seneca always feels energetic, fresh, robust. His philosophy of rest and relaxation—intermixed with his rigorous study and other Stoic rituals—probably had a lot to do with it.

The mind is a muscle, and like the rest, it can be strained, overworked, even injured. Our physical health is also worn down by overcommitment, a lack of rest, and bad habits. Remember the tall tale about John Henry—the man who challenged the machine? He died of exhaustion at the end. Don't forget that.

Today, you may face things that try your patience, require considerable focus or clarity, or demand creative breakthroughs. Life is a long haul—it will mean many such moments. Are you going to be able to handle them if you've burned the candle at both ends? If you've been abusing and overworking your body?

December 26th
LIFE IS LONG—IF YOU KNOW HOW TO USE IT

"It's not at all that we have too short a time to live, but that we squander a great deal of it. Life is long enough, and it's given in sufficient measure to do many great things if we spend it well. But when it's poured down the drain of luxury and neglect, when it's employed to no good end, we're finally driven to see that it has passed by before we even recognized it passing. And so it is—we don't receive a short life, we make it so."

—SENECA, *ON THE BREVITY OF LIFE*, 1.3–4a

No one knows how long they have to live, but sadly, we can be sure of one thing: we'll waste far too much of life. Waste it sitting around, waste it chasing the wrong things, waste it by refusing to take the time to ask ourselves what's actually important to us. Far too often, we're like the overconfident academics that Petrarch criticized in his classic essay on ignorance—the types who "fritter away their powers incessantly in caring for things outside of them and seek themselves there." Yet they have no idea this is what they're doing.

So today, if you find yourself rushed or uttering the words "I just don't have enough time," stop and take a second. Is this actually true? Or have you just committed to a lot of unnecessary things? Are you actually being efficient, or have you assumed a great deal of waste into your life? The average American spends something like forty hours a year in traffic. That's *months* over the course of a life. And for "traffic," you can substitute so many activities—from fighting with others to watching television to daydreaming.

Your life is plenty long—just use it properly.

December 27th
DON'T LET YOUR SOUL GO FIRST

"It's a disgrace in this life when the soul surrenders first while the body refuses to."

—MARCUS AURELIUS, *MEDITATIONS*, 6.29

Despite his privileges, Marcus Aurelius had a difficult life. The Roman historian Cassius Dio mused that Marcus "did not meet with the good fortune that he deserved, for he was not strong in body and was involved in a multitude of troubles throughout practically his entire reign." At one point, he was so sick that a rumor spread that he had died—and matters were made worse when his most trusted general used it as an opportunity to declare himself the new emperor.

But throughout these struggles—the years at war, the crippling illnesses, his troubled son—he never gave up. It's an inspiring example for us to think about today if we get tired, frustrated, or have to deal with some crisis. Here was a guy who had every reason to be angry and bitter, who could have abandoned his principles and lived in luxury or ease, who could have put his responsibilities aside and focused on his own health.

But he never did. His soul stayed strong even after his body became weak. He didn't give up, right up to the second until his body finally did—when he died near Vienna in 180 AD.

December 28th
ON BEING REMEMBERED

"Everything lasts for a day, the one who remembers and the re-membered."

—MARCUS AURELIUS, *MEDITATIONS*, 4.35

Take a walk down Forty-first Street toward the beautiful New York City Public Library, with its majestic stone lions. On your way up "Library Way," you'll pass a gold placard laid into the cement, part of a series of quotations from great writers throughout history. This one is from Marcus Aurelius: "Everything is only for a day, both that which remembers and that which is remembered."

The library itself was designed by the firm of John Merven Carrère, one of the twentieth century's most accomplished architects. It combines the collections of such luminaries and philanthropists as Samuel Tilden, John Jacob Astor, and James Lenox, and their names are carved into the stone. Today, the naming rights go to hedge fund manager Stephen A. Schwarzman. The opening of the library in 1911 was attended by President William Howard Taft, Governor John Alden Dix, and New York City mayor William Jay Gaynor. The plaques you pass on your way were designed by the excellent Gregg LeFevre.

Marcus's quote makes us ponder: How many of these people have we even heard of? The people involved in the story of the library were some of the most famous men in the world, masters of their respective crafts, rich beyond imagination in some cases. Even along "Library Way," many of the famous authors are unfamiliar to the modern reader. They are all long gone, as are the people who remembered them.

All of us, including Marcus—who is passed over by just as many unaware pedestrians—last for just a day, at most.

December 29th
GIVE THANKS

"In all things we should try to make ourselves be as grateful as possible. For gratitude is a good thing for ourselves, in a manner in which justice, commonly held to belong to others, is not. Gratitude pays itself back in large measure."

—SENECA, *MORAL LETTERS*, 81.19

Think of all the things you can be grateful for today. That you are alive, that you live in a time primarily of peace, that you have enough health and leisure to read this book. What of the little things? The person who smiled at you, the woman who held the door open, that song you like on the radio, the pleasant weather.

Gratitude is infectious. Its positivity is radiant.

Even if today was your last day on earth—if you knew in advance that it was going to end in a few short hours—would there still be plenty to be grateful for? How much better would your life be if you kicked off every day like that? If you let it carry through from morning to night and touch every part of your life?

December 30th
TAKING THE BITE OUT OF IT

"To bear trials with a calm mind
robs misfortune of its strength and burden."
—SENECA, *HERCULES OETAEUS*, 231–232

The people you admire, the ones who seem to be able to successfully handle and deal with adversity and difficulty, what do they have in common? Their sense of equilibrium, their orderly discipline. On the one-yard line, in the midst of criticism, after a heartbreaking tragedy, during a stressful period, they keep going.

Not because they're better than you. Not because they're smarter. But because they have learned a little secret. You can take the bite out of any tough situation by bringing a calm mind to it. By considering it and meditating on it in advance.

And this is true not just for our day-to-day adversities but for the greatest and most unavoidable trial of all: our own eventual death. It could come tomorrow, it could come in forty years. It could be quick and painless, or it could be excruciating. Our greatest asset in that ordeal will not be religion, it will not even be the wise words of the philosophers. It will be, simply, our calm and reasoned mind.

December 31st
GET ACTIVE IN YOUR OWN RESCUE

"Stop wandering about! You aren't likely to read your own note-books, or ancient histories, or the anthologies you've collected to enjoy in your old age. Get busy with life's purpose, toss aside empty hopes, get active in your own rescue—if you care for yourself at all—and do it while you can."

—MARCUS AURELIUS, *MEDITATIONS*, 3.14

The purpose of all our reading and studying is to aid us in the pursuit of the good life (and death). At some point, we must put our books aside and take action. So that, as Seneca put it, the "words become works." There is an old saying that a "scholar made is a soldier spoiled." We want to be both scholars and soldiers—soldiers in the good fight.

That's what's next for you. Move forward, move onward. Another book isn't the answer. The right choices and decisions are. Who knows how much time you have left, or what awaits us tomorrow?

STAYING STOIC

We hope this book has lasted you a year (though we won't fault you if you read through it without regard to the date. In fact, we'd be flattered). So what's next? We hope that you get involved with Stoicism and make it a daily practice in your life. To that end, we've created **DailyStoic.com**—a site full of interviews with Stoic practitioners, articles, exercises, and a daily email where you can get more Stoic wisdom delivered to your inbox every single day.

You can go to DailyStoic.com right now or email hello@DailyStoic.com to get a special package of Stoic bonuses, including what books to read next and more material that we couldn't fit in this book.

Hope to see you there soon!

A MODEL OF LATE STOIC PRACTICE AND GLOSSARY OF KEY TERMS AND PASSAGES

Late Stoic thought of the second century, as articulated in the writings of Epictetus and Marcus Aurelius, paints a vivid picture of the work of philosophy in producing both self-coherence and progress on the path to virtue. As suggested in the work of Pierre Hadot and A. A. Long (see Suggestions for Further Reading), we have developed and formalized Epictetus's three disciplines into a chart that presents the progressive nature of the late Stoic prescription for handling ourselves and our actions in the world. This chart brings together the three *topoi* (topics, or fields of study) and three different levels of training (*askêsis*) suggested by Epictetus and shows how they correlate (noted in Hadot) to the pursuit of virtue as expressed by Marcus Aurelius. The chart itself comes from these key passages in Epictetus:

> "There are three areas in which the person who would be wise and good must be trained. *The first has to do with desires and aversions*—that a person may never miss the mark in desires nor fall into what repels them. *The second has to do with impulses to act and not to act*—and more broadly, with duty—that a person may *act deliberately for good reasons and not carelessly. The third has to do with freedom from deception and composure and the whole area of judgment, the assent our mind gives to its perceptions.* Of these areas, the chief and most urgent is the first which has to do with the passions, for strong emotions arise only when we fail in our desires and aversions."
>
> —EPICTETUS, *DISCOURSES*, 3.2.1–3a

> "That's why the philosophers warn us not to be satisfied with mere *learning*, but to add *practice* and then *training*. For as time passes

we forget what we learned and end up doing the opposite, and hold opinions the opposite of what we should."

—EPICTETUS, DISCOURSES, 2.9.13–14

We have placed key terms in each level of the chart. There is progress (*prokopê*) upward out of deception, false opinion, and error—through impulse control—to more clear judgments and knowledge (self-coherence); and there is progress across the levels of training (study/*manthanô*, practice/*meletaô*, hard training/*askeô*) through the remediation of habit, acting more appropriately, and improving judgment toward living the virtues. We offer an annotated glossary of key Stoic terms and passages following the chart.

A MODEL OF LATE STOIC PRACTICE

	Three Disciplines for Action		
Three Parts of Self	1. Study/Learn μανθάνω (*manthanô*)	2. Practice μελετάω (*meletaô*)	3. Train ἀσκέω (*askeô*)
3. Will: Assent/Rejection συγκατάθεσις/ανανεύω (*synkatathesis/ananeuô*) Freedom from deception; composure	Logic: what is ours, for the common good, and true κατάληψις (*katalêpsis*)	Judgment and Truth ἐπιστήμη (*epistêmê*)	Wisdom φρόνησις (*phronêsis*)
2. Action: Impulse to Do/ Refuse to Do ὁρμή/ἀφορμή (*hormê/aphormê*) Acting deliberately and not carelessly	Ethics: what is ours and for the common good κοινωνικόν (*koinônikon*)	Duty and Appropriate Action καθῆκον (*kathêkon*)	Justice and Courage δικαιοσύνη, ἀνδρεία (*dikaiosunê, andreia*)
1. Perception: Desire/ Aversion ὄρεξις/ἔκκλισις (*orexis/ekklisis*) Removing false opinion (οἴησις/*oiêsis*) and passion (πάθος/*pathos*)	Physics: what is ours, not ours, and indifferent ἐφ᾽ ἡμῖν/οὐκ ἐφ᾽ ἡμῖν/ ἀδιάφορα (*eph' hêmin/ouk eph' hêmin/adiaphora*)	Habit and Disposition ἔθος/ἕξις (*ethos/hexis*)	Self-Control σωφροσύνη (*sôphrosunê*)

Adiaphora (ἀδιάφορα): indifferent things; neither good nor bad in an absolute moral sense. In Stoic thought, all things outside our sphere of reasoned choice (see *prohairesis*) are indifferent. In a relative sense, some of the things outside our control are preferred or dispreferred goods (*proêgmena/aproêgmena*). Marcus says (5.20) that people who thwart the progress of our reasoned choice, although normally our natural concern, also become indifferent to us. The term appears in Epictetus's *Discourses* seventeen times and once in *Enchiridion*; see *Discourses* 2.19.12b–13 and 3.3.1. In Marcus it appears six times; see also 8.56 (my *prohairesis* is indifferent to that of others, and vice versa).

Agathos (ἀγαθός): good, or a proper object of desire. Epictetus upholds the classic Stoic position when he says that the good (and evil) are only to be found in us, in our *prohairesis*, not in external things (*Discourses* 2.16.1), and when he says, "God laid down this law, saying: if you want some good, get it from yourself" (1.29.4). "Protect your own good in all that you do" (4.3.11).

Anthrôpos (ἄνθρωπος): a human being, human beings in general. For Epictetus (*Discourses* 2.10.1), above all we are human beings whose power of reasoned choice (*prohairesis*) supervises all and is completely free. A "beautiful human being" possesses the virtues (*Discourses* 3.1.6b–9). We must be a "unified human being" (*Discourses* 3.15.13), what Hadot calls self-coherence (*The Inner Citadel*, pp. 130–31). In Marcus (see 5.1, 5.20, 8.1, 8.5, 8.26), the term is used in conjunction with an emphasis on what our proper concern and work should be.

Apatheia (ἀπάθεια): passionless calm, peace of mind. In verb form, ἀπαθέω means to free from passion. Epictetus: *Discourses* (seven times noun, eleven times verb), see 4.3.8; twice in *Enchiridion*. Marcus uses it in verb form four times; see 6.16.2b–4a. In its single use as a noun, he says that the closer a person is to *apatheia*, the stronger they are (11.18.5b). See *pathos*.

Aphormê (ἀφορμή): avoidance, disinclination, the impulse not to act (as a result of *ekklisis*). Opposite of *hormê*. *Hormê/Aphormê* is the second of the three areas of training for Epictetus (3.2.1–3a), and the term appears frequently in the *Discourses*. Marcus doesn't use the term in this sense, only *hormê*.

Apotynchanô (ἀποτυγχάνω): to fail in gaining, hitting, achieving; to miss one's purpose or to err. It appears twenty-four times in Epictetus, often with *orexis/oregô*; see especially 3.2.1–3a. Diogenes Laertius says Zeno defined "want" as failing to gain what we yearn for or reach out for (*Lives of the Eminent Philosophers* 7.1.113). The term doesn't appear in Marcus. This experience is a fundamental source of disturbance in life. See also *hamartanô*.

Aproêgmena (ἀπροηγμένα): dispreferred things; indifferent in an absolute moral sense, but things of relative negative value and naturally undesirable things, such as illness. Opposite of *proêgmena*. These terms don't appear in either Epictetus or Marcus, but we know from Diogenes Laertius that they were common Stoic teaching from Zeno and Chrysippus through Posidonius (*Lives of the Eminent Philosophers* 7.1.102ff). Cicero rehearses Zeno's use of the terms and offers the Latin equivalents of *reiecta/praeposita* (*On the Ends of Good and Evil* and *Academica*, 1.X.36–39). Seneca does not follow Cicero in this use, but uses *commoda/incommoda* (advantageous/disadvantageous). "There are things in life which are advantageous and disadvantageous—both beyond our control" (*Moral Letters* 92.16). Cicero makes it a subclass of *reiecta/praeposita* (*On the Ends of Good and Evil* 3.21).

Aretê (ἀρετή): Virtue, goodness, and human excellence; the source of absolute value. Hadot notes that the four cardinal virtues of Plato are not fully present in Arrian's presentation of Epictetus (*The Inner Citadel*, p. 238), but that in Marcus, who followed Epictetus closely, they have a clear articulation and correlation to what Hadot calls "the three acts of the soul" (see chart). Diogenes Laertius says that the four cardinal virtues were primary for

THE DAILY STOIC

the Stoics (*Lives of the Eminent Philosophers,* "Zeno," 7.92b): σωφροσύνη/*sôphrosunê*/self-control, δικαιοσύνη/*dikaiosunê*/justice, ἀνδρεία/*andreia*/courage, φρόνησις/*phronêsis*/wisdom. Chrysippus said that experiencing wisdom (*phronimos*) for even a moment is equal to an eternity of exercising *aretê* (Plutarch, *Moralia* 1062). Musonius Rufus said, "The human being is born with an inclination toward virtue" (*Lectures* 1.7.1–2). Marcus mentions all four virtues in 3.6.1 and 5.12, and three (without courage) in 7.63, 8.32, and 12.15. We present them here as the aims of moral progress to which all our activity in the world is directed. Marcus says we should let our virtues shine until we are extinguished (12.15). Epictetus does cite justice and self-control together in his discussion of virtue in 3.1.6b–9, where his use of σωφροσύνη is milder in the "even-tempered" sense (contrasted by him with "undisciplined"), and his preferred term for self-control here (and elsewhere, appearing with wisdom/φρονίμῳ in 2.21.9) is ἐγκρατεῖς/*enkrateis*/mastery, or exercising control over (contrasted with ἀκρατεῖς/*akrateis*/uncontrolled). Seneca uses the Latin *virtus* and says that "virtue is the only good" and is nothing less than "true and steadfast judgment" (*Moral Letters* 71.32).

Askêsis (ἄσκησις): exercise, practice, disciplined training designed to achieve virtue. Epictetus sees three areas of training (*Discourses* 3.2.1–3a, 3.12.8)—the famous doctrine of three topics (*topoi*) that scholars think was Epictetus's unique contribution to late Stoicism (see Long's *Epictetus: A Stoic and Socratic Guide to Life,* pp. 112–118; Hadot's *The Inner Citadel,* pp. 89–100). Before Epictetus, Seneca affirms the long-standing Stoic division of philosophy into three parts, which he calls "the moral, the natural, and the rational" (*Moral Letters* 89.9). Epictetus, we argue, also sees three levels of discipline, moving from learning/study (μανθάνω/*manthanô,* appearing seventy-nine times) to practice (μελετάω/*meletaô,* appearing fifty-four times; see *Discourses* 2.19.29–34, where he says "learn and diligently practice") to more rigorous training (ἀσκέω/ἄσκησις, appearing forty times). For the three levels of discipline, see 2.9.13–14. For Epictetus, the exercise and training analogies run from wrestling and athletics (see the "invincible athlete" in 1.18.21–23; "true athlete in rigorous training" in 2.18.27–2), to the *pankration* (3.10.6–7), and the ultimate "hard winter training" (χειμασκῆσαι/*cheimaskêsai*) of soldiers (1.2.32, 4.8.35–37). While each of these three areas of training and three levels of discipline reach into and inform one another, there is a clear sense of hierarchy in the acts of the soul, moving up from desire through action to assent, and of making forward progress in our actions in the world, from study to practice to hard training, toward virtue (see chart). For Marcus, who is often derisive of mere study, books, and displays of learning (2.2, 3.14, 5.5, 5.9), these words scarcely appear. He seems more interested in simply getting straight to putting things to the test in everyday life by following the dictates of our guiding reason (*hêgemonikon*). In this way he is very much in tune with Epictetus's memorable admonition against spouting what you've learned without having digested it (see *Discourses* 3.21.1–3). For Marcus, the point of it all is to use our reason to produce in action the virtues of self-control, courage, justice, and wisdom, which correlate to the *topoi* of Epictetus (see chart).

Ataraxia (ἀταραξία): tranquility, freedom from disturbance by external things. It is the fruit of following philosophy, according to Epictetus (*Discourses* 2.1.21–22). It appears fourteen times in the *Discourses* and twice in the *Enchiridion;* see *Discourses* 2.2 (Arrian's caption of section), 2.18.28, 4.3.6b–8, and 4.6.34–35. It appears once in Marcus (9.31; not here).

Axia (ἀξία): the true value or worth of things; the relative value of things preferential; of people, meaning reputation or what's deserved. It appears eighteen times in Marcus; see 4.32, 5.1, 5.36, 9.1.1, and 12.1. Marcus quotes Epictetus on this concept in discussing how to use the power of assent in the area of our impulses (11.37). For Epictetus, the term appears twenty-nine times in the *Discourses* and twice in *Enchiridion* (36; not here). See *Discourses*

GLOSSARY OF TERMS AND PASSAGES

1.2.5–7, 4.1.170, 4.3.6–8, and 4.5.34–37. Overall, the idea is that we too often trade things of great value for things of very little value, an idea that goes back to the teachings of Diogenes of Sinope, the founder of the Cynic school, as described by Diogenes Laertius (*Lives of the Eminent Philosophers* 6.2.35b).

Daimôn (δαίμων): **divine spirit within humans; our individual genius.** Chrysippus held that a happy and well-flowing life was the result "when the affairs of life are in every way tuned to the harmony between the individual divine spirit and the will of the director of the universe" (*Lives of the Eminent Philosophers* 7.1.88). Epictetus tells us never to worry because we are never alone: God is always within, as is our own *daimôn* (*Discourses* 1.14.14; not here).

Diairesis (διαίρεσις): **analysis, division into parts.** Used when distinguishing what is subject to our power of choice from what is not.

Dianoia (διανοία): **thought, intelligence, purpose, faculty of mind.** Haines notes: "not affected by the motions of the pneuma."

Dikaiosunê (δικαιοσύνη): **justice, righteousness.** Diogenes Laertius noted that for the Stoics, it meant "being in harmony with the law and tending to bring people together" (*Lives of the Eminent Philosophers* 7.99; not here). It is one of the four cardinal virtues (i.e., self-control, justice, courage, and wisdom). The word is used seventeen times in Marcus, always in the spirit Diogenes Laertius outlines, where it appears with the other virtues (see especially 3.6, 5.12, 7.63, and 12.15). Epictetus is notable in 3.1.6b–9, where he speaks of "the just" as the kind of person we should strive to be.

Dogma (δόγμα): **that which seems to one; opinion or belief; philosophically, *dogma* are principles or judgments established by reason and experience.** Haines notes that "what the sensations are to the body and impulses to the soul, *dogmata* are to the intelligence." Epictetus takes aim at the untested form of *dogmata* by framing them as τὰ πονηρὰ δόγματα, or oppressive or worthless opinions that must be rooted out by our reasoned choice (*Discourses* 3.3.18–19; see also 3.19.2–3) before they destroy our inner fortress (4.1.86). The term appears more than one hundred times in Epictetus (see *Enchiridion* 5, where he says that it's not things that disturb us, but our judgments/*dogmata* about them) and twenty-three times in Marcus (see especially 4.49, 7.2, 8.1, 8.22, and 8.47, where he often talks about straightening out your principles). Marcus and Epictetus also use the word *krima* (κρῖμα) when talking about decisions and judgment (Marcus, *Meditations* 11.11, 8.47; Epictetus, *Discourses* 4.11.7).

Dokimazein (δοκιμάζω): **to assay; to put to the test; to thoroughly examine.** This is a key verb in understanding Epictetus's Stoicism (found ten times in the *Discourses* and once in the opening of the *Enchiridion*), but it was not used by Marcus. The word carries the meaning of the assayist, one who tests fine metals and coins to verify their authenticity. In one of the most memorable passages in Epictetus, he compares our need to test impressions to what is done with coins and how the skilled merchant can hear a counterfeit coin cast upon a table just as a musician would detect a sour note (*Discourses* 1.20.7–11ff). See also the exercises he gives for handling impressions (*Discourses* 2.18.24; *Enchiridion* 1.5). As sense impressions need to be put to the test, so too our judgments (*dogmata/theôrêma*) need a tough cross-examination (ἐλέγχω; used by both Epictetus and Marcus) to be fully tested.

Doxa (δόξα): **belief, opinion.**

Ekklisis (ἔκκλισις): **aversion; inclination away from a thing.** The opposite of, but often appearing with, *orexis*. This is the first level of self-coherence (see chart). Epictetus warns repeatedly that with aversions we must be careful to apply them only to our own concerns and not to those controlled by others (see *Discourses* 4.1.81–82ff; not here). The word appears fifty-three times in the *Discourses*. In a vivid metaphor of a sparring match, Marcus tells us we can avoid people who might have ill intent without being suspicious toward them (6.20). In step with Epictetus, Marcus urges us to limit our aversion to only those things in our power (8.7). See *orexis*.

Ekpyrôsis (ἐκπύρωσις): **cyclical conflagration (birth and rebirth) of the universe.** This idea, central to Stoic physics and cosmology, goes back to Heraclitus (Marcus 3.3; not here). Stoics equate this fire with the all-permeating reason (*logos spermatikos*) of the universe (see Marcus 6.24).

Eleutheria (ἐλευθερία): **freedom, liberty.** The masses say that only the free can be educated, but the Stoic says that only the educated can be free (*Discourses* 2.1.21–22). Including the adjectival form, it appears more than one hundred times in the *Discourses*. Marcus uses the noun five times (see 5.9).

Eph' hêmin (ἐφ' ἡμῖν): **what is up to us; what is in our control; our correct use of impressions, impulses, and judgments.** The *Enchiridion* (or *Handbook*) *of Epictetus* opens with this most famous of all Stoic phrases. Epictetus says when we want something outside our control, we are stricken with anxiety (*Discourses* 2.13.1). Our judgments about what is up to us determine our freedom (3.26.34–35).

Epistêmê (ἐπιστήμη): **certain and true knowledge, over and above that of *katalêpsis*.**

Ethos (ἔθος): **custom or habit.** See also *hexis*. In late Stoic practice, there is a great focus on habit. Musonius Rufus's ideas about education were aimed at addressing the upbringing, environment, and habits that vary from person to person (*Lectures* 1.1). Epictetus carries this focus on habit forward: "Since habit is such a powerful influence, and we're used to pursuing our impulses to gain and avoid outside our own choice, we should set a contrary habit against that, and where appearances are really slippery, use the counterforce of our training" (*Discourses* 3.12.6). He also talks about the importance of using a contrary, opposing habit in 1.27.4. The term appears seventeen times in Epictetus's *Discourses*. Marcus uses this term four times.

Eudaimonia (εὐδαιμονία): **happiness, flourishing, well-being.** Epictetus says that God made human beings to be happy and stable/serene (εὐσταθεῖν/*eustathein*; *Discourses* 3.24. 2b–3). *Eudaimonia* appears thirteen times in the *Discourses* and once in the *Enchiridion*. Epictetus holds that it is incompatible with yearning for what we don't have (*Discourses* 3.24.17). It appears twice in Marcus (7.67) in conjunction with "life," which, he says, depends on the fewest possible things (see also 7.17). Marcus has one other equivalent word in his use of εὐζωήσεις/*euzôêseis*, or "happy in life" (3.12; none of these three reproduced here).

Eupatheia (εὐπάθεια): **good passions or emotions (as contrasted with *pathos*), the result of correct judgments and virtuous actions.** Diogenes Laertius says, "The Stoics assert there are three good emotional states (*eupatheia*): joy, caution, and wishing . . . joy is rational elation . . . caution is rational avoidance . . . wishing is rational inclination . . . under wishing they place goodwill, benevolence, friendliness and affection; under caution, respect and modesty; under joy, delight, good cheer and contentment" (*Lives of the Eminent Philosophers* 7.116).

Hamartanô (ἁμαρτάνω): **to do wrong, err, fail one's purpose.** The verb appears twenty-eight times in Epictetus and thirty-four times in Marcus. Also, *hamartia* (ἁμαρτία)—a failure, fault, error, to do wrong to another—appears three times in Marcus, notably in 10.30, when he talks about seeing another's wrongdoing from the standpoint of our own failings. Both Epictetus and Musonius Rufus often use the obverse as the ideal, being free from error, *anamartêtos* (ἀναμάρτητος), which, although not possible, is what we should strive for (see especially *Discourses* 4.12.19; *Lectures* 2.5.1). Since Aristotle's *Poetics*, the concept had been the fatal flaw or decision that leads to a tragic demise. The Stoics part ways with any tragic thinking, on the one hand, and, on the other, with any notion of original sin—all sin is the result of bad habit, following common opinion, and bad judgments. Philosophy is meant to help us scrape the accumulated errors of existence from our souls.

Hêgemonikon **(ἡγεμονικόν): ruling or guiding reason; ruling principle. A. A.** Long says the term, meaning "suited to command," was borrowed from Isocrates, the Athenian rhetorician, and was taken up by the early Stoics to represent the intellectual part of the soul as distinct from the senses (*Greek Models of Mind and Self*, p. 89). Long notes that by the time of the late Stoics, Epictetus had applied it even to the souls of animals, which lack rationality (*Epictetus: A Stoic and Socratic Guide to Life*, p. 211), and said it means "the governing faculty of the mind." Hadot calls it the superior or guiding part of the soul. Marcus uses it as a unique property of human beings (especially in 12.1 and 12.33). Epictetus's *Discourses* (twenty-six references): 1.26.15, 1.20.11, 4.4.43, 4.5.5. Marcus Aurelius (forty-six references): 3.9, 4.38, 5.11, 8.48, 8.56, 9.22, 9.26, 12.1, 12.33. Whereas Epictetus leans heavily on *prohairesis*, Marcus prefers *hêgemonikon*: "How does your ruling reason manage itself? For in that is the key to everything. Whatever else remains, be it in the power of your choice or not, is but a corpse and smoke" (12.33).

Heimarmenê **(εἱμαρμένη): fate, destiny.** Stoics were compatibilists about the free will and determinism question—all things are determined, but our response is entirely our own. See *pronoia*.

Hexis **(ἕξις): abstract noun built on *echein*, to have, possess; a state of mind or habit, disposition toward something; of physical things, a natural property or tendency.** Epictetus says that habits must be "first weakened and then obliterated" (*Discourses* 2.18.11b–14); otherwise, they become fuel for personal destruction (2.18.4–5). See *ethos*.

Hormê **(ὁρμή): positive impulse or appetite toward an object (as a result of *orexis* and our assent) that leads to action; the opposite of *aphormê*.** These can be irrational impulses to act or a reasoned choice to act or exert effort toward an end. Quoting Epictetus, Marcus says that we "must pay special attention to the sphere of our impulses—that they are subject to reservation (μέθ᾽ ὑπεξαίρεσις), to the common good (κοινωνικαί), and that they are in proportion to actual worth (ἀξίαν)" (11.37). This is the second level of self-coherence that gives rise to our actions (see chart). Marcus repeatedly ties the discipline of *hormê* to acts for the common good (see also 8.7) and the claims of justice (4.22). It appears thirty-four times in Epictetus's *Discourses*, three times in the *Enchiridion*, and thirty-five times in Marcus. Seneca uses the Latin equivalent *impetus* seventy-nine times in his letters (see *Moral Letters* 71.32, where he says virtue resides in our judgment, which gives rise to impulse and clarifies all appearances that give rise to impulse).

Hulê **(ὕλη): matter, material.** This is a very common reference in Epictetus, appearing more than forty times, usually with the analogy of the material that craftspeople use as a way of talking about where our own focus should be, and where the evidence of our progress will be seen in the art of living (*Discourses* 1.15.2). He calls external things the raw material of our *prohairesis* (1.29.1–4a); elsewhere he says, "The raw material for the work of a good and excellent person is their own guiding reason (*hêgemonikon*)" (3.3.1). The term appears nineteen times in Marcus; see especially 8.35, where he talks about how we can "convert any obstacle into the raw material for our own purpose." Sometimes used interchangeably with *ousia*.

Hypolêpsis (ὑπόληψις): literally "taking up" an opinion, assumption, conception, notion, understanding. Hadot translates the term as "value judgment" and sees a movement upward into higher-level value judgments, from *prolêpsis* to *hypolêpsis* to *katalêpsis*. See Marcus 4.3.4b and 9.13, where he talks about how our own assumptions can crush us, so we must throw them out. He also says that "everything turns on our assumptions" (12.22), and we should hold our power for understanding, or forming opinions, sacred (3.9). The term appears eight times in Epictetus's *Discourses* (see 2.19.13–14, where he says we hold opinions the opposite of what we should) and three times in the *Enchiridion* (see 20, where he talks about how our own opinions or assumptions are what fuel anger).

Kalos (καλός): beautiful; in the moral sense, noble, virtuous. Seneca's equivalent term, used quite frequently, is *honestum*.

Katalêpsis (κατάληψις): true comprehension, clear perception, and firm conviction needed for right conduct. Hadot translates the term as "perception" or "objective representation." This is a prominent term for Epictetus and stands in contrast to the Skeptic's notion that nothing could be known with certainty (ἀκατάληπτος). Epictetus says that true progress (*prokopê*) is about giving assent (see *synkatathesis*) only where there is *katalêpsis* (*Discourses* 3.8.4). Marcus uses the term in praising the character of Antoninus and his zeal for "getting a true grasp of affairs" (6.30.2), as well as in 4.22, where he says every impulse should be subject to the claims of justice and keeping our convictions clear.

Kathêkon (καθῆκον): duty, appropriate action on the path to virtue. Diogenes Laertius says that Zeno was the first philosopher to use the term as relating to conduct in the sense of being incumbent upon an actor (*Lives of the Eminent Philosophers*, "Zeno," 7.108). Marcus says that every duty in life is a sum of acts that deserve methodical attention (6.26).

Koinos (κοινός): common, shared in common. As Haines noted, this term and its cognates appear more than eighty times in Marcus, and it is a very central part of his thinking and ethical orientation. Community, partnership, fellowship, neighborliness, and cooperation are all heavily emphasized in terms ranging from κοινωνία (5.16, and "action for the common good in the present moment" in 9.6) to his own coined word κοινονοημοσύνη, regard for the feelings of others (1.16). In 6.30, Marcus tells us, "Life is short—the fruit of this life is a good character and acts for the common good." See also his morning ritual to remind ourselves that we've "been made by nature for the purpose of working with others" (8.12). A related common term appearing in both Marcus and Epictetus is the word ἀλλήλων/*allêlôn*, which stresses how we are made "for each other" or "for one another" (twenty-six times in Marcus, especially 5.16 and 6.38; and twenty times in Epictetus, notably 2.20).

Kosmos (κόσμος): all-encompassing order, world, universe.

Logos/Logikos (λόγος/λογικός): reason or rational; the ordering principle of the cosmos. *Logos spermatikos* (λόγος σπερματικός) is the generative principle of the universe, which creates and takes back all things (see Marcus 6.24).

Nomos (νόμος): law, custom.

Oiêsis (οἴησις): conceit, self-deception, illusion, arrogant opinion or notion. Epictetus says (3.14.8) that two things must be rooted out of every human being: self-deception and mistrust/timidity (*apistia*). Our conceit, arrogance, and false opinions are what must be removed (2.17.1), along with passion (*pathos*). Epictetus sees a movement from preconception (*prolêpsis*) through conception (*hypolêpsis*) to our more firmly formed convictions (*katalêpsis*), and all can be subject to error (*hamartia*). Heraclitus called self-deception "an awful disease" (Diogenes Laertius, *Lives of the Eminent Philosophers*, 9.7), and the Stoics offered their practices for overcoming it.

Oikeiôsis (οἰκείωσις): **self-ownership, appropriation to the individual's or species' needs.** There is only one instance of this noun in Epictetus (*Discourses* 1.19.15), which pertains to self-preservation, although it appears in a discussion of "the common interest." Marcus also has one use, and it moves explicitly to the other pole of appropriation—namely, to that which lends to the "care for others" or human fellowship (3.9), and our ruling reason is what enables us to keep in accord with nature and effect such appropriation. The related verbal and adjectival forms of "appropriating" and being "fitting or appropriate" are more common to both.

Orexis (ὄρεξις): **desire, inclination toward a thing.** The opposite of *ekklisis*. In Aristotle this was understood as "appetence" and was something shared with animals and different from purposive choice (*prohairesis*), which involved both reason and deliberation. Epictetus says if we want to be free, we shouldn't desire something in someone else's control (*Discourses* 1.4. 18–22). *Orexis/ekklisis* are the subject of the first of the three *topoi*, or areas of training that produce self-coherence, the other two being *hormê/aphormê* and *synkatathesis* (3.2.1–3a). The word appears fifty-six times in the *Discourses* and seven times in the *Enchiridion*. It appears five times in Marcus, once in saying principles need to be the source of desire and action (8.1.5) and be limited to only what's in our control (8.7). The verb form, ὀρέγω/*oregô*, meaning to reach out for, yearn for, often appears and in many instances it occurs with "not missing the mark"; see *hamartanô* and *apotynchanô*.

Ousia (οὐσία): **substance or being, sometimes used interchangeably with** *hulê* (**matter, material**). Marcus speaks vividly of substance being "like a river's unending flow, its activities constantly changing and causes infinitely shifting so that almost nothing at all stands still" (5.23), harkening back to Heraclitus (*Lives of the Eminent Philosophers*, 9.8).

Paideia (παιδεία): **training, teaching, and education.** *Askeô*, *manthanô*, and *meletaô* (see chart) are each a part of getting an education as outlined by Epictetus in *Discourses* 2.9.13–14. The daily disciplines are central to being educated for the Stoic, and only the educated are truly free (2.1.21–23 and 1.22.9–10a). Working over our preconceptions (*prolêpsin*) is the point of education (1.2.5–7).

Pathos (πάθος): **passion or emotion, often excessive and based on false judgments.** Haines places passion as the "affect" following from *hormê* that lead to acts against nature. The four passions divide into two types: (1) for things not in present possession or anticipated in the future, which are desire (ἐπιθυμία) and fear (φόβος); and (2) for things presently engaging a person, which are pleasure (ἡδονή) and distress (λύπη). Epictetus states the Stoic position most clearly in *Discourses* 4.1.175: "Freedom isn't secured by filling up on your heart's desire but by removing your desire." Diogenes Laertius says that Zeno defined passion/emotion as an irrational and unnatural movement in the soul, or as excessive *hormê* (*Lives of the Eminent Philosophers* 7.110). Despite the popular misconception, the Stoics did celebrate certain passions as good (*eupatheia*), if in rational bounds: in particular, joy, caution, and wishing (*Lives of the Eminent Philosophers* 7.116).

Phantasia (φαντασία): **impression, appearance, perception.** Epictetus says (1.1.7–9) that the gods gave us one power that governs all the rest—"the ability to make the right use of

THE DAILY STOIC

appearances." He also says that the first and greatest task of the philosopher is to test (δοκιμάζω, "to assay") and separate appearances (see also 2.18.24). He uses the metaphors of sweeping currents, battle, and the rigorous training of an athlete for the work we must do to hold our own against impressions (2.18.27–28). "The task of the good and excellent person is to handle their impressions in harmony with nature" (3.3.1). There are more than two hundred references to *phantasia* in the *Discourses* and nine in the *Enchiridion* (34). The term appears about forty times in Marcus's *Meditations* (5.2, 5.16, 6.13, 8.7, 8.26, 8.28–29). Marcus has a great exercise for not telling yourself more than initial impressions ("report" in 8.49).

Phronēsis (φρόνησις): **practical wisdom, one of the four cardinal virtues.** The term is used repeatedly by Marcus, most memorably in 4.37, where he says that "wisdom and acting justly are one and the same," and in 5.9, where he says "there is nothing so pleasing as wisdom itself." See *arête.*

Physis (φύσις): **nature, the natural order; of things, species, or kind: characteristic.** Both Epictetus and Marcus repeatedly state that we must use our ruling principle to keep ourselves in harmony with nature (*Discourses* 4.4.43; Marcus 3.9). In Stoic thought, God and nature are one.

Pneuma (πνεῦμα): **air, breath, spirit; a principle in Stoic physics.** The part of the soul set into disturbance by desires and aversions, which Haines calls the inferior part of the soul, distinct from *nous* (mind). Epictetus has a memorable image in *Discourses* 3.3.20–22, where he talks about the movement of a disturbed bowl of water being like the spirit in which things exist.

Proēgmena (προηγμένα): **preferred things; indifferent in an absolute moral sense, but of relative positive value, naturally desirable things, such as health.** Opposite of *aproēgmena.*

Prohairesis (προαίρεσις): **reasoned or deliberative choice, our free will to choose, the sphere of choice.** The term goes back to Aristotle's *Ethics* and has been traditionally translated there as "purposive choice." A. A. Long, in an attempt to free it from modern moral concepts, translates it as "volition," a term we find too remote from everyday understanding— for generations prior it was translated as "moral purpose" (W. A. Oldfather, George Long, and others). We are avoiding loading the term with either the *moral* sense of Christian tradition or the modernist sense of *will*, so heavily colored since Schopenhauer and Nietzsche. A. A. Long sees this as Epictetus's preferred term for what distinguishes human beings from animals (which also have *hēgemonikon* in his reading of Epictetus; *Epictetus: A Stoic and Socratic Guide to Life*, p. 211), something not even the gods can touch (*Discourses* 1.1.23). The term is used sixty-nine times in the *Discourses* (1.4.18–22, 1.18.21–23, 1.22.10, 1.29.1–4a, 2.1.12–13, 2.5. 4–5, 2.6.25, 2.10.1, 2.16.1–2a, 2.22.19–20, 3.1.39b–40a, 3.3.18–19, 3.7.5, 3.10.18, 3.19.2–3, 3.21.1–3, 3.22.13, 4.4.23, 4.5.34–37) and six times in the *Enchiridion* (13). Marcus uses it five times in the negative (ἀπροαίρετα), or outside of our choice, and three times in the positive sense of deliberate choice (3.6, 6.41, 8.56, 12.3, 12.33). Where this is the focal point of Epictetus's system, Marcus leans heavily to *hēgemonikon.*

Prokopē (προκοπή): **progress or improvement; on the path toward the virtues of self-control, courage, justice, and wisdom.** See Epictetus, *Discourses* 1.4, captioned "on progress," especially 1.4.18–22; also 3.19.2–3. The word appears fourteen times in Epictetus (most often in 1.4). Hanging out with the wrong people can limit our progress, according to Epictetus (4.2.1–5), and Musonius Rufus reminds us of the same (*Lectures* 11.53.21–22; losing our soul).

Prolēpsis (πρόληψις): **a primary conception, or preconception, possessed by all rational beings.** Epictetus talks about keeping them ready like polished weapons (*Discourses* 4–5a,

6b). See also 1.22 and 1.2.5–7, where he talks about working over our preconceptions and the true meaning of education.

Pronoia (πρόνοια): foreknowledge, foresight, divine providence. Epictetus says we can praise providence if we have two qualities: seeing things clearly and gratitude (1.6.1–2). Marcus talks about entrusting the future to providence in 12.1. The word appears ten times in Epictetus (see 3.17.1) and twelve times in Marcus.

Prosochê (προσοχή): attention, diligence, soberness. See especially *Discourses* 4.12.1–21. In 1.20.8–11, Epictetus says it is particularly needed for things that might steer us wrongly. Marcus uses the term once in the body of his *Meditations* in speaking about what a short time we have in life to keep indifferent things from consuming our attention (11.16; not here).

Psychê (ψυχή): state of mind, soul, life, living principle. It appears forty-three times in the *Discourses*, and the laconic Marcus uses it sixty-nine times in his *Meditations*. Marcus has a beautiful image of the rational soul as a sphere in 11.12 (not here); Epictetus sees it as a bowl of water in 3.3.20–22. Seneca's term is *animus*, the rational soul. The Stoics were materialists, so the soul itself has substance.

Sophos (σοφός): wise person, virtuous sage, and the ethical ideal of a practicing Stoic.

Sympatheia (συμπάθεια): sympathy, affinity of parts to the organic whole, mutual interdependence.

Synkatathesis (συγκατάθεσις): assent; approval to impressions, conceptions, and judgments, enabling action to take place. See Marcus quoting Epictetus in 11.37 (in verb form) and how it relates to *katalêpsis*; also, in 5.10 Marcus talks about how every assent to impressions is subject to error. This is the third level of self-coherence, concerning the will and judgment and what we choose to reject (see chart). It appears eight times in noun form and twenty-one times in verb form in Epictetus: 3.2.1–3a, 3.8.4, and 4.11.6–7.

Technê (τέχνη): craft, art in the sense of profession or vocation. Marcus says our *technê* is to be a good human being (11.5). Epictetus uses the analogies of crafts and trades quite often, particularly in drawing focus to the proper material of our work as human beings.

Telos (τέλος): the end goal or objective of life.

Theôrêma (θεώρημα): general principle or perception, a truth of science; used interchangeably with *dogmata* in discussing the mind's store of judgments.

Theos (θεός): god; the divine, creative power that orders the universe and gives human beings their reason and freedom of choice. As far as theology goes, despite reflecting the polytheism of their culture and making references to gods of all stripes, the late Stoics were monists and pantheists: God = nature. Further, they were materialists, so even the divine spark in us—and the soul—are corporeal. Epictetus was a Phrygian by birth and had a very vivid, personalistic view of God. He referred to God as a kindly father (see particularly *Discourses* 1.6, 3.24). A. A. Long, the foremost scholar of Epictetus, put it this way: "Whether [Epictetus] speaks of Zeus or God or Nature or the gods, he is completely committed to the belief that the world is providentially organized by a divine power whose creative agency reaches its highest manifestation in human beings" (*Epictetus: A Stoic and Socratic Guide to Life*, p. 134). Long thinks Epictetus was reviving Cleanthes's (successor to Zeno) strong religious sense. There is no transcendent god for any of the Stoics—a key difference from Christianity. Epictetus says we must seek to bind up our choice with the will of God (*Discourses*

4.1.89). Marcus tends to refer to the divine in a looser, often more polytheistic way (see 9.1.1), but he shares Epictetus's views, especially when he says, "hold sacred your capacity for understanding," a gift from God requiring obedience to God (3.9). Seneca, too, speaks often of the divine in plural, but all three are agreed that we must accept fate and seek to correct our own faults rather than blame others or the gods (*Moral Letters* 107.12).

Tonos (τόνος): **tension, a principle in Stoic physics accounting for attraction and repulsion; a way of seeing what gives rise to virtue and vice in the soul.**

A WORD ON THE TRANSLATIONS, REFERENCES, AND SOURCES

All the translations in this volume were rendered with the aid of two primary and indispensable sources. The first is the incomparable treasure of the Loeb Classical Library (Harvard University Press), which has been the standard resource for the original language texts for generations. Today, in addition to the handsome green and red printed volumes loved by many, the full Greek and Latin texts are now available via online subscription, with terrific search capabilities in both languages, as well as in English for the general reader, at www.loebclassics.com. I have found this service to be a godsend in organizing and managing my work. From a lexical standpoint, the resources at www.perseus.tufts.edu have proved to be invaluable, offering, in addition to search capabilities, links to the superlative lexicon of Liddell and Scott (Greek) and the dictionary of Lewis and Short (Latin), along with comparative usage statistics and occurrences across authors and time periods. I also used extensively the print editions of both works (Oxford University Press) for particularly challenging passages and for source texts not available online (Musonius Rufus). Of course, the translations were informed by the excellent work of Loeb translators W. A. Oldfather, C. R. Haines, Richard M. Gummere, John W. Basore, and others. In the case of Epictetus, I especially enjoyed consulting the works of Thomas Wentworth Higginson, a fellow Harvard divinity graduate, and George Long (both available in print and at www.perseus.tufts.edu). There have been quite a few more recent translations of Marcus Aurelius, and among them Ryan and I both enjoy the lyrical Gregory Hays (Modern Library); for a more literal modern rendering, particularly for precision with philosophical terms, the Robin Hard translation (Oxford University Press) is hard to beat.

With regard to the translations, the goal was to make the work of these late Stoic thinkers as accessible, digestible, and coherent as possible. In the major terms of Stoic thought and its development in Epictetus and Marcus, my effort has been placed on consistency and avoiding anachronism while pointing out any places of difference in emphasis or use as necessary. Apart from the core terminology, the translations have been made with an aim to remain as literal as possible, with only a few liberties taken when needed to make a point stand out or to avoid repeated images or phrases. A special thanks to Amanda C. Gregory for her review of my glossary and translations.

All source and line references given, unless otherwise noted, are to the original texts as found on www.perseus.tufts.edu, and most of the remaining ones are to the Loeb texts (online version, which occasionally differs from the printed editions in line numbering). The pieces from Musonius Rufus came from an edition of the Greek text in Cora Lutz's 1947 work, *Musonius Rufus, Lectures and Fragments* (Yale), which I procured from a reprinter in India (but it contains only the *Lectures* and is missing her introduction, the *Fragments*, and much of the textual notes). I have spoken with the director of Yale University Press about possibly bringing that work back into print, and it will be reissued in February 2020.

SUGGESTIONS FOR FURTHER READING

In addition to the Loeb Classics and online resources at www.perseus.tufts.edu and the other printed translations mentioned previously, there are a handful of exceptional recent works by accessible scholars that you should read:

Hadot, Pierre. *The Inner Citadel: The Meditations of Marcus Aurelius*, translated by Michael Chase (Cambridge, MA: Harvard University Press, 2001).

———. *What Is Ancient Philosophy?* Translated by Michael Chase (Cambridge, MA: Harvard University Press, new edition, 2004).

Long, A. A. *Epictetus: A Stoic and Socratic Guide to Life* (New York: Oxford University Press, 2004).

———. *Greek Models of Mind and Self* (Cambridge, MA: Harvard University Press, 2015).

Nussbaum, Martha. *The Therapy of Desire: Theory and Practice in Hellenistic Ethics* (Princeton, NJ: Princeton University Press, reissued 2009).

Robertson, Donald. *The Philosophy of Cognitive Behavioural Therapy* (London: Karnac Books, 2010).

Join millions of other readers with these #1 bestsellers!

This journal belongs to

_____

If found, please do the right thing!

The
DAILY
STOIC
JOURNAL

366 Days of Writing and Reflection on the Art of Living

Make time

RYAN HOLIDAY

AND STEPHEN HANSELMAN

THE PAINTED PORCH BOOKSHOP

PENGUIN

Make time

INTRODUCTION

In his tent at the front near the Granua River in the distant territory of Germania, the Emperor Marcus Aurelius rose at dawn. It was a struggle for him to get up this early, but he did anyway; his job required it. In the lamplight, he sat at the table and began to write in Greek in his journal about what the day ahead held in store for him. "I will encounter busybodies, ingrates, egomaniacs, liars, the jealous and cranks," he wrote to himself, preparing mentally for the inevitable difficulties of the life of an emperor, particularly one faced with leading an army and overseeing the empire from abroad.

But don't assume this was a complaint. There was not a note of frustration or resentment in his tone.

Marcus Aurelius was practicing with pleasure the philosophy he'd come to love and depend on, Stoicism. He was not writing off his fellow men and his subjects. On the contrary, in the completion of that thought, he would say of those busybodies and ingrates "that none can do me harm, or implicate me in ugliness—nor can I be angry at my relatives or hate them. For we are made for cooperation." And so he went about the rest of his morning journaling, writing little notes for himself on how to think, how to live, what to be grateful for, and then he proceeded on to meet the day, not simply as a philosopher, but as a true *philosopher king.*

If we can go back in time a little further, almost exactly one century and one evening before Marcus's morning meditation, we'd find another Stoic philosopher doing something quite similar. His name was Seneca, and he was alternatively a powerbroker, a playwright, and public intellectual serving at the highest levels in the court of Nero. Instead of journaling in the morning, he preferred to do his at night, putting, as he said, each day up for review. Seneca would look back on the day just then coming to a close and ask himself whether his actions had been just, what he could have done better, what habits he could curb, how he might improve himself. "We reflect upon that which we are about to do," he would tell his older brother about this nightly routine, "and yet our plans for the future descend from the past."

Reviewing the previous day is what helped Seneca prepare for the one that he would face the following morning.

Epictetus, another famous Stoic, was a former slave who lived a life not nearly as cushy or powerful as Seneca or Marcus, and would repeatedly remind his students to rehearse their lessons, to write them down for their own use. In *Discourses*, he says, "Every day and night keep thoughts like these at hand—write them, read them aloud, talk to yourself and others about them."

These then, the morning preparation and the evening review, are two of the most essential and intertwining exercises in Stoic philosophy and a tradition now more than two thousand years old. It's a tradition that you, in holding *The Daily Stoic Journal*, are now an heir to and can continue twice per day in your pursuit of the good life.

Unlike many other philosophies, Stoicism wasn't designed simply to be some explanation of the universe. It wasn't overly interested in complicated questions about where we came from or theoretical discussions of this issue or that one. Stoicism was designed by the Greeks and perfected by the Romans for the living and the *doing* of daily life for the man and woman trying to make it in a confusing world. As such, it was much more than a set of teachings or long-ago written sentences. It was instead a set of timeless practical exercises—systems for reducing fear, thoughts for battling destructive thoughts, reminders of things we take for granted, tools for resisting temptation, pillars of strength for tough moments. This meant that Stoicism wasn't something to be learned once or read once. It was meant to be studied and practiced.

Consider the title of Marcus Aurelius's only work, *Meditations*. He was *meditating*, to himself, for himself, on the philosophic principles he was still learning and practicing even in old age. A peek at Seneca's letters finds the same thing—he is writing to someone else, yes, but clearly the intended audience is also himself. He is thinking out loud. Epictetus, too, survives in the form of notes written by his student Arrian, and they read as if his day was spent trying to answer the endless questions of his students: What do I do about this? How can I handle something like that? Any advice for when I _____?

In our book *The Daily Stoic*, we tried to bring a collection of this wisdom to busy readers in a digestible and accessible way. Instead of translating and republishing the Stoics in their original form (which has been done quite well, many times), we created the first ever single-volume collection of all the great Stoics, arranged to highlight a thought from one each day. The response to the book was humbling and surprising. The book spent three months on the national bestseller lists and debuted in the form of a keynote address at what was likely the largest single gathering of Stoics in two thousand years. Our accompanying daily e-mail at DailyStoic.com was inundated with sign-ups, meaning that each morning tens of thousands of aspiring Stoics were all reading the same thing at the same time. We also began to see photos online from readers who had filled up the pages of *The Daily Stoic* and Moleskine journals with thoughts inspired by each day's meditation.

In response, we set out to create this journal, a companion guide to *The Daily Stoic* and a resource to anyone trying to practice the philosophy. We're honored that you now hold it in your hands.

HOW TO USE THIS JOURNAL

This book presents fifty-two Stoic disciplines or practices, one for each week of the year. Each practice is presented with some direction about its significance and application, along with a few quotes from the great Stoics to help focus your attention on the practice for the week—the first quote about each weekly practice is taken directly from that same week in *The Daily Stoic*. Each day presents a question to help you focus your morning preparations or evening review (or both). The questions will work for you whether you are reading along with *The Daily Stoic*, using our daily e-mail readings, or any other source.

We have not written a set of commandments or a step-by-step system that must be adhered to unthinkingly (if you don't want to respond to the prompts, ignore them and write about whatever you feel would be most beneficial. We also have suggestions at the back for other sources to use). As Seneca said: "The ones who pioneered these paths aren't our masters, but our guides. Truth stands open to everyone; it hasn't been monopolized."

The reason these Stoic practices have been so enduring (and are enjoying a modern-day resurgence) is that they are relentlessly focused on the situations that we face on a daily basis, what Richard Sorabji calls "the ordinary ups and downs of life, on bereavement, loss of office, promotion, the rat race, money, invasions, the sacking of cities, exile, worries about health." As the American philosopher Brand Blanshard marveled at Marcus Aurelius's legacy:

"Few care now about the marches and countermarches of the Roman commanders. What the centuries have clung to is a notebook of thoughts by a man whose real life was largely unknown who put down in the midnight dimness not the events of the day or the plans of the morrow, but something of far more permanent interest, the ideals and aspirations that a rare spirit lived by."

The Roman Stoics focused not on words, but action. As Seneca memorably put it, "Philosophy teaches us how to act, not how to talk." This bias toward improving our actions on a daily basis was something Epictetus made central to his teaching, summarized in his warning "not to be satisfied with mere learning, but to add practice and then training."

This journal is a place to focus your attention (*prosochē*) and practice (*meletē*) as you try to remember and apply what you are learning on the path to progress (*prokopē*). When you pursue the Stoic disciplines presented in this journal, each morning you will ask, as the great modern Stoic Pierre Hadot put it, "What principles will guide and inspire my actions?" And each evening you will examine where you fell short of those principles, as well as where you have made progress. You can begin on any calendar date you choose and proceed until the book is complete.

Together, the fifty-two ideals and aspirations offer something for every situation. Whether it's dealing with bad habits like complaining (Week XXXI), procrastination (Week XXXV), or panic (Week XXXIX), or finding less destructive alternatives to anger (Week XXIX), fear of the future (Week XXXIV), or dealing with haters (Week XXXVIII), you will find practical tools to put to use. You will gain powerful perspective by learning the exercise of taking "the view from above" (Week XXII), or learning to see things as others do (Week XI), and by taking on a role model (Week XXIII). You'll train yourself in the Stoic basics like the dichotomy of control (Week I), focus on the present moment (Week V), or how to test your impressions (Week XV).

It's important to remember this isn't a contest to see if you can live like some perfect sage or escape the correction of someone farther along the path than you. Anyone who uses philosophy that way is decidedly un-Stoic! As Seneca reminded us, "Let philosophy scrape off your own faults, rather than be a way to rail against the faults of others." Think of this journal as a brush for your own soul, just like brushing your teeth each morning and each evening.

The final lesson at the end of this book is the most essential one of all of Stoic philosophy: learning how to turn words into works. We hope you will make it that far, and if you do, we encourage you to start the same journey once again the following year, for you will be, as Heraclitus said, no longer the same person nor will this be the same book.

WEEK I
WHAT'S UP TO US, WHAT'S NOT UP TO US

Epictetus's handbook (the *Enchiridion*) begins with the most power-ful exercise in all of Stoicism: the distinction between the things that are "up to us" (in our control) and the things that are "not up to us." It is this, the dichotomy of control, that is the first principle in the entire philosophy. We don't control many of the things we pursue in life—yet we become angry, sad, hurt, scared, or jealous when we don't get them. In fact, those emotions—those reactions—are about the only thing that we do control. If that is the only lesson you journal about or remember for this year, consider it a year well and philosophically lived.

"The chief task in life is simply this: to identify and separate mat-ters so that I can say clearly to myself which are externals not under my control, and which have to do with the choices I actu-ally control. Where then do I look for good and evil? Not to uncontrollable externals, but within myself to the choices that are my own . . ."

—EPICTETUS, *DISCOURSES*, 2.5.4–5

"Some things are in our control, while others are not. We control our opinion, choice, desire, aversion, and, in a word, everything of our own doing. We don't control our body, property, reputa-tion, position, and, in a word, everything not of our own doing. Even more, the things in our control are by nature free, unhin-dered, and unobstructed, while those not in our control are weak, slavish, can be hindered, and are not our own."

—EPICTETUS, *ENCHIRIDION*, 1.1–2

"We control our reasoned choice and all acts that depend on that moral will. What's not under our control are the body and any of its parts, our possessions, parents, siblings, children, or country—anything with which we might associate."

—EPICTETUS, *DISCOURSES*, 1.22.10

January 1st   What things are truly in my control?

MORNING REFLECTION

EVENING REFLECTION

January 2nd   What am I learning and studying for?

MORNING REFLECTION

EVENING REFLECTION

January 3rd   What can I say no to so I can say yes to what matters?

MORNING REFLECTION

EVENING REFLECTION

January 4th   Am I seeing clearly? Acting generously? Accepting what I can't change?

MORNING REFLECTION

EVENING REFLECTION

January 5th   What is my purpose in life?

MORNING REFLECTION

EVENING REFLECTION

January 6th   Who am I and what do I stand for?

MORNING REFLECTION

EVENING REFLECTION

January 7th   How can I keep my mind clear from pollution?

MORNING REFLECTION

EVENING REFLECTION

WEEK II
THE SPHERE OF CHOICE

If the first step is to discern what is or isn't in our control, the second is to focus our energy on the things we have a choice about. The Stoics viewed the soul as a sphere that, when well tuned, well directed, was an invincible fortress against any trial or circumstance. Protected by our reason, this sphere of choice (*prohairesis*) is like a sacred temple and is the only thing we truly possess in life. We are the product of our choices, so it is essential then that we choose well. This week, consider and reflect on the choices you have: about your emotions, your actions, your beliefs, and your priorities.

"Keep this thought at the ready at daybreak, and through the day and night—there is only one path to happiness, and that is in giving up all outside of your sphere of choice, regarding nothing else as your possession, surrendering all else to God and Fortune."

—EPICTETUS, *DISCOURSES*, 4.4.39

"Who then is invincible? The one who cannot be upset by anything outside their reasoned choice."

—EPICTETUS, *DISCOURSES*, 1.18.21

"The soul is a sphere, true to itself. It neither projects itself toward any external thing nor does it collapse on itself, but instead radiates a light which it shows itself the truth of all things and the truth in itself."

—MARCUS AURELIUS, *MEDITATIONS*, 11.12

January 8th   What am I addicted to?

MORNING REFLECTION

EVENING REFLECTION

January 9th   If I don't control what happens to me, what is left?

MORNING REFLECTION

EVENING REFLECTION

January 10th   Where can I find steadiness?

MORNING REFLECTION

EVENING REFLECTION

January 11th   What are sources of unsteadiness in my life?

MORNING REFLECTION

_____

_____

_____

_____

_____

_____

_____

_____

_____

EVENING REFLECTION

_____

_____

_____

_____

_____

_____

_____

_____

_____

January 12th   Where is the path to serenity?

MORNING REFLECTION

_____

_____

_____

_____

_____

_____

_____

_____

EVENING REFLECTION

January 13th   What can I put outside my circle of control?

MORNING REFLECTION

EVENING REFLECTION

January 14th   What jerks me around?

MORNING REFLECTION

EVENING REFLECTION

WEEK III
THE WAKE UP

E ach day you write in this journal, you'll be following in the footsteps of Epictetus, Marcus Aurelius, and all the other great Stoics. The Stoics did not face each day on a whim, but instead with preparation and discipline. They spent real time thinking and anticipating what was to come over the course of a day, a week, a year. Each morning activity—journaling included—was designed to make them ready to face the day. And with your work in this book, so you will be, too.

"Ask yourself the following first thing in the morning:

- What am I lacking in attaining freedom from passion?
- What for tranquility?
- What am I? A mere body, estate-holder, or reputation? None of these things.
- What, then? A rational being.
- What then is demanded of me? Meditate on your actions.
- How did I steer away from serenity?
- What did I do that was unfriendly, unsocial, or uncaring?
- What did I fail to do in all these things?"

—Epictetus, *Discourses*, 4.6.34–35

"On those mornings you struggle with getting up, keep this thought in mind—I am awakening to the work of a human being. Why then am I annoyed that I am going to do what I'm made for, the very things for which I was put into this world? Or was I made for this, to snuggle under the covers and keep warm? It's so pleasurable. Were you then made for pleasure? In short, to be coddled or to exert yourself?"

—Marcus Aurelius, *Meditations*, 5.1

January 15th   Am I staying the course or being steered away?

MORNING REFLECTION

EVENING REFLECTION

January 16th   What assumptions have I left unquestioned?

MORNING REFLECTION

EVENING REFLECTION

January 17th   Am I doing work that matters?

MORNING REFLECTION

EVENING REFLECTION

January 18th   Can I find grace and harmony in places others overlook?

MORNING REFLECTION

EVENING REFLECTION

January 19th   Good or bad, high or low, do I still have choices?

MORNING REFLECTION

EVENING REFLECTION

January 20th   How can I rekindle my principles and start living today?

MORNING REFLECTION

EVENING REFLECTION

January 21st   What am I getting out of my journaling ritual?

MORNING REFLECTION

EVENING REFLECTION

∽

WEEK IV
A LITTLE BETTER EVERY DAY

The Stoics saw their lives as works in progress. They didn't believe they were born perfect but they believed that with work, and dedication, they could get a little better every day. There is real delight in this progress, as Epictetus quoted by way of Socrates. Marcus Aurelius avidly pursued his own education and improvement, eagerly looking for advice from books, mentors, and historical examples. Follow that example this week, and see how you get a little better as each day passes.

We must keep constant watch over ourselves and, as Seneca phrased it, put each day up for review. Looking back on our day helps us to better understand where we may have fallen short and gives us tangible feedback for how to improve and grow. Only what you measure and record can be monitored; only what you put up for reflection can be learned from.

"I will keep constant watch over myself and—most usefully—will put each day up for review. For this is what makes us evil—that none of us looks back upon our own lives. We reflect upon only that which we are about to do. And yet our plans for the future descend from the past."

—SENECA, *MORAL LETTERS*, 83.2

"From Rusticus . . . I learned to read carefully and not be satisfied with a rough understanding of the whole, and not to agree too quickly with those who have a lot to say about something."

—MARCUS AURELIUS, *MEDITATIONS*, 1.7.3

"But what does Socrates say? 'Just as one person delights in improving his farm, and another his horse, so I delight in attending to my own improvement day by day.'"

—EPICTETUS, *DISCOURSES*, 3.5.14

January 22nd   What bad habit did I curb today?

MORNING REFLECTION

EVENING REFLECTION

January 23rd   Which of my possessions own me?

MORNING REFLECTION

EVENING REFLECTION

January 24th   Am I doing deep work?

MORNING REFLECTION

EVENING REFLECTION

January 25th   What do I truly prize?

MORNING REFLECTION

EVENING REFLECTION

January 26th   What is my mantra today?

MORNING REFLECTION

EVENING REFLECTION

January 27th   What am I studying, practicing, and training?

MORNING REFLECTION

EVENING REFLECTION

January 28th   What ruler do I measure myself against?

MORNING REFLECTION

EVENING REFLECTION

WEEK V
FOCUS ON THE PRESENT MOMENT

Marcus Aurelius ruled at a particularly turbulent time. Wars erupted on multiple fronts. Terrible plagues ravaged Rome. His rule was certainly one of constant, unrelenting pressure. But he never let it overwhelm him. From the Stoics and from the example of his adoptive father, the Emperor Antoninus Pius, Marcus found a coping strategy in always sticking close to the present moment and the duties at hand. When our own stress boils over, we can remember his practices and exercises, to stick with what is in front of us and not everything it might mean.

"At every moment keep a sturdy mind on the task at hand, as a Roman and human being, doing it with strict and simple dignity, affection, freedom, and justice—giving yourself a break from all other considerations. You can do this if you approach each task as if it is your last, giving up every distraction, emotional subversion of reason, and all drama, vanity, and complaint over your fair share. You can see how mastery over a few things makes it possible to live an abundant and devout life."

—MARCUS AURELIUS, *MEDITATIONS*, 2.5

"Were you to live three thousand years, or even a countless multiple of that, keep in mind that no one ever loses a life other than the one they are living, and no one ever lives a life other than the one they are losing. The longest and the shortest life, then, amount to the same, for the present moment lasts the same for all and is all anyone possesses. No one can lose either the past or the future, for how can someone be deprived of what's not theirs?"

—MARCUS AURELIUS, *MEDITATIONS*, 2.14

"Don't let your reflection on the whole sweep of life crush you. Don't fill your mind with all the bad things that might still happen. Stay focused on the present situation and ask yourself why it's so unbearable and can't be survived."

—MARCUS AURELIUS, *MEDITATIONS*, 8.36

January 29th   Am I keeping a sturdy mind on the task at hand?

MORNING REFLECTION

EVENING REFLECTION

January 30th   Am I content to be clueless about things that don't matter?

MORNING REFLECTION

EVENING REFLECTION

January 31st   What healing can philosophy help me find today?

MORNING REFLECTION

EVENING REFLECTION

February 1st How can I conquer my temper?

MORNING REFLECTION

_____

_____

_____

_____

_____

_____

_____

_____

EVENING REFLECTION

_____

_____

_____

_____

_____

_____

_____

_____

February 2nd What impulses rob me of self-control?

MORNING REFLECTION

_____

_____

_____

_____

_____

_____

_____

_____

EVENING REFLECTION

February 3rd   Am I in control or is my anxiety?

MORNING REFLECTION

EVENING REFLECTION

February 4th   Am I cultivating the invincibility of my power to choose?

MORNING REFLECTION

_____

_____

_____

_____

_____

_____

_____

_____

_____

EVENING REFLECTION

_____

_____

_____

_____

_____

_____

_____

_____

WEEK VI
SUSPEND YOUR OPINIONS

E pictetus would teach that opinions were "the cause of a troubled mind." Opinions about the way we think things should be, need to be. One of the Stoic words for "opinion" is "dogma." The practice of Stoicism begins with a relentless attempt to suspend this dogmatic way of living—a cessation of the belief that you can force your opinions and expectations onto the world.

> "We have the power to hold no opinion about a thing and to not let it upset our state of mind—for things have no natural power to shape our judgments."
>
> —MARCUS AURELIUS, *MEDITATIONS*, 6.52

> "Today I escaped from the crush of circumstances, or better put, I threw them out, for the crush wasn't from outside me but in my own assumptions."
>
> —MARCUS AURELIUS, *MEDITATIONS*, 9.13

> "There are two things that must be rooted out in human beings— arrogant opinion and mistrust. Arrogant opinion expects that there is nothing further needed, and mistrust assumes that under the torrent of circumstance there can be no happiness."
>
> —EPICTETUS, *DISCOURSES*, 3.14.8

> "Throw out your conceited opinions, for it is impossible for a person to begin to learn what he thinks he already knows."
>
> —EPICTETUS, *DISCOURSES*, 2.17.1

February 5th   Am I thinking before I act?

MORNING REFLECTION

EVENING REFLECTION

February 6th   What needless conflict can I avoid?

MORNING REFLECTION

EVENING REFLECTION

February 7th How can I conquer fear and worry—before they conquer me?

MORNING REFLECTION

EVENING REFLECTION

February 8th   Do my outbursts ever make things better?

MORNING REFLECTION

EVENING REFLECTION

February 9th   What if I didn't have an opinion about this?

MORNING REFLECTION

EVENING REFLECTION

February 10th   What parts of my life are driven by anger?

MORNING REFLECTION

EVENING REFLECTION

February 11th   Is my soul a good ruler or a tyrant?

MORNING REFLECTION

EVENING REFLECTION

WEEK VII
WATCH OVER YOUR PERCEPTIONS

Every moment brings a flood of impressions of the world around us, and our minds are filled with the perceptions that arise with them. The Stoics teach us that we must keep a constant watch on this flood, as if we are standing guard to protect something of vital importance. What is it that we are protecting? Our peace of mind, clarity, and freedom—all of which are anchored in our perceptions. Epictetus reminds us that we need to pay attention to what matters and to learn how to ignore so many of the relentless provocations that come our way.

"Keep constant guard over your perceptions, for it is no small thing you are protecting, but your respect, trustworthiness and steadiness, peace of mind, freedom from pain and fear, in a word your freedom. For what would you sell these things?"

—EPICTETUS, *DISCOURSES*, 4.3.6B–8

"An important place to begin in philosophy is this: a clear perception of one's own ruling principle."

—EPICTETUS, *DISCOURSES*, 1.26.15

"I don't agree with those who plunge headlong into the middle of the flood and who, accepting a turbulent life, struggle daily in great spirit with difficult circumstances. The wise person will endure that, but won't choose it—choosing to be at peace, rather than at war."

—SENECA, *MORAL LETTERS*, 28.7

February 12th   For what have I sold my peace of mind?

MORNING REFLECTION

EVENING REFLECTION

February 13th   Which of my pleasures are really punishments?

MORNING REFLECTION

EVENING REFLECTION

February 14th   How can I do a better job listening to the little voice inside me?

MORNING REFLECTION

EVENING REFLECTION

February 15th   Do these strong emotions even make sense?

MORNING REFLECTION

EVENING REFLECTION

February 16th   What am I making harder than it needs to be?

MORNING REFLECTION

EVENING REFLECTION

February 17th   What happiness am I putting off that I could have right now?

MORNING REFLECTION

EVENING REFLECTION

February 18th   Am I in rigorous training against false impressions?

MORNING REFLECTION

EVENING REFLECTION

WEEK VIII
REDUCE WANTS, INCREASE HAPPINESS

The Stoics knew that wanting less increases gratitude, just as wanting more obliterates it. Epictetus focused much of his teaching on helping his students reduce the destructive habit of wanting more. In it he saw the key to a happy life and relationships. By practicing the art of wanting less and being grateful for the portion that we already have before us, we are hopping off the so-called hedonic treadmill and taking a real step on the path to a life of real contentment.

> "Remember to conduct yourself in life as if at a banquet. As something being passed around comes to you, reach out your hand and take a moderate helping. Does it pass you by? Don't stop it. It hasn't yet come? Don't burn in desire for it, but wait until it arrives in front of you. Act this way with children, a spouse, toward position, with wealth—one day it will make you worthy of a banquet with the gods."
>
> —EPICTETUS, *ENCHIRIDION*, 15

> "When children stick their hand down a narrow goody jar they can't get their full fist out and start crying. Drop a few treats and you will get it out! Curb your desire—don't set your heart on so many things and you will get what you need."
>
> —EPICTETUS, *DISCOURSES*, 3.9.22

> "Freedom isn't secured by filling up on your heart's desire but by removing your desire."
>
> —EPICTETUS, *DISCOURSES*, 4.1.175

February 19th   Am I happy with my portion at the banquet of life?

MORNING REFLECTION

EVENING REFLECTION

February 20th   Are the pleasures I'm chasing actually worth it?

MORNING REFLECTION

EVENING REFLECTION

February 21st   What can I stop yearning for?

MORNING REFLECTION

EVENING REFLECTION

February 22nd   Am I certain what I want to say isn't better left unsaid?

MORNING REFLECTION

EVENING REFLECTION

February 23rd   Why get angry at things, if anger doesn't change it?

MORNING REFLECTION

EVENING REFLECTION

February 24th   Why am I telling myself that I've been harmed?

MORNING REFLECTION

EVENING REFLECTION

February 25th   Will I even remember this fight in a few months?

MORNING REFLECTION

EVENING REFLECTION

WEEK IX
CULTIVATE INDIFFERENCE

Some people spend their lives chasing good things: health, wealth, pleasure, achievement. Others try to avoid the bad things with equal energy: sickness, poverty, pain. These look like two drastically different approaches but in the end, they are the same. The Stoics continually reminded themselves that so many of the things we desire and avoid are beyond our control. Instead of chasing impossibilities, the Stoics trained to be equally prepared and equally suited to thrive in either condition. They trained to be indifferent. This is a great power and the cultivation of this skill is a very powerful exercise.

"Of all the things that are, some are good, others bad, and yet others indifferent. The good are virtues and all that share in them; the bad are the vices and all that indulge them; the indifferent lie in between virtue and vice and include wealth, health, life, death, pleasure, and pain."

—Epictetus, *Discourses*, 2.19.12b–13

"My reasoned choice is as indifferent to the reasoned choice of my neighbor, as to his breath and body. However much we've been made for cooperation, the ruling reason in each of us is master of its own affairs. If this weren't the case, the evil in someone else could become my harm, and God didn't mean for someone else to control my misfortune."

—Marcus Aurelius, *Meditations*, 8.56

"There are things in life which are advantageous and disadvantageous—both beyond our control."

—Seneca, *Moral Letters*, 92.16

February 26th   Why do I need to care that someone else screwed up?

MORNING REFLECTION

EVENING REFLECTION

February 27th   How can I cultivate indifference to unimportant things?

MORNING REFLECTION

EVENING REFLECTION

February 28th What would happen if I took a second to cool down?

MORNING REFLECTION

EVENING REFLECTION

February 29th
A Leap Year Day Mantra: You Can't Always Be Getting What You Want

March 1st   How often do I question the things others take for granted?

MORNING REFLECTION

EVENING REFLECTION

March 2nd   Do I see and assess myself accurately?

MORNING REFLECTION

EVENING REFLECTION

_____

_____

_____

_____

_____

_____

_____

_____

March 3rd   Am I standing with the philosopher or the mob?

MORNING REFLECTION

_____

_____

_____

_____

_____

_____

_____

_____

EVENING REFLECTION

_____

_____

_____

_____

_____

_____

_____

_____

March 4th   How many of my limitations are really self-imposed?

MORNING REFLECTION

_____

_____

_____

_____

_____

_____

_____

_____

_____

EVENING REFLECTION

_____

_____

_____

_____

_____

_____

_____

_____

WEEK X
WHAT EXPENSIVE THINGS COST

From the Cynics, the Stoics learned the powerful practice of focusing on the true worth (*axia*) of things. That the cost of an item isn't simply what it's sold for, but what it costs the owner to own. So much of our desire for material goods comes at the great price of both anxiety and the loss of our serenity—and even when gained, these things often leave us more anxious and less serene. This week, spend some time reflecting on what the things you buy actually cost. See if they are really worth what you have been paying.

"So, concerning the things we pursue, and for which we vigorously exert ourselves, we owe this consideration—either there is nothing useful in them, or most aren't useful. Some of them are superfluous, while others aren't worth that much. But we don't discern this and see them as free, when they cost us dearly."

—SENECA, *MORAL LETTERS*, 42.6

"If a person gave away your body to some passerby, you'd be furious. Yet you hand over your mind to anyone who comes along, so they may abuse you, leaving it disturbed and troubled—have you no shame in that?"

—EPICTETUS, *ENCHIRIDION*, 28

"Diogenes of Sinope said we sell things of great value for things of very little, and vice versa."

—DIOGENES LAERTIUS,
LIVES OF THE EMINENT PHILOSOPHERS, 6.2.35B

March 5th   Do I really need these things I work so hard for?

MORNING REFLECTION

EVENING REFLECTION

March 6th   Where am I a loud mouth?

MORNING REFLECTION

EVENING REFLECTION

March 7th   Can I test my own opinion before trusting it?

MORNING REFLECTION

EVENING REFLECTION

March 8th   Am I protecting my time and attention?

MORNING REFLECTION

EVENING REFLECTION

March 9th   Does my social circle make me better or worse?

MORNING REFLECTION

EVENING REFLECTION

March 10th   Who is my role model? Why?

MORNING REFLECTION

EVENING REFLECTION

March 11th   Where have I traded away freedom? How can I get it back?

MORNING REFLECTION

EVENING REFLECTION

WEEK XI
THINK ABOUT IT FROM THE OTHER PERSON'S PERSPECTIVE

We tend to assume the best about our own intentions and the worst about other people's. Then we wonder why life is so full of conflict! The Stoics flipped this habit around, reminding themselves to be suspicious about their own first reaction and to approach others first with sympathy. Powerful people are often surprisingly terrible at behaving this way, but Marcus Aurelius, the most powerful man on earth during his reign, was renowned for his humanity in dealing with others. He told himself to always take a moment to remember his own failings and to contemplate how another might see a situation. He reminded himself, as we should, that most people are trying their best, even though that's easy to lose sight of in the rough and tumble of daily life. Let's remember that this week and think about each interaction from more than just our own point of view.

"Whenever someone has done wrong by you, immediately consider what notion of good or evil they had in doing it. For when you see that, you'll feel compassion, instead of astonishment or rage. For you may yourself have the same notions of good and evil, or similar ones, in which case you'll make an allowance for what they've done. But if you no longer hold the same notions, you'll be more readily gracious for their error."

—MARCUS AURELIUS, *MEDITATIONS*, 7.26

"When your sparring partner scratches or head-butts you, you don't then make a show of it, or protest, or view him with suspicion or as plotting against you. And yet you keep an eye on him, not as an enemy or with suspicion, but with a healthy avoidance. You should act this way with all things in life. We should give a pass to many things with our fellow trainees. For, as I've said, it's possible to avoid without suspicion or hate."

—MARCUS AURELIUS, *MEDITATIONS*, 6.20

March 12th What would change if I looked for other people's good intentions?

MORNING REFLECTION

EVENING REFLECTION

March 13th Instead of calling it bad luck, can I come to see it as inevitable?

MORNING REFLECTION

EVENING REFLECTION

March 14th   How is my arrogance preventing me from learning?

MORNING REFLECTION

EVENING REFLECTION

March 15th   What would it be like if I focused entirely on the present moment?

MORNING REFLECTION

EVENING REFLECTION

March 16th   Do I appreciate this mind I have been given?

MORNING REFLECTION

EVENING REFLECTION

March 17th   Are my choices beautiful?

MORNING REFLECTION

EVENING REFLECTION

March 18th   What bad assumptions can I cast out?

MORNING REFLECTION

EVENING REFLECTION

WEEK XII
THE PORTABLE RETREAT

I t is in the future—on a vacation, on our day off, when we plan to get out into nature—that we think we'll find peace and release from the crush of the everyday demands of life. Yet this never seems to really happen as often as we think, does it? And when we do get that peace, it is difficult to keep once we're back in the fray. For a Stoic, all of this is madness. The true retreat is to the freedom of our own mind and soul, to consider the gifts we already have that can be our refuge for all time. If we take the time, daily, to do so.

"People seek retreats for themselves in the country, by the sea, or in the mountains. You are very much in the habit of yearning for those same things. But this is entirely the trait of a base person, when you can, at any moment, find such a retreat in yourself. For nowhere can you find a more peaceful and less busy retreat than in your own soul—especially if on close inspection it is filled with ease, which I say is nothing more than being well-ordered. Treat yourself often to this retreat and be renewed."

—MARCUS AURELIUS, *MEDITATIONS*, 4.3.1

"Remember that it's not only the desire for wealth and position that debases and subjugates us, but also the desire for peace, leisure, travel, and learning. It doesn't matter what the external thing is, the value we place on it subjugates us to another . . . where our heart is set, there our impediment lies."

—EPICTETUS, *DISCOURSES*, 4.4.1–2; 15

"Remember that your ruling reason becomes unconquerable when it rallies and relies on itself, so that it won't do anything contrary to its own will, even if its position is irrational. How much more unconquerable if its judgments are careful and made rationally? Therefore, the mind freed from passions is an impenetrable fortress—a person has no more secure place of refuge for all time."

—MARCUS AURELIUS, *MEDITATIONS*, 8.48

March 19th   What is the real cause of my irritations—external things or my opinions?

MORNING REFLECTION

EVENING REFLECTION

March 20th   Am I cultivating the virtue that makes adversity bearable?

MORNING REFLECTION

EVENING REFLECTION

March 21st   What if I sought peace where I am right now instead of in distant lands?

MORNING REFLECTION

EVENING REFLECTION

March 22nd   Have I confused schooling and *education*?

MORNING REFLECTION

_____

_____

_____

_____

_____

_____

_____

_____

EVENING REFLECTION

_____

_____

_____

_____

_____

_____

_____

_____

March 23rd   How can I treat my greedy vices? How can I heal my sickness?

MORNING REFLECTION

_____

_____

_____

_____

_____

_____

_____

_____

EVENING REFLECTION

March 24th   What philosophical lessons can I find in ordinary things?

MORNING REFLECTION

EVENING REFLECTION

March 25th   Would I feel wealthier if I decreased my wants?

MORNING REFLECTION

EVENING REFLECTION

WEEK XIII
SAY NO TO THE NEED TO IMPRESS

If the desire to impress and be liked by others is innate to humans as a species, then every generation born before social media got off lucky. Today we face an unending stream of status updates demanding to be filled with all the impressive things we are doing, the trials we are overcoming, announcements of our dangers averted and triumphs realized. It's exhausting. Centuries ago, Epictetus saw this pride and narcissism even in his (computerless) students and reminded them it wasn't so innocent. In fact, he told them that it would destroy their life's purpose, it would distract and fatigue them. Seneca, too, saw this seeking of the approval of spectators as one of life's disgraces. Watch those impulses this week, notice how much you seem to need your phone and status updates and then ask: Is this the kind of person I want to be? Is this what a philosopher would do?

> "If you should ever turn your will to things outside your control in order to impress someone, be sure that you have wrecked your whole purpose in life. Be content, then, to be a philosopher in all that you do, and if you wish also to be seen as one, show yourself first that you are and you will succeed."
>
> —EPICTETUS, *ENCHIRIDION*, 23

> "In public avoid talking often and excessively about your accomplishments and dangers, for however much you enjoy recounting your dangers, it's not so pleasant for others to hear about your affairs."
>
> —EPICTETUS, *ENCHIRIDION*, 33.14

> "How disgraceful is the lawyer whose dying breath passes while at court, at an advanced age, pleading for unknown litigants and still seeking the approval of ignorant spectators."
>
> —SENECA, *ON THE BREVITY OF LIFE*, 20.2

March 26th   Am I keeping watch?

MORNING REFLECTION

EVENING REFLECTION

March 27th   What valuable things do I sell too cheaply?

MORNING REFLECTION

EVENING REFLECTION

March 28th   Is my training designed to help me rise to the occasion?

MORNING REFLECTION

EVENING REFLECTION

March 29th   Why do I care so much about impressing people?

MORNING REFLECTION

EVENING REFLECTION

March 30th   If I'm not ruled by reason, what am I ruled by?

MORNING REFLECTION

EVENING REFLECTION

March 31st　Can I stop chasing the impossible today?

MORNING REFLECTION

EVENING REFLECTION

April 1st   What thoughts are coloring my world?

MORNING REFLECTION

_____

_____

_____

_____

_____

_____

_____

_____

_____

EVENING REFLECTION

_____

_____

_____

_____

_____

_____

_____

_____

WEEK XIV
WHAT CAN GO WRONG . . . MIGHT

W e call the people who dwell on what might go wrong "pessimists." Some even think that bad thoughts attract bad events. The Stoics found this all to be nonsense. In fact, they had a practice of *praemeditatio malorum* (premeditation of evils) that specifically encouraged musing on the so-called worst-case scenario. Marcus would begin his day thinking about all the ugliness he would see on display at court—not for the purpose of working himself up, but precisely the opposite, to calm and focus himself to be prepared to act in the proper way rather than to react. Seneca, too, practiced meditating in advance, not only about what normally happens, but what could happen. Epictetus went as far as to imagine losing a loved one every time he would kiss them. The Stoics believed all that we have is on loan from Fortune, and that negative visualization helps increase our awareness of the unexpected—don't shy away from this in your thoughts.

> "When you first rise in the morning tell yourself: I will encounter busybodies, ingrates, egomaniacs, liars, the jealous and cranks. They are all stricken with these afflictions because they don't know the difference between good and evil. Because I have understood the beauty of good and the ugliness of evil, I know that these wrongdoers are still akin to me . . . and that none can do me harm, or implicate me in ugliness—nor can I be angry at my relatives or hate them. For we are made for cooperation."
>
> —MARCUS AURELIUS, *MEDITATIONS*, 2.1

> "Being unexpected adds to the weight of a disaster, and being a surprise has never failed to increase a person's pain. For that reason, nothing should ever be unexpected by us. Our minds should be sent out in advance to all things and we shouldn't just consider the normal course of things, but what could actually happen. For is there anything in life that Fortune won't knock off its high horse if it pleases her?"
>
> —SENECA, *MORAL LETTERS*, 91.3A–4

April 2nd   What can I do today to keep drama away?

MORNING REFLECTION

EVENING REFLECTION

April 3rd   Are my plans at war with my other plans?

MORNING REFLECTION

EVENING REFLECTION

April 4th   Can I fight to be the person philosophy wants me to be today?

MORNING REFLECTION

EVENING REFLECTION

April 5th   What would happen if I stopped to verify my opinions and initial reactions?

MORNING REFLECTION

EVENING REFLECTION

April 6th   Despite the worst things people do, can I love them anyway?

MORNING REFLECTION

EVENING REFLECTION

April 7th   Where are my opinions part of the problem?

MORNING REFLECTION

EVENING REFLECTION

April 8th   What bad assumptions, habits, or advice have I accepted?

MORNING REFLECTION

_____

_____

_____

_____

_____

_____

_____

_____

EVENING REFLECTION

_____

_____

_____

_____

_____

_____

_____

_____

WEEK XV
TEST YOUR IMPRESSIONS

One of Epictetus's key teachings was about testing all our impressions—any experience, perception, or circumstance that we find in front of us. He uses a key verb to emphasize this practice, *dokimázō*, ten times in the *Discourses* and once in the opening of the *Enchiridion*. The word carries the meaning of the assayer, one who tests fine metals and coins to verify their authenticity. In one of the most memorable uses Epictetus compares our need to test impressions to what is done with coins and how the skilled merchant can hear a counterfeit coin cast upon a table just as a musician would detect a sour note. This week, let us go through the exercise of assaying everything that comes before us, assuming it all to be counterfeit or misleading until we can prove otherwise.

"When it comes to money, where we feel our clear interest, we have an entire art where the tester uses many means to discover the worth . . . just as we give great attention to judging things that might steer us badly. But when it comes to our own ruling principle, we yawn and doze off, accepting any appearance that flashes by without counting the cost."

—EPICTETUS, *DISCOURSES*, 1.20.8; 11

"First off, don't let the force of the impression carry you away. Say to it, 'hold up a bit and let me see who you are and where you are from—let me put you to the test.' . . ."

—EPICTETUS, *DISCOURSES*, 2.18.24

"From the very beginning, make it your practice to say to every harsh impression, 'you are an impression and not at all what you appear to be.' Next, examine and test it by the rules you possess, the first and greatest of which is this—whether it belongs to the things in our control or not in our control, and if the latter, be prepared to respond, 'It is nothing to me.'"

—EPICTETUS, *ENCHIRIDION*, 1.5

April 9th Can I step back and test my impressions? What would I find if I did?

MORNING REFLECTION

EVENING REFLECTION

April 10th How do my judgments cause me anguish?

MORNING REFLECTION

EVENING REFLECTION

April 11th   Can I stop thinking I already know and learn something here?

MORNING REFLECTION

EVENING REFLECTION

April 12th What's the truth about so-called "honors" and "riches"?

MORNING REFLECTION

EVENING REFLECTION

April 13th What would *less* look like?

MORNING REFLECTION

EVENING REFLECTION

April 14th   Do I balance my life better than the balance sheet of my business?

MORNING REFLECTION

EVENING REFLECTION

April 15th   Life is full of taxes—am I prepared to pay them?

MORNING REFLECTION

EVENING REFLECTION

WEEK XVI
IMPULSE CONTROL

I f something is making you upset, write it here and look at it. What happened? Who caused it? Now think about your reaction: What did you say? What did you feel? Did this make it better or worse? Marcus Aurelius, as emperor, clearly had many people and causes to be upset about. He also had real power and authority. Even so we find that he would tell himself, "You have power over your mind—not outside events. Realize this, and you will find strength." So, too, with what has happened to you—you did not control what happened, but you do control which impulses you follow in the wake of it.

"Epictetus says we must discover the missing art of assent and pay special attention to the sphere of our impulses—that they are subject to reservation, to the common good, and that they are in proportion to actual worth."

—MARCUS AURELIUS, *MEDITATIONS*, 11.37

"You say, good fortune used to meet you at every corner. But the fortunate person is the one who gives themselves a good fortune. And good fortunes are a well-tuned soul, good impulses, and good actions."

—MARCUS AURELIUS, *MEDITATIONS*, 5.36

"Frame your thoughts like this—you are an old person, you won't let yourself be enslaved by this any longer, no longer pulled like a puppet by every impulse, and you'll stop complaining about your present fortune or dreading the future."

—MARCUS AURELIUS, *MEDITATIONS*, 2.2

April 16th   What can I pay closer attention to today?

MORNING REFLECTION

EVENING REFLECTION

April 17th   Can I stop feeling hurt by every little thing?

MORNING REFLECTION

EVENING REFLECTION

April 18th   Do I need to have an opinion about this?

MORNING REFLECTION

EVENING REFLECTION

April 19th   Am I leaving room for what might happen?

MORNING REFLECTION

EVENING REFLECTION

April 20th   What are the few real goods?

MORNING REFLECTION

EVENING REFLECTION

April 21st   How long can I go without letting my attention slide?

MORNING REFLECTION

EVENING REFLECTION

April 22nd   Am I self-aware, self-critical, and self-determining?

MORNING REFLECTION

EVENING REFLECTION

WEEK XVII
THE FREEDOM OF CONTEMPT

The language we use to describe things imputes value to those things. We often embellish our language with superlatives to help make our choices of what to buy, wear, eat, or drink seem much better than they really are. As emperor, Marcus Aurelius could have the finest Falernian wine at his table at any meal—but he preferred to remind himself it was only grape juice. As emperor, he was the only Roman allowed to wear a purple cloak, but he took pains to point out that his cloak was like any other, just dyed with shellfish blood to produce the purple hue. This week, practice cutting your own luxuries and the things you yearn for down to size with a little contempt. Describe them with the bluntest language you can—and see how much their power over you diminishes.

> "Just as when meat or other foods are set before us we think, this is a dead fish, a dead bird or pig; and also, this fine wine is only the juice of a bunch of grapes, this purple-edged robe just sheep's wool dyed in a bit of blood from a shellfish; or of sex, that it is only rubbing private parts together followed by a spasmic discharge—in the same way our impressions grab actual events and permeate them, so we see them as they really are."
>
> —MARCUS AURELIUS, *MEDITATIONS*, 6.13

> "Keep a list before your mind of those who burned with anger and resentment about something, of even the most renowned for success, misfortune, evil deeds, or any special distinction. Then ask yourself, how did that work out? Smoke and dust, the stuff of simple myth trying to be legend . . ."
>
> —MARCUS AURELIUS, *MEDITATIONS*, 12.27

> "You know what wine and liqueur tastes like. It makes no difference whether a hundred or a thousand bottles pass through your bladder—you are nothing more than a filter."
>
> —SENECA, *MORAL LETTERS*, 77.16

April 23rd   How am I caring for my mind?

MORNING REFLECTION

EVENING REFLECTION

April 24th   Nice cars, jewels, fine wine—what are these things really?

MORNING REFLECTION

EVENING REFLECTION

April 25th　Am I willing to admit when I'm wrong?

MORNING REFLECTION

EVENING REFLECTION

April 26th   How can I learn from my sparring partners?

MORNING REFLECTION

EVENING REFLECTION

April 27th   How long does praise really last anyway?

MORNING REFLECTION

EVENING REFLECTION

April 28th   What power does all my wanting take from me?

MORNING REFLECTION

EVENING REFLECTION

April 29th   What do I feel when I look up at the sky?

MORNING REFLECTION

_____

_____

_____

_____

_____

_____

_____

_____

_____

EVENING REFLECTION

_____

_____

_____

_____

_____

_____

_____

_____

_____

WEEK XVIII
SHOW, DON'T TELL

The art of living isn't a set of teachings or a formula we can memorize. It's a practice that requires constant work. Epictetus was constantly reminding his students not to parrot back what they'd heard in the lecture hall or read in books, but to put it to work in practice. He knew that progress you could see was better than any proclaimed. Let your writing this week exhibit what you have done and what you are doing, not on what you plan to do or think you are. Let it be a catalog of your actions—good actions.

"Those who receive the bare theories immediately want to spew them, as an upset stomach does its food. First digest your theories and you won't throw them up. Otherwise they will be raw, spoiled, and not nourishing. After you've digested them, show us the changes in your reasoned choices, just like the shoulders of gymnasts display their diet and training, and as the craft of artisans show in what they've learned."

—Epictetus, *Discourses*, 3.21.1–3

"First practice not letting people know who you are—keep your philosophy to yourself for a bit. In just the manner that fruit is produced—the seed buried for a season, hidden, growing gradually so it may come to full maturity. But if the grain sprouts before the stalk is fully developed, it will never ripen. . . . That is the kind of plant you are, displaying fruit too soon, and the winter will kill you."

—Epictetus, *Discourses*, 4.8.35b–37

April 30th   Do my actions match my character?

MORNING REFLECTION

EVENING REFLECTION

May 1st   Do my actions—and my mind—match my philosophy?

MORNING REFLECTION

EVENING REFLECTION

May 2nd   What kind of person do I want to be?

MORNING REFLECTION

EVENING REFLECTION

May 3rd   Am I showing or telling?

MORNING REFLECTION

EVENING REFLECTION

May 4th   Where can I spend money to help others?

MORNING REFLECTION

EVENING REFLECTION

May 5th　Have I made myself a lifelong project?

MORNING REFLECTION

EVENING REFLECTION

May 6th   Am I seeking the beauty of human excellence?

MORNING REFLECTION

EVENING REFLECTION

WEEK XIX
WE ARE A PRODUCT OF OUR HABITS

The Roman Stoics put a heavy emphasis on dealing with habitual behavior in order to make progress in the art of living. The great Roman Stoic educator Musonius Rufus held that all the theory in the world couldn't trump good habits (or overcome bad habits). Epictetus followed Musonius in this focus on habit, with an eye to not reinforcing bad habits—such as anger—and finding a way to replace them with better ones. We all recognize bad habits when we see them in others, but it's a little harder to see them in ourselves. This week meditate on the habits or recurring behaviors that are holding you back—even ask someone close to you to help.

"Every habit and capability is confirmed and grows in its corresponding actions, walking by walking, and running by running . . . therefore, if you want to do something, make a habit of it; if you don't want to do that, don't, but make a habit of something else instead. The same principle is at work in our state of mind. When you get angry, you've not only experienced that evil, but you've also reinforced a bad habit, adding fuel to the fire."

—EPICTETUS, *DISCOURSES*, 2.18.1–5

"If you don't wish to be a hothead, don't feed your habit. Try as a first step to remain calm and count the days you haven't been angry. I used to be angry every day, now every other day, then every third or fourth . . . if you make it as far as thirty days, thank God! For habit is first weakened and then obliterated. When you can say 'I didn't lose my temper today, or the next day, or for three or four months, but kept my cool under provocation,' you will know you are in better health."

—EPICTETUS, *DISCOURSES*, 2.18.11B–14

"What assistance can we find in the fight against habit? Try the opposite!"

—EPICTETUS, *DISCOURSES*, 1.27.4

May 7th   What is some good I can get from myself today?

MORNING REFLECTION

EVENING REFLECTION

May 8th   What evil comes from my own choices?

MORNING REFLECTION

EVENING REFLECTION

May 9th   Will I seize this day?

MORNING REFLECTION

EVENING REFLECTION

May 10th   What bold thing can I do today?

MORNING REFLECTION

EVENING REFLECTION

May 11th   Where does my lack of self-control create problems?

MORNING REFLECTION

EVENING REFLECTION

May 12th   What would happen if I responded with kindness, no matter what?

MORNING REFLECTION

EVENING REFLECTION

May 13th   Which bad habits am I fueling?

MORNING REFLECTION

EVENING REFLECTION

WEEK XX
COUNT YOUR BLESSINGS

It's easy to complain about the things missing in our lives, and so much harder to appreciate how much we already have. Seneca reminded us that everything we need to be happy is right in front of us, while the luxuries we might be missing would themselves come at great cost—at the cost of what we already have. Marcus agreed, and reminded himself to count those blessings present in our lives and to imagine what it would be like to not have them (and how much we would miss them). List your blessings this week, take conscious note of what you are fortunate to have and enjoy, so you can see clearly, as Epictetus put it, where they came from and feel a sense of gratitude for that.

"Don't set your mind on things you don't possess as if they were yours, but count the blessings you actually possess and think how much you would desire them if they weren't already yours. But watch yourself, that you don't value these things to the point of being troubled if you should lose them."

—MARCUS AURELIUS, *MEDITATIONS*, 7.27

"The founder of the universe, who assigned to us the laws of life, provided that we should live well, but not in luxury. Everything needed for our well-being is right before us, whereas what luxury requires is gathered by many miseries and anxieties. Let us use this gift of nature and count it among the greatest things."

—SENECA, *MORAL LETTERS*, 119.15B

"It is easy to praise providence for anything that may happen if you have two qualities: a complete view of what has actually happened in each instance and a sense of gratitude. Without gratitude what is the point of seeing, and without seeing what is the object of gratitude?"

—EPICTETUS, *DISCOURSES*, 1.6.1–2

May 14th   Are my actions contributing to my well-being?

MORNING REFLECTION

EVENING REFLECTION

May 15th   What blessings can I count right now?

MORNING REFLECTION

EVENING REFLECTION

May 16th   How am I creating momentum for my good habits?

MORNING REFLECTION

EVENING REFLECTION

May 17th   Am I on the path to progress?

MORNING REFLECTION

EVENING REFLECTION

May 18th   Is my attention actually on the things at hand?

MORNING REFLECTION

EVENING REFLECTION

May 19th　Where am I doing the opposite of what I should?

MORNING REFLECTION

EVENING REFLECTION

May 20th   What are the seeds I'm planting and what will they grow?

MORNING REFLECTION

EVENING REFLECTION

WEEK XXI
PRACTICE TRUE JOY

The Stoics held joy (*chara*) to be one of the good passions, worthy of practice in everyday life. But Stoic joy isn't about the delights of the senses or material pleasure. To Marcus, joy was being kind to others. To Seneca, it was freedom from fear of suffering and death. Let's laugh with Democritus, as Seneca says, and engage in our "proper human work" with joy. Consider in your writing this week where you might find joy and what good you might do with it.

"Joy for human beings lies in proper human work. And proper human work consists in: acts of kindness to other human beings, disdain for the stirrings of the senses, identifying trustworthy impressions, and contemplating the natural order and all that happens in keeping with it."

—MARCUS AURELIUS, *MEDITATIONS*, 8.26

"Trust me, real joy is a serious thing. Do you think someone can, in the charming expression, blithely dismiss death with an easy disposition? Or swing open the door to poverty, keep pleasures in check, or meditate on the endurance of suffering? The one who is comfortable with turning these thoughts over is truly full of joy, but hardly cheerful. It's exactly such a joy that I would wish for you to possess, for it will never run dry once you've laid claim to its source."

—SENECA, *MORAL LETTERS*, 23.4

"Heraclitus would shed tears whenever he went out in public— Democritus laughed. One saw the whole as a parade of miseries, the other of follies. And so, we should take a lighter view of things and bear them with an easy spirit, for it is more human to laugh at life than to lament it."

—SENECA, *ON TRANQUILITY OF MIND*, 15.2

May 21st   Can I take a blow and stay in the ring?

MORNING REFLECTION

EVENING REFLECTION

May 22nd   Can I be a good person right here, right now?

MORNING REFLECTION

EVENING REFLECTION

May 23rd   Can I start living right here, right now?

MORNING REFLECTION

EVENING REFLECTION

May 24th   How can I make my own good fortune?

MORNING REFLECTION

EVENING REFLECTION

May 25th   What kind or selfless things will bring me joy?

MORNING REFLECTION

EVENING REFLECTION

May 26th   What if I stopped caring what others thought?

MORNING REFLECTION

EVENING REFLECTION

May 27th   What small stuff should I sweat?

MORNING REFLECTION

_____

_____

_____

_____

_____

_____

_____

_____

EVENING REFLECTION

_____

_____

_____

_____

_____

_____

_____

_____

WEEK XXII
THE VIEW FROM ABOVE

The way to escape petty concerns and worries of daily existence requires taking some time out and getting what Stoics like to call "the view from above." This was something Marcus Aurelius reminded himself to do regularly. He had learned from Heraclitus that everything in the world was constantly changing and that remembering this can eliminate so many stresses and concerns. This week don't just look at what you're dealing with in your life up close; try to see it from far away, too. Try to describe what another, larger perspective would look like—of your problems, of your worries, of your obsessions.

"How beautifully Plato put it. Whenever you want to talk about people, it's best to take a bird's-eye view and see everything all at once—of gatherings, armies, farms, weddings and divorces, births and deaths, noisy courtrooms or silent spaces, every foreign people, holidays, memorials, markets—all blended together and arranged in a pairing of opposites."
—MARCUS AURELIUS, *MEDITATIONS*, 7.48

"Watch the stars in their courses and imagine yourself running alongside them. Think constantly on the changes of the elements into each other, for such thoughts wash away the dust of earthly life."
—MARCUS AURELIUS, *MEDITATIONS*, 7.47

"The cosmic order—the same for everyone—wasn't made by any god or human, but always was and always will be. An eternal fire, kindled in measures, and extinguished in measures."
—HERACLITUS (AS QUOTED BY CLEMENT OF ALEXANDRIA)

May 28th   What should I think about before I take action?

MORNING REFLECTION

EVENING REFLECTION

May 29th   What work nourishes my mind?

MORNING REFLECTION

EVENING REFLECTION

May 30th   Is my hard work for the right end?

MORNING REFLECTION

EVENING REFLECTION

May 31st   If my vocation is to be a good person, am I doing a good job?

MORNING REFLECTION

EVENING REFLECTION

June 1st   Do I have a backup option in mind for all things?

MORNING REFLECTION

EVENING REFLECTION

June 2nd   Where have I lost the forest for the trees?

MORNING REFLECTION

EVENING REFLECTION

June 3rd   Do I have a backup plan for my backup plan?

MORNING REFLECTION

EVENING REFLECTION

WEEK XXIII
ROLE MODELS

Adoption was a widespread practice in Roman society, especially in the senatorial class and as a provision for imperial succession. Marcus Aurelius himself was the adopted son of Emperor Antoninus Pius, who himself was adopted by the Emperor Hadrian so that Marcus would one day succeed them both to the purple. While Seneca was never adopted, his brother Novatus was, becoming Gallio who in the New Testament refused to press charges on Saint Paul. But Seneca liked to look at the phenomenon of adoption the other way around, saying we can always choose whose children we want to be. For him, Cato, the towering, resolute Stoic who railed against Julius Caesar in defense of the Republic, was always standing by in his mind. The first book in Marcus Aurelius's *Meditations* is a catalog of all the people he had learned from and the lessons he had taken from their lives. Use this week to think of models that you can follow, wise and admirable people you can measure yourself against.

"We like to say that we don't get to choose our parents, that they were given by chance—yet we can truly choose whose children we'd like to be."

—SENECA, *ON THE BREVITY OF LIFE*, 15.3A

"We can remove most sins if we have a witness standing by as we are about to go wrong. The soul should have someone it can respect, by whose example it can make its inner sanctum more inviolable. Happy is the person who can improve others, not only when present, but even when in their thoughts!"

—SENECA, *MORAL LETTERS*, 11.9

June 4th   Do I realize how tough and strong I am capable of being?

MORNING REFLECTION

EVENING REFLECTION

June 5th   Can I blow my own nose—instead of asking someone to do it for me?

MORNING REFLECTION

EVENING REFLECTION

June 6th   Is this a time to stick or to quit?

MORNING REFLECTION

EVENING REFLECTION

June 7th   What mentors do I follow—alive or dead?

MORNING REFLECTION

EVENING REFLECTION

June 8th   If I took things patiently, step by step, what could I conquer?

MORNING REFLECTION

EVENING REFLECTION

June 9th What do I need to nip in the bud right now?

MORNING REFLECTION

EVENING REFLECTION

June 10th   If someone else was strong enough to do it, why can't I?

MORNING REFLECTION

EVENING REFLECTION

WEEK XXIV
TRY THE OTHER HANDLE

Epictetus offered a powerful tool in his handbook, the *Enchiridion*, which Stoics use as an exercise in decision-making about difficult events. Everything, Epictetus said, has two interpretations, or handles by which they can be grabbed: one that will make it harder, one that will make it easier. Do you take offense? Or do you focus on common ground? Do you focus on all that has gone wrong? Or what has gone right? Ask yourself these questions about everything you see and feel this week. Make sure you are using the right handle.

> "Every event has two handles—one by which it can be carried, and one by which it can't. If your brother does you wrong, don't grab it by his wronging, because this is the handle incapable of lifting it. Instead, use the other—that he is your brother, that you were raised together, and then you will have hold of the handle that carries."
>
> —EPICTETUS, *ENCHIRIDION*, 43

> "No, it is events that give rise to fear—when another has power over them or can prevent them, that person becomes able to inspire fear. How is the fortress destroyed? Not by iron or fire, but by judgments . . . here is where we must begin, and it is from this front that we must seize the fortress and throw out the tyrants."
>
> —EPICTETUS, *DISCOURSES*, 4.1.85–86; 87A

June 11th   How often is anger more destructive than what caused it?

MORNING REFLECTION

EVENING REFLECTION

June 12th   Am I learning to be adaptable?

MORNING REFLECTION

EVENING REFLECTION

June 13th   Am I fulfilling my post in this campaign of life, or sleeping on duty?

MORNING REFLECTION

EVENING REFLECTION

June 14th   Do I have a hold on the right handle of this situation?

MORNING REFLECTION

EVENING REFLECTION

June 15th   Can I listen more and talk less today?

MORNING REFLECTION

EVENING REFLECTION

June 16th   Where do I need help? Who can I ask for it?

MORNING REFLECTION

EVENING REFLECTION

June 17th   What am I blaming on chance or luck that's really on me?

MORNING REFLECTION

EVENING REFLECTION

WEEK XXV
TAKE A WALK

Seneca believed we should take frequent wandering walks, because constant work will fracture our minds. (As a writer he must have agreed with the novelist Helen Dunmore, "A problem with a piece of writing often clarifies itself if you go for a long walk.") Take some good walks this week and watch the dullness and feebleness depart. Enjoy the scenery, enjoy being away from your work. Make them part of your morning and evening writing routine. Return with a stimulated mind that's ready to journal about and follow the philosophy you know. You think that it's taking a "break," but really you end up smarter and clearer than you were when you left.

"We should take wandering outdoor walks, so that the mind might be nourished and refreshed by the open air and deep breathing."

—SENECA, *ON TRANQUILITY OF MIND*, 17.8

"Pass through this brief patch of time in harmony with nature, and come to your final resting place gracefully, just as a ripened olive might drop, praising the earth that nourished it and grateful to the tree that gave it growth."

—MARCUS AURELIUS, *MEDITATIONS*, 4.48.2

"The mind must be given relaxation—it will rise improved and sharper after a good break. Just as rich fields must not be forced—for they will quickly lose their fertility if never given a break—so constant work on the anvil will fracture the force of the mind. But it regains its powers if it is set free and relaxed for a while. Constant work gives rise to a certain kind of dullness and feebleness in the rational soul."

—SENECA, *ON TRANQUILITY OF MIND*, 17.5

June 18th   Am I ready and able?

MORNING REFLECTION

EVENING REFLECTION

June 19th   How can I better keep myself in the present moment?

MORNING REFLECTION

EVENING REFLECTION

_____
_____
_____
_____
_____
_____
_____
_____
_____

June 20th   Am I the calm one in the room or the one who needs to be calmed?

MORNING REFLECTION

_____
_____
_____
_____
_____
_____
_____

EVENING REFLECTION

_____
_____
_____
_____
_____
_____
_____
_____

June 21st   How can I refresh my mind today?

MORNING REFLECTION

EVENING REFLECTION

June 22nd   Am I actually learning from my failures?

MORNING REFLECTION

EVENING REFLECTION

June 23rd   Where am I standing in my own way?

MORNING REFLECTION

EVENING REFLECTION

June 24th   Do I really need to argue and quarrel so much?

MORNING REFLECTION

EVENING REFLECTION

WEEK XXVI

WHAT'S IN YOUR WAY *IS* THE WAY

Obstacles are a fact of life. Even the most powerful and lucky of us are not exempt from this reality, but we have a superpower at our hands through Stoic philosophy in that our purposes, intentions, and attitudes can adapt to any conditions to find a way forward. The Stoics had a word for this, *hupexhairesis*, meaning acting with a kind of "reserve-clause" or "reverse-clause" that allows us to reconsider and set a new course of action as needed. Marcus Aurelius tells us that any obstacle can actually become the raw material for a new purpose! How might the obstacles you're facing reveal a new path?

"While it's true that someone can impede our actions, they can't impede our intentions and our attitudes, which have the power of being conditional and adaptable. For the mind adapts and converts any obstacle to its action into a means of achieving it. That which is an impediment to action is turned to advance action. The obstacle on the path becomes the way."

—Marcus Aurelius, *Meditations*, 5.20

". . . just as nature turns to its own purpose any obstacle or any opposition, sets its place in the destined order, and co-opts it, so every rational person can convert any obstacle into the raw material for their own purpose."

—Marcus Aurelius, *Meditations*, 8.35

"You must build up your life action by action, and be content if each one achieves its goal as far as possible—and no one can keep you from this. But there will be some external obstacle! Perhaps, but no obstacle to acting with justice, self-control, and wisdom. But what if some other area of my action is thwarted? Well, gladly accept the obstacle for what it is and shift your attention to what is given, and another action will immediately take its place, one that better fits the life you are building."

—Marcus Aurelius, *Meditations*, 8.32

June 25th Am I expecting the possible, and not just what I *want*?

MORNING REFLECTION

EVENING REFLECTION

June 26th What thing do I always do that fails and what if I tried the opposite?

MORNING REFLECTION

EVENING REFLECTION

June 27th   What can this adversity show me?

MORNING REFLECTION

EVENING REFLECTION

June 28th   What can I stop beating myself up over?

MORNING REFLECTION

EVENING REFLECTION

June 29th   What can I stop making excuses for?

MORNING REFLECTION

EVENING REFLECTION

June 30th   How can I use this obstacle as an opportunity?

MORNING REFLECTION

EVENING REFLECTION

July 1st   As a Stoic, what is my job?

MORNING REFLECTION

_____

_____

_____

_____

_____

_____

_____

_____

_____

EVENING REFLECTION

_____

_____

_____

_____

_____

_____

_____

_____

_____

WEEK XXVII
PROTECT YOUR OWN GOOD

Musonius Rufus, one of Epictetus's teachers, taught that human beings are all born with an innate goodness, or, as he put it, with an inclination to virtue. It's our choices that decide whether that goodness comes out or not. We're not bad people, essentially, though we might sometimes do bad things. The purpose of Stoicism then is to remind us of that goodness and to help us work hard to protect it. Spend some time writing about the choices you can make this week—the actions you can take—to do just that.

> "Protect your own good in all that you do, and as concerns everything else take what is given as far as you can make reasoned use of it. If you don't, you'll be unlucky, prone to failure, hindered, and stymied."
>
> —EPICTETUS, *DISCOURSES*, 4.3.11

> "Dig deep within yourself, for there is a fountain of goodness ever ready to flow if you will keep digging."
>
> —MARCUS AURELIUS, *MEDITATIONS*, 7.59

July 2nd   What is the harder choice I'm avoiding?

MORNING REFLECTION

EVENING REFLECTION

July 3rd   What if I saw opportunities instead of obligation?

MORNING REFLECTION

EVENING REFLECTION

July 4th   Am I keeping the flame of virtue burning?

MORNING REFLECTION

EVENING REFLECTION

July 5th   Am I doing the honorable thing?

MORNING REFLECTION

EVENING REFLECTION

July 6th   Am I dragging my feet or am I doing my job as a human being?

MORNING REFLECTION

EVENING REFLECTION

July 7th　Can I show Odysseus-like determination and perseverance?

MORNING REFLECTION

EVENING REFLECTION

July 8th   What painful things can I take responsibility for?

MORNING REFLECTION

EVENING REFLECTION

WEEK XXVIII
DON'T LOOK FOR THE THIRD THING

The Stoics teach us that doing well is its own reward. To do the right thing, and to see someone helped by it, is enough. To go around expecting thanks—what Marcus Aurelius described as the "third thing"—on top of it? That's being greedy. Keeping score not only misses the purpose of being good, it's foolish. It sets you up for disappointment. If you are going to do some accounting, look at it from the other direction. How many people have helped us—and what do we owe them in return? Think about clearing your debts this week, and consider forgiving any notion of others owing you.

"One person, on doing well by others, immediately accounts the expected favor in return. Another is not so quick, but still considers the person a debtor and knows the favor. A third kind of person acts as if not conscious of the deed, rather like a vine producing a cluster of grapes without making further demands, like a horse after its race, or a dog after its walk, or a bee after making its honey. Such a person, having done a good deed, won't go shouting from rooftops but simply moves on to the next deed just like the vine produces another bunch of grapes in the right season."

—MARCUS AURELIUS, *MEDITATIONS*, 5.6

"When you've done well and another has benefited by it, why like a fool do you look for a third thing on top—credit for the good deed or a favor in return?"

—MARCUS AURELIUS, *MEDITATIONS*, 7.73

July 9th   Am I on the philosopher's path or winging it?

MORNING REFLECTION

EVENING REFLECTION

July 10th   Am I dedicated to my craft?

MORNING REFLECTION

EVENING REFLECTION

___

July 11th   How will I improve myself today?

MORNING REFLECTION

___

EVENING REFLECTION

___

July 12th   What principles govern my behavior?

MORNING REFLECTION

EVENING REFLECTION

July 13th   Am I ready to be a leader? Ready to do my job?

MORNING REFLECTION

EVENING REFLECTION

_____

_____

_____

_____

_____

_____

_____

_____

_____

July 14th　Am I becoming more humble or less humble?

MORNING REFLECTION

_____

_____

_____

_____

_____

_____

_____

_____

EVENING REFLECTION

_____

_____

_____

_____

_____

_____

_____

_____

July 15th   Can I do the right thing—even without the promise of rewards?

MORNING REFLECTION

EVENING REFLECTION

WEEK XXIX
PRACTICE GENTLENESS INSTEAD OF ANGER

I t's easy to imagine Marcus Aurelius losing his temper. His responsibilities were vast and his job required him to work with many frustrating, difficult people. As such, he had an acute sense of the problem of anger, knowing just how counterproductive it can be and how miserable it can make its users. He often repeated a simple exercise designed to preserve goodwill for others by simply replacing anger with gentleness. We can't allow ourselves to desert our goodwill, and we must remind ourselves that no one makes a mistake willingly. Each time you feel anger this week, remember Marcus and see how you might replace it with gentleness—and write these examples down.

"As you move forward along the path of reason, people will stand in your way. They will never be able to keep you from doing what's sound, so don't let them knock out your goodwill for them. Keep a steady watch on both fronts, not only for well-based judgments and actions, but also for gentleness with those who would obstruct our path or create other difficulties. For getting angry is also a weakness, just as much as abandoning the task or surrendering under panic."

—MARCUS AURELIUS, *MEDITATIONS*, 11.9

"As Plato said, every soul is deprived of truth against its will. The same holds true for justice, self-control, goodwill to others, and every similar virtue. It's essential to constantly keep this in your mind, for it will make you more gentle to all."

—MARCUS AURELIUS, *MEDITATIONS*, 7.63

"Keep this thought handy when you feel a fit of rage coming on— it isn't manly to be enraged. Rather, gentleness and civility are more human, and therefore manlier. A real man doesn't give way to anger and discontent, and such a person has strength, courage, and endurance. . . ."

—MARCUS AURELIUS, *MEDITATIONS*, 11.18.5B

July 16th   To what service am I committed?

MORNING REFLECTION

EVENING REFLECTION

July 17th   Where have I abandoned others?

MORNING REFLECTION

EVENING REFLECTION

July 18th   Can I mind my own business and not be distracted by others?

MORNING REFLECTION

EVENING REFLECTION

July 19th   What would forgiveness feel like?

MORNING REFLECTION

_____
_____
_____
_____
_____
_____
_____
_____
_____

EVENING REFLECTION

_____
_____
_____
_____
_____
_____
_____

July 20th   Am I living a just life?

MORNING REFLECTION

_____
_____
_____
_____
_____
_____
_____

EVENING REFLECTION

July 21st   How can I work better with others?

MORNING REFLECTION

EVENING REFLECTION

July 22nd   Am I acting nobly or grudgingly?

MORNING REFLECTION

_____

_____

_____

_____

_____

_____

_____

_____

_____

EVENING REFLECTION

_____

_____

_____

_____

_____

_____

_____

_____

WEEK XXX
KEEPING "THE NEWS" IN CHECK

Even the ancients felt inundated with gossip and news. This week you will face a barrage like they couldn't have imagined—from texts, calls, e-mails to the incessant grind of the 24/7 news machine. Instead of responding to every status update, urgent call, or the latest trending incendiary news story, take a moment to remember three ways the Stoics used to keep their focus on their purpose and duty in the present moment: (1) Step away from the noise. (2) Remember that no news can throw you off the purpose of your present choices. (3) Don't add something negative (or positive) to what is being reported.

> "Are you distracted by breaking news? Then take some leisure time to learn something good, and stop bouncing around. But when you do, keep in mind the other mistake, to be so distracted by getting control that you wear yourself out and lose a purpose by which you can direct your impulses and thoughts."
>
> —Marcus Aurelius, *Meditations*, 2.7

> "Whenever disturbing news is delivered to you, bear in mind that *no news can ever be relevant to your reasoned choice.* Can anyone break news to you that your assumptions or desires are wrong? No way! But they can tell you someone died—even so, what is that to you?"
>
> —Epictetus, *Discourses*, 3.18.1–2

> "*Don't tell yourself anything more than what the initial impressions report.* It's been reported to you that someone is speaking badly about you. This is the report—the report wasn't that you've been harmed. I see that my son is sick—but not that his life is at risk. So always stay within your first impressions, and don't add to them in your head—this way nothing can happen to you."
>
> —Marcus Aurelius, *Meditations*, 8.49

July 23rd   How can I make sure none of it goes to my head—good or bad?

MORNING REFLECTION

EVENING REFLECTION

July 24th   Can I keep my cool when receiving disturbing news?

MORNING REFLECTION

EVENING REFLECTION

July 25th   Where do I let work diminish my quality of life?

MORNING REFLECTION

EVENING REFLECTION

July 26th   Where can I pitch in? How can I help?

MORNING REFLECTION

EVENING REFLECTION

July 27th   What is better than virtue?

MORNING REFLECTION

EVENING REFLECTION

July 28th　Where have I been privileged—and what am I doing with it?

MORNING REFLECTION

EVENING REFLECTION

July 29th   Where can I find confidence?

MORNING REFLECTION

EVENING REFLECTION

∞

WEEK XXXI
A WEEK WITHOUT COMPLAINING

Epictetus spoke often to his students about the need to give up blaming and complaining—in fact, he saw it as one of the primary measuring sticks of progress in the art of living. How much of life is wasted pointing fingers? Has complaining ever solved a single problem? Marcus Aurelius would say, "Blame yourself—or no one." This week, try constructive feedback over complaining and responsibility over blame. And if something goes wrong, spend some time reflecting on what the true causes were. Don't waste a minute with complaints—in this journal or out loud.

"You must stop blaming God, and not blame any person. You must completely control your desire and shift your avoidance to what lies within your reasoned choice. You must no longer feel anger, resentment, envy, or regret."

—Epictetus, *Discourses*, 3.22.13

"For nothing outside my reasoned choice can hinder or harm it— my reasoned choice alone can do this to itself. If we would lean this way whenever we fail, and would blame only ourselves and remember that nothing but opinion is the cause of a troubled mind and uneasiness, then by God, I swear we would be making progress."

—Epictetus, *Discourses*, 3.19.2–3

"But if you deem as your own only what is yours, and what belongs to others as truly not yours, then no one will ever be able to coerce or to stop you, you will find no one to blame or accuse, you will do nothing against your will, you will have no enemy, no one will harm you, because no harm can affect you."

—Epictetus, *Enchiridion*, 1.3

July 30th   Can I seek joy today in purpose, excellence, and duty?

MORNING REFLECTION

EVENING REFLECTION

July 31st   Am I neglecting the personal for the professional?

MORNING REFLECTION

EVENING REFLECTION

August 1st   Where does my idealism hold me back?

MORNING REFLECTION

EVENING REFLECTION

August 2nd   How can I make do with the tough situations I face?

MORNING REFLECTION

_____

_____

_____

_____

_____

_____

_____

EVENING REFLECTION

_____

_____

_____

_____

_____

_____

_____

August 3rd   Can I get the most out of where I am right here, right now?

MORNING REFLECTION

_____

_____

_____

_____

_____

_____

_____

EVENING REFLECTION

August 4th   How can I avoid fruitless emotions today?

MORNING REFLECTION

EVENING REFLECTION

August 5th   Can I hold my tongue today?

MORNING REFLECTION

_____

_____

_____

_____

_____

_____

_____

_____

_____

EVENING REFLECTION

_____

_____

_____

_____

_____

_____

_____

_____

WEEK XXXII
WHAT LITTLE WINS CAN YOU FIND?

Zeno of Citium, the Phoenician merchant who founded the Stoic school on the painted porch (*stoa poikilē*) of the Agora after a shipwreck, said that happiness was a matter of small steps. While the Stoics believed in the perfectibility of human beings, they knew much stood in the way of realizing that potential. So they would be skeptical of the so-called epic wins and quantum leaps that our culture obsesses over today. Instead, they would urge you to focus on your daily duties, on making incremental progress. Spend your writing time this week thinking about the small wins you can rack up, what little gains can be had from this improvement or that one, a decision here or a decision there. Be satisfied with each small step. Keep moving and don't give up.

"Do now what nature demands of you. Get right to it if that's in your power. Don't look around to see if people will know about it. Don't await the perfection of Plato's *Republic*, but be satisfied with even the smallest step forward and regard the outcome as a small thing."

—MARCUS AURELIUS, *MEDITATIONS*, 9.29

"We don't abandon our pursuits because we despair of ever perfecting them."

—EPICTETUS, *DISCOURSES*, 1.2.37B

"Well-being is realized by small steps, but is truly no small thing."

—ZENO, QUOTED IN DIOGENES LAERTIUS,
LIVES OF THE EMINENT PHILOSOPHERS, 7.1.26

August 6th   Do I think through my problems to apply the right pressure?

MORNING REFLECTION

EVENING REFLECTION

August 7th   Can I live well no matter how trying the environment?

MORNING REFLECTION

EVENING REFLECTION

August 8th   What's the smallest step I can take toward a big thing today?

MORNING REFLECTION

EVENING REFLECTION

August 9th   Can I keep things simple today? Straightforward?

MORNING REFLECTION

EVENING REFLECTION

August 10th   Where is perfectionism holding me back?

MORNING REFLECTION

EVENING REFLECTION

August 11th   Are my habits getting better?

MORNING REFLECTION

EVENING REFLECTION

August 12th   Am I making this philosophy my own by putting it into practice?

MORNING REFLECTION

EVENING REFLECTION

WEEK XXXIII
ALWAYS ASK YOURSELF THIS QUESTION

M uch of what we do and say during the course of a week is completely unnecessary. Meetings, material possessions, confrontations, pursuits—pointless distractions and problems. They take us away from tranquility and purpose. A Stoic cuts through these temptations and obligations by asking this question, a question that you should lead your journaling with this week. Try it. Before speaking, acting, or buying something, ask simply: "Is this one of the necessary things?"

"It is said that if you would have peace of mind, busy yourself with little. But wouldn't a better saying be do what you must and as required of a rational being created for public life? For this brings not only the peace of mind of doing few things, but the greater peace of doing them well. Since the vast majority of our words and actions are unnecessary, corralling them will create an abundance of leisure and tranquility. As a result, we shouldn't forget at each moment to ask, is this one of the unnecessary things? But we must corral not only unnecessary actions but unnecessary thoughts, too, so needless acts don't tag along after them."

—MARCUS AURELIUS, *MEDITATIONS*, 4.24

"I was shipwrecked before I even boarded . . . the journey showed me this—how much of what we have is unnecessary, and how easily we can decide to rid ourselves of these things whenever it's necessary, never suffering the loss."

—SENECA, *MORAL LETTERS*, 87.1

August 13th   What troubles can I solve in advance?

MORNING REFLECTION

EVENING REFLECTION

August 14th   How will philosophy help steer my course today?

MORNING REFLECTION

EVENING REFLECTION

August 15th   Will decisions I make today be based on true judgments?

MORNING REFLECTION

EVENING REFLECTION

August 16th   How will I turn today's adversities into advantages?

MORNING REFLECTION

EVENING REFLECTION

August 17th   Can I go a whole day without blaming others?

MORNING REFLECTION

EVENING REFLECTION

August 18th   Where can I better play to my strengths?

MORNING REFLECTION

EVENING REFLECTION

August 19th   What inessential things can I eliminate from my life?

MORNING REFLECTION

EVENING REFLECTION

WEEK XXXIV
JUST SAY NO TO FUTURE MISERY

How often we make ourselves miserable . . . in advance. Out of fear of this, out of desperate hope for that. When we focus on pining for or avoiding a certain future, we make ourselves miserable here in the present. Hecato of Rhodes, the great student of the great middle-Stoic scholar Panaetius, taught that this misery is always tied to hopes or fears we give to imagined future outcomes. From this Seneca reminds us this week to say no to both, because indulging them robs us of the ability to enjoy the present. As you write, don't think about the future—what you hope will happen, what you fear might—just focus on right now. What you're doing and thinking right now.

"It's ruinous for the soul to be anxious about the future and miserable in advance of misery, engulfed by anxiety that the things it desires might remain its own until the very end. For such a soul will never be at rest—by longing for things to come it will lose the ability to enjoy present things."
—SENECA, *MORAL LETTERS*, 98.5B–6A

"But there is no reason to live and no limit to our miseries if we let our fears predominate."
—SENECA, *MORAL LETTERS*, 13.12B

"Hecato says, 'Cease to hope and you will cease to fear.'. . . The primary cause of both these ills is that instead of adapting ourselves to present circumstances we send out thoughts too far ahead."
—SENECA, *MORAL LETTERS*, 5.7B–8

August 20th   How well is my soul dressed?

MORNING REFLECTION

EVENING REFLECTION

August 21st   What if I stopped worrying about the future and enjoyed the present?

MORNING REFLECTION

EVENING REFLECTION

August 22nd   What small stuff can I stop sweating?

MORNING REFLECTION

EVENING REFLECTION

August 23rd   Where do I have too much of a good thing?

MORNING REFLECTION

EVENING REFLECTION

August 24th   What can I learn from others—even the people I don't like?

MORNING REFLECTION

EVENING REFLECTION

August 25th   What new path can I blaze today?

MORNING REFLECTION

EVENING REFLECTION

August 26th   What potential losses can I anticipate in advance?

MORNING REFLECTION

EVENING REFLECTION

WEEK XXXV
A CURE FOR PROCRASTINATION

To the Stoic, procrastination almost looks like a form of delusion and entitlement. Who is to say you'll even be around next month or next week to deal with it? If it's important, they'd say, don't wait. Do it now. As Seneca says, if it needs to be done, do it with "courage and promptness." Procrastination seems like it makes things easier, but it damns us to a low-grade, gnawing state of anxiety. Is that how you'd want to spend this week? Any week? Your last week? Ask yourself: What am I avoiding? What can I handle today instead of tomorrow? What can I do promptly and bravely, right now?

> "Anything that must yet be done, virtue can do with courage and promptness. For anyone would call it a sign of foolishness for one to undertake a task with a lazy and begrudging spirit, or to push the body in one direction and the mind in another, to be torn apart by wildly divergent impulses."
> —SENECA, *MORAL LETTERS*, 74.31b–32

> "This is the mark of perfection of character—to spend each day as if it were your last, without frenzy, laziness, or any pretending."
> —MARCUS AURELIUS, *MEDITATIONS*, 7.69

> "You get what you deserve. Instead of being a good person today, you choose instead to become one tomorrow."
> —MARCUS AURELIUS, *MEDITATIONS*, 8.22

August 27th   Where can I learn to laugh rather than cry?

MORNING REFLECTION

EVENING REFLECTION

August 28th   What luxuries can I practice not needing?

MORNING REFLECTION

EVENING REFLECTION

August 29th   What wants can I eliminate today?

MORNING REFLECTION

EVENING REFLECTION

August 30th   Can I do today's duties with both courage and confidence?

MORNING REFLECTION

EVENING REFLECTION

August 31st   Where have I done others wrong?

MORNING REFLECTION

EVENING REFLECTION

September 1st　Am I working to make my soul stronger than any Fortune?

MORNING REFLECTION

EVENING REFLECTION

September 2nd   What's the most painful part of Stoicism for you?

MORNING REFLECTION

EVENING REFLECTION

WEEK XXXVI
A HARD WINTER TRAINING

The art of living has three levels of discipline: study, practice, and hard training. Reading the Stoics, that's study. Trying out the lessons and reflecting on them in this journal, that's practice. What's left is the hard training. Epictetus liked to use the analogy of the Roman army's practice of training hard in the off months of winter so they would be prepared to meet any challenge when they returned to battle in the spring. Seneca would spend time each month exposing himself to tougher than usual conditions. He, too, used a military analogy, pointing to the way soldiers are tasked with hard jobs so they would be strong when the enemy eventually came. What are you doing this week to push yourself beyond mere study and practice?

"We must undergo a hard winter training and not rush into things for which we haven't prepared."

—EPICTETUS, *DISCOURSES*, 1.2.32

"Here's a lesson to test your mind's mettle: take part of a week in which you have only the most meager and cheap food, dress scantly in shabby clothes, and ask yourself if this is really the worst that you feared. It is when times are good that you should gird yourself for tougher times ahead, for when Fortune is kind the soul can build defenses against her ravages. So it is that soldiers practice maneuvers in peacetime, erecting bunkers with no enemies in sight and exhausting themselves under no attack so that when it comes they won't grow tired."

—SENECA, *MORAL LETTERS*, 18.5–6

"When a challenge confronts you, remember that God is matching you with a younger sparring partner, as would a physical trainer. Why? Becoming an Olympian takes sweat! I think no one has a better challenge than yours, if only you would use it like an athlete would that younger sparring partner."

—EPICTETUS, *DISCOURSES*, 1.24.1–2

September 3rd   How am I preparing in the off-season for what is to come?

MORNING REFLECTION

EVENING REFLECTION

September 4th   How can I see these difficulties as a lesson and a test?

MORNING REFLECTION

EVENING REFLECTION

September 5th   What is truly mine?

MORNING REFLECTION

EVENING REFLECTION

September 6th   If I lost my freedom, would it break me?

MORNING REFLECTION

EVENING REFLECTION

September 7th   How will I use the power of choice today?

MORNING REFLECTION

EVENING REFLECTION

September 8th   Am I prepared for my bubble to be burst?

MORNING REFLECTION

EVENING REFLECTION

September 9th   Do I rule my fears, or do they rule me?

MORNING REFLECTION

EVENING REFLECTION

WEEK XXXVII
A NEW WAY TO PRAY

We often pray for the things we desire and, in the process, excuse ourselves from the equation. We're hoping the heavens will magically gift us with the outcome we want—whether it's for a promotion or the speedy recovery of a loved one. The Stoics would urge you to stop doing this. Marcus Aurelius reminded himself not to present the gods with a list of demands for pleasures or comforts, but instead to ask for help not needing those things. In a sense then, he was really asking for inner strength. He was asking *himself*. Think about all the things you want—that you're praying or hoping for this week—and try turning them around like that. See what you come up with instead.

"Try praying differently, and see what happens: Instead of asking for 'a way to sleep with her,' try asking for 'a way to stop desiring to sleep with her.' Instead of 'a way to get rid of him,' try asking for 'a way to not crave his demise.' Instead of 'a way to not lose my child,' try asking for 'a way to lose my fear of it.'"

—MARCUS AURELIUS, *MEDITATIONS*, 9.40.(6)

"We cry to God Almighty, how can we escape this agony? Fool, don't you have hands? Or could it be God forgot to give you a pair? Sit and pray your nose doesn't run! Or rather just wipe your nose and stop seeking a scapegoat."

—EPICTETUS, *DISCOURSES*, 2.16.13

"But I haven't at any time been hindered in my will, nor forced against it. And how is this possible? I have bound up my choice to act with the will of God. God wills that I be sick, such is my will. He wills that I should choose something, so do I. He wills that I reach for something, or something be given to me—I wish for the same. What God doesn't will, I do not wish for."

—EPICTETUS, *DISCOURSES*, 4.1.89

September 10th   How can I prepare for the losses I fear?

MORNING REFLECTION

EVENING REFLECTION

September 11th   Where can I do with less today?

MORNING REFLECTION

EVENING REFLECTION

September 12th   Where am I putting on airs?

MORNING REFLECTION

EVENING REFLECTION

September 13th   How strong is my Inner Citadel?

MORNING REFLECTION

EVENING REFLECTION

September 14th   Are you praying—or *demanding*?

MORNING REFLECTION

EVENING REFLECTION

September 15th   Are you sizzle or steak?

MORNING REFLECTION

EVENING REFLECTION

September 16th   Will I triumph over the disasters and panics of the day?

MORNING REFLECTION

EVENING REFLECTION

WEEK XXXVIII
ON HANDLING HATERS

The Stoics taught that kindness trumps hate. They believed that those who engage in hate are prisoners to a destructive passion—one that hurts the practitioner, not the intended target. There's no reason to hate a hater; they are already suffering enough. In fact, when you see them this way, it makes it easier to be kind, good-natured, genuine, and useful. Remember the line in the Bible about how loving your enemies is like pouring hot coals on them, because it's so unexpected? Who can you surprise like that this week? Whose enmity can you meet with kindness and compassion? How much better do you feel having done so?

"What if someone despises me? Let them see to it. But I will see to it that I won't be found doing or saying anything contemptible. What if someone hates me? Let them see to that. But I will see to it that I'm kind and good-natured to all, and prepared to show even the hater where they went wrong. Not in a critical way, or to show off my patience, but genuinely and usefully."

—MARCUS AURELIUS, *MEDITATIONS*, 11.13

"Kindness is invincible, but only when it's sincere, with no hypocrisy or faking. For what can even the most malicious person do if you keep showing kindness and, if given the chance, you gently point out where they went wrong—right as they are trying to harm you?"

—MARCUS AURELIUS, *MEDITATIONS*, 11.18.5.9A

"Keep in mind that it isn't the one who has it in for you and takes a swipe that harms you, but rather the harm comes from your own belief about the abuse. So when someone arouses your anger, know that it's really your own opinion fueling it. Instead, make it your first response not to be carried away by such impressions, for with time and distance self-mastery is more easily achieved."

—EPICTETUS, *ENCHIRIDION*, 20

September 17th   Can I resist giving in to haters—and hating them in return?

MORNING REFLECTION

EVENING REFLECTION

September 18th   Can I let the pains of life pass without adding to them?

MORNING REFLECTION

EVENING REFLECTION

September 19th   Am I flexible enough to change my mind and accept feedback?

MORNING REFLECTION

EVENING REFLECTION

September 20th   How ready am I for unexpected attacks?

MORNING REFLECTION

EVENING REFLECTION

September 21st   Can I keep life's rhythm no matter the interruption?

MORNING REFLECTION

EVENING REFLECTION

September 22nd   How will today's difficulties show my character?

MORNING REFLECTION

EVENING REFLECTION

September 23rd   How is my training coming?

MORNING REFLECTION

EVENING REFLECTION

WEEK XXXIX
PANIC IS SELF-INFLICTED HARM

Name one situation that is improved by panicking. Go ahead—write it down if you've got one! Seneca mused often about the problem of panic both in his letters and essays. It creates danger and limits our ability to function effectively. It prevents us from finding success and seeing objectively. Worse, it makes us weaker over time because we've never truly faced the danger we are so worried about. Meditate on the scary things that might make you panic. Think about what is so overwhelming about them. Come to understand them. Get familiar with them.

"For even peace itself will supply more reason for worry. Not even safe circumstances will bring you confidence once your mind has been shocked—once it gets in the habit of blind panic, it can't provide for its own safety. For it doesn't really avoid danger, it just runs away. Yet we are exposed to greater danger with our backs turned."

—SENECA, *MORAL LETTERS*, 104.10B

"Success comes to the lowly and to the poorly talented, but the special characteristic of a great person is to triumph over the disasters and panics of human life."

—SENECA, *ON PROVIDENCE*, 4.1

"The unprepared are panic-stricken by the smallest things."

—SENECA, *MORAL LETTERS*, 107.4

September 24th   Have I thought about *all* that might happen?

MORNING REFLECTION

EVENING REFLECTION

September 25th   What am I a slave to?

MORNING REFLECTION

EVENING REFLECTION

September 26th   What idle leisure can I replace with something more fulfilling?

MORNING REFLECTION

EVENING REFLECTION

September 27th   What do prosperity and difficulty each reveal about me?

MORNING REFLECTION

EVENING REFLECTION

September 28th   How will I respond to the things that happen today?

MORNING REFLECTION

EVENING REFLECTION

September 29th   Where are my eyes bigger than my stomach?

MORNING REFLECTION

EVENING REFLECTION

September 30th   How can I strengthen my Inner Citadel?

MORNING REFLECTION

EVENING REFLECTION

∽∞

WEEK XL
PRACTICE SILENCE

S ocial media teaches us to have an opinion about everything. Silence beckons us to speak. We live in a loud culture and we try to keep up by being louder in return. How much trouble does that cause us? How much might we learn if we spent more time listening to others than we do trying to sandwich our opinions in at every turn? How much of what we say have we come to regret? The truly loud thing to say is nothing. Write your thoughts down here this week, but see how many of them you can keep to yourself. Be bold in your silence, in how much you hold your tongue this week.

"Better to trip with the feet than with the tongue."

—ZENO, QUOTED IN DIOGENES LAERTIUS,
LIVES OF THE EMINENT PHILOSOPHERS, 7.1.26

"To the youngster talking nonsense Zeno said, 'The reason why we have two ears and only one mouth is so we might listen more and talk less.'"

—DIOGENES LAERTIUS,
LIVES OF THE EMINENT PHILOSOPHERS, 7.1.23

"Cato practiced the kind of public speech capable of moving the masses, believing proper political philosophy takes care like any great city to maintain the warlike element. But he was never seen practicing in front of others, and no one ever heard him rehearse a speech. When he was told that people blamed him for his silence, he replied, 'Better they not blame my life. I begin to speak only when I'm certain what I'll say isn't better left unsaid.'"

—PLUTARCH, *CATO THE YOUNGER*, 4

"Silence is a lesson learned from the many sufferings of life."

—SENECA, *THYESTES*, 309

October 1st   How will I let my virtues shine today?

MORNING REFLECTION

EVENING REFLECTION

October 2nd   If wisdom is the most valuable asset, how have I invested in it?

MORNING REFLECTION

EVENING REFLECTION

October 3rd Do I live as if we are all one—all part of the same whole?

MORNING REFLECTION

EVENING REFLECTION

October 4th   Will my actions today be good for all concerned?

MORNING REFLECTION

EVENING REFLECTION

October 5th   What do I say that's better left unsaid?

MORNING REFLECTION

EVENING REFLECTION

October 6th   Who else can I root for—other than myself?

MORNING REFLECTION

EVENING REFLECTION

October 7th   Why does my wrongdoing hurt me most of all?

MORNING REFLECTION

EVENING REFLECTION

WEEK XLI
PRACTICE LOVE

The Stoic notion of *sympatheia*, that we all are part of an organic whole, connected by mutual interests and affinities, is greater than the Golden Rule. Don't treat others how you would like to be treated, treat them like you treat yourself, because we are all one. Seneca said that whenever he encountered another human being he saw an opportunity for kindness. He had learned from Hecato that if you want to be loved there is only one thing to do: love others. Who can you give love to this week? What kindness can you expend? How can you show how you feel—strangers, friends, and family? How can you show them that you believe we are all part of the same whole?

"Hecato says, 'I can teach you a love potion made without any drugs, herbs, or special spell—if you would be loved, love.'"

—SENECA, *MORAL LETTERS*, 9.6

"A benefit should be kept like a buried treasure, only to be dug up in necessity. . . . Nature bids us to do well by all. . . . Wherever there is a human being, we have an opportunity for kindness."

—SENECA, *ON THE HAPPY LIFE*, 24.2–3

"Nature produced us as a family, since we all sprang from the same source and toward the same end. Nature bestowed upon us mutual love, and joined us together as friends."

—SENECA, *MORAL LETTERS*, 95.52

October 8th   What is more pleasing than wisdom?

MORNING REFLECTION

EVENING REFLECTION

October 9th   Have I set my standards and am I using them?

MORNING REFLECTION

EVENING REFLECTION

October 10th   What do my principles tell me about persisting and resisting?

MORNING REFLECTION

EVENING REFLECTION

October 11th   Is honesty my default setting?

MORNING REFLECTION

EVENING REFLECTION

October 12th   Instead of seeking love can I give it first?

MORNING REFLECTION

EVENING REFLECTION

October 13th   Has revenge ever made anything better?

MORNING REFLECTION

EVENING REFLECTION

October 14th   What if instead of getting mad, I offered to help?

MORNING REFLECTION

EVENING REFLECTION

WEEK XLII
MAKE HONESTY YOUR ONLY POLICY

As emperor, Marcus Aurelius did not see the best of humanity. At court there would have been backbiting, people who sold their friends out when they saw an opportunity to advance themselves, avarice, and deceit. But he especially didn't like faux attempts at honesty. His point: if you have to say "I'm going to be honest with you here," you're casually saying that honesty is the exception and not the rule. How sad is that? It's time to think about what those little statements say about us—and make sure that our default policy is honesty and straightforwardness.

"How rotten and fraudulent when people say they intend to give it to you straight. What are you up to, dear friend? It shouldn't need your announcement, but be readily seen, as if written on your forehead, heard in the ring of your voice, a flash in your eyes—just as the beloved sees it all in the lover's glance. In short, the straightforward and good person should be like a smelly goat—you know when they are in the room with you. A calculated 'giving it to you straight' is like a dagger. There's nothing worse than a wolf befriending sheep. Avoid false friendship at all costs. If you are good, straightforward, and well-meaning it should show in your eyes and not escape notice."

—MARCUS AURELIUS, *MEDITATIONS*, 11.15

"It's in keeping with Nature to show our friends affection and to celebrate their advancement, as if it were our very own. For if we don't do this, virtue, which is strengthened only by exercising our perceptions, will no longer endure in us."

—SENECA, *MORAL LETTERS*, 109.15

October 15th   Will I give people the benefit of the doubt?

MORNING REFLECTION

EVENING REFLECTION

October 16th   How can I share this philosophy that has helped me so much?

MORNING REFLECTION

EVENING REFLECTION

October 17th   Where can I show other people kindness?

MORNING REFLECTION

EVENING REFLECTION

October 18th   Am I avoiding false friendships and bad influences?

MORNING REFLECTION

EVENING REFLECTION

October 19th   Which good habit can I use today to drive out a bad one?

MORNING REFLECTION

EVENING REFLECTION

October 20th   Do my principles show themselves in my life?

MORNING REFLECTION

EVENING REFLECTION

October 21st   Can I do the right thing and not care about credit?

MORNING REFLECTION

EVENING REFLECTION

∞

WEEK XLIII
BUILD UP, DON'T TEAR DOWN

Is there a worse environment to work in than one where bullying and one-upmanship is the norm? Sometimes leaders seem to think that that is part of the job description—that they are there to regulate and keep people in line. In truth, tearing people down is incredibly counterproductive. Pete Carroll, coach of the Seattle Seahawks, poses a question: If self-confidence is so important for players, why would a coach ever do anything to damage it? Marcus Aurelius, who had the power to take down anyone at will, almost never did. Instead, he reminded himself that it was better to build up—be community-minded, modest, prepared, and tolerant of others. We are made for cooperation (*synergia*) and to render works held in common (*praxeis koinonikas apodidonai*). Let's think about that going forward: How can we help build the self-confidence of others? How can we find some of our own in doing so?

"So someone's good at taking down an opponent, but that doesn't make them more community-minded, or modest, or well-prepared for any circumstance, or more tolerant of the faults of others."

—Marcus Aurelius, *Meditations*, 7.52

"Whenever you have trouble getting up in the morning, remind yourself that you've been made by nature for the purpose of working with others. . . . And it's our own natural purpose that is more fitting and more satisfying."

—Marcus Aurelius, *Meditations*, 8.12

October 22nd   Am I actually improving—or am I just chasing vanity?

MORNING REFLECTION

EVENING REFLECTION

October 23rd   Am I displaying my best qualities?

MORNING REFLECTION

EVENING REFLECTION

October 24th   What goodness can I find inside myself? Can I bring it to the surface?

MORNING REFLECTION

EVENING REFLECTION

October 25th   What are my tasks in this life?

MORNING REFLECTION

EVENING REFLECTION

October 26th   Are my goals natural, moral, and rational?

MORNING REFLECTION

EVENING REFLECTION

October 27th　What bad behaviors or choices have come back to haunt me?

MORNING REFLECTION

EVENING REFLECTION

October 28th   What can I do to be part of something bigger than myself?

MORNING REFLECTION

EVENING REFLECTION

WEEK XLIV
ACCEPTING WHAT IS

Reinhold Niebuhr's Serenity Prayer is a mantra for many: "God grant me the serenity to accept the things I cannot change; courage to change the things I can; and wisdom to know the difference." The Stoics wanted to push past simply "accepting" what is—they wanted to be grateful and happy with what it is. Epictetus taught that we get a well-flowing life when we wish for what is going to happen not what we want to happen, and Marcus added that we should meet anything that comes our way with gratitude. Not "I wish this was different, but I'll tolerate it"; instead "I am glad it happened this way. It is for the best." Try that on for size this week.

> "Don't seek for everything to happen as you wish it would, but rather wish that everything happens as it actually will—then your life will flow well."
>
> —EPICTETUS, *ENCHIRIDION*, 8

> "To be truly educated means this—learning to wish that each thing happens exactly as it does."
>
> —EPICTETUS, *DISCOURSES*, 1.12.15

> "All you need are these: certainty of judgment in the present moment; action for the common good in the present moment; and an attitude of gratitude in the present moment for anything that comes your way."
>
> —MARCUS AURELIUS, *MEDITATIONS*, 9.6

October 29th   How can I improve my character?

MORNING REFLECTION

EVENING REFLECTION

October 30th   What time can I claw back for myself—and how will I use it?

MORNING REFLECTION

EVENING REFLECTION

October 31st　What good turns can be done today?

MORNING REFLECTION

EVENING REFLECTION

November 1st   Can I love *everything* that happens today?

MORNING REFLECTION

EVENING REFLECTION

November 2nd   Can I make my choices and accept whatever will be?

MORNING REFLECTION

EVENING REFLECTION

November 3rd   How can this be exactly what I needed?

MORNING REFLECTION

EVENING REFLECTION

November 4th   Is change really so bad? Is the status quo really so good?

MORNING REFLECTION

EVENING REFLECTION

WEEK XLV
THE REAL POWER YOU HAVE

There is fleeting power and there is real power. Fleeting power can be taken away, while real power is in our minds and our bones. The former tends to be along the lines of wealth, fame, high position, and the leverage all those things give us over others. The Stoics thought this kind of power was inferior to the real power that each person possesses—the power of our minds to reason and make judgments and choices based on the real worth of things. You can have both kinds of power, too, but only if you keep the first kind of power subject to the kind of power the Stoics cared about.

"This is the very thing which makes up the virtue of the happy person and a well-flowing life—when the affairs of life are in every way tuned to the harmony between the individual divine spirit and the will of the director of the universe."

—CHRYSIPPUS, QUOTED IN DIOGENES LAERTIUS,
LIVES OF THE EMINENT PHILOSOPHERS, 7.1.88

"Don't trust in your reputation, money, or position, but in the strength that is yours—namely, your judgments about the things that you control and don't control. For this alone is what makes us free and unfettered, that picks us up by the neck from the depths and lifts us eye to eye with the rich and powerful."

—EPICTETUS, DISCOURSES, 3.26.34–35

"Understand at last that you have something in you more powerful and divine than what causes the bodily passions and pulls you like a mere puppet. What thoughts now occupy my mind? Is it not fear, suspicion, desire, or something like that?"

—MARCUS AURELIUS, MEDITATIONS, 12.19

November 5th   Is my character producing a well-flowing life?

MORNING REFLECTION

_____

_____

_____

_____

_____

_____

_____

_____

_____

EVENING REFLECTION

_____

_____

_____

_____

_____

_____

_____

_____

November 6th   Am I prepared for the randomness of fate and luck?

MORNING REFLECTION

_____

_____

_____

_____

_____

_____

_____

_____

EVENING REFLECTION

November 7th   Are you trying to master yourself—or other people?

MORNING REFLECTION

EVENING REFLECTION

November 8th   What's my role in the play of life?

MORNING REFLECTION

EVENING REFLECTION

November 9th   What principles will steer me through the flow of change?

MORNING REFLECTION

EVENING REFLECTION

November 10th What will remain when all else passes away?

MORNING REFLECTION

EVENING REFLECTION

November 11th   What false judgment can I wipe away today?

MORNING REFLECTION

EVENING REFLECTION

WEEK XLVI
JUDGE YOURSELF, NOT OTHERS

There is nothing less philosophical than being a know-it-all. This is especially true of those who use their knowledge to scold others for their mistakes while proclaiming the superiority of their knowledge or insight. The Stoics taught that behaving this way was to miss the entire purpose of philosophy—as a tool for self-correction, medicine for our own souls, not a weapon for putting others down. Seneca's letters twice employ the metaphor of scrubbing down or scraping off our faults. We need to see ourselves as "in the care of philosophy's principles," or, as Epictetus put it later when referring to the philosopher's lecture hall, we need to see it as a hospital for our own therapy. Don't let yourself write down a single complaint or problem of another person in this journal this week—focus on what ails you.

"When philosophy is wielded with arrogance and stubbornly, it is the cause for the ruin of many. Let philosophy scrape off your own faults, rather than be a way to rail against the faults of others."

—SENECA, *MORAL LETTERS*, 103.4B–5A

"Some people with exceptional minds quickly grasp virtue or produce it within themselves. But other dim and lazy types, hindered by bad habits, must have their rusty souls constantly scrubbed down. . . . The weaker sorts will be helped and lifted from their bad opinions if we put them in the care of philosophy's principles."

—SENECA, *MORAL LETTERS*, 95.36–37

"Men, the philosopher's lecture-hall is a hospital—you shouldn't walk out of it feeling pleasure, but pain, for you aren't well when you enter it."

—EPICTETUS, *DISCOURSES*, 3.23.30

November 12th   Can the buck stop with me today?

MORNING REFLECTION

EVENING REFLECTION

November 13th   Does complaining accomplish anything?

MORNING REFLECTION

EVENING REFLECTION

November 14th　Will I add negative thoughts on top of my troubles?

MORNING REFLECTION

EVENING REFLECTION

November 15th   Will I embrace the flow of change today?

MORNING REFLECTION

EVENING REFLECTION

November 16th   Can I cease both hoping for and fearing certain outcomes?

MORNING REFLECTION

EVENING REFLECTION

November 17th   Is it really my place to judge other people?

MORNING REFLECTION

EVENING REFLECTION

November 18th   Am I practicing good Stoic thoughts?

MORNING REFLECTION

_____

_____

_____

_____

_____

_____

_____

_____

EVENING REFLECTION

_____

_____

_____

_____

_____

_____

_____

_____

We suffer when we lose things we love, and we suffer most when we lose people we love—a natural and unavoidable part of life. The Stoics say this suffering is increased by our belief that we possess the objects of our love—that they are, as we like to say, "a part of us." This belief doesn't increase our love and care for them, but rather is a form of clinging that ignores the simple fact that we don't control what will happen, not to our own bodies, let alone to the ones we love. Epictetus taught a powerful exercise that every time you wish a dear child, family member, or friend good night, remember that these people are like a precious breakable glass, and remember how dramatically things could change while you sleep. Marcus, too, struggled to practice this with his own family as he tucked them in at night. The point isn't to be morbid but to create a sense of appreciation and a kind of humility. Don't take anyone—especially someone you love—for granted this week.

"Whenever you experience the pangs of losing something, don't treat it like a part of yourself but as a breakable glass, so when it falls you will remember that and won't be troubled. So, too, whenever you kiss your child, sibling, or friend, don't layer on top of the experience all the things you might wish, but hold them back and stop them, just as those who ride behind triumphant generals remind them they are mortal. In the same way, remind yourself that your precious one isn't one of your possessions, but something given for now, not forever."

—EPICTETUS, *DISCOURSES*, 3.24.84–86A

"But the wise person can lose nothing. Such a person has everything stored up for themselves, leaving nothing to Fortune, their own goods are held firm, bound in virtue, which requires nothing from chance, and therefore can't be either increased or diminished."

—SENECA, *ON THE FIRMNESS OF THE WISE*, 5.4

November 19th   Will I accept the situation and still fight to do and be good?

MORNING REFLECTION

EVENING REFLECTION

November 20th   Where can I find timelessness in every moment?

MORNING REFLECTION

EVENING REFLECTION

November 21st How can I make this minute—right now—be enough?

MORNING REFLECTION

EVENING REFLECTION

November 22nd   What am I irrationally afraid of losing?

MORNING REFLECTION

EVENING REFLECTION

November 23rd   Why is my power to choose so resilient and adaptable?

MORNING REFLECTION

EVENING REFLECTION

November 24th   How can I see my loved ones as gifts not possessions?

MORNING REFLECTION

EVENING REFLECTION

November 25th   Is more money really going to make things better?

MORNING REFLECTION

EVENING REFLECTION

WEEK XLVIII
BALANCE THE BOOKS OF LIFE DAILY

We journal as a way of gathering up life's experiences, insights, frustrations, unexpected struggles and triumphs, and more. In all of this we are making a reckoning of our progress on life's way. Seneca, whose father-in-law was in charge of keeping the books on Rome's granary, liked the metaphor of balancing life's books each day. Rather than postpone, our impulse each day should be to bring things, as much as possible, to completion. Why? Because we never know what tomorrow might bring. Epictetus, too, would tell his students that the important thing was that they had begun: begun to practice, learn, get better. Give yourself credit this week for the journey you are on—and reflect on how far you have come (and how far there is left to go).

"Let us prepare our minds as if we'd come to the very end of life. Let us postpone nothing. Let us balance life's books each day. Life's greatest flaw is that it's always imperfect, and a certain portion of it is postponed. The one who puts the finishing touches on their life each day is never short of time."

—SENECA, *MORAL LETTERS*, 101.7B–8A

"Believe me, it's better to produce the balance-sheet of your own life than that of the grain market."

—SENECA, *ON THE BREVITY OF LIFE*, 18.3B

"I am your teacher and you are learning in my school. My aim is to bring you to completion, unhindered, free from compulsive behavior, unrestrained, without shame, free, flourishing, and happy, looking to God in things great and small—your aim is to learn and diligently practice all these things. Why then don't you complete the work, if you have the right aim and I have both the right aim and right preparation? What is missing? . . . The work is quite feasible, and is the only thing in our power. . . . Let go of the past. We must only begin. Believe me and you will see."

—EPICTETUS, *DISCOURSES*, 2.19.29–34

November 26th   What petty comparisons am I bothering myself with?

MORNING REFLECTION

EVENING REFLECTION

November 27th   What sources of unrest can I tune out?

MORNING REFLECTION

EVENING REFLECTION

November 28th   What's bothering me that I haven't spoken up about?

MORNING REFLECTION

EVENING REFLECTION

November 29th   How can I be less agitated—and complain about it less, too?

MORNING REFLECTION

EVENING REFLECTION

November 30th   Am I ready to accept the pull of the universe?

MORNING REFLECTION

EVENING REFLECTION

December 1st   If I lived today as if it were my last, what would I do?

MORNING REFLECTION

EVENING REFLECTION

December 2nd   How can I make my actions count?

MORNING REFLECTION

EVENING REFLECTION

WEEK XLIX
BE STINGY WITH TIME

One of the most common sayings we hear is "life is short." It is—but as Seneca remarked, it's also plenty long if you know how to use it. The first step to that? Not giving so much of it away to other people. Becoming miserly about our time is a powerful exercise, which can keep us from squandering this nonrenewable resource. What in your life consumes a lot of time for no good purpose? What amusements and desires consume our time without giving us any good return? As you review that list, make a commitment to doing something about it. Life is short, after all; you don't have too much to spare.

"Were all the geniuses of history to focus on this single theme, they could never fully express their bafflement at the darkness of the human mind. No person would give up even an inch of their estate, and the slightest dispute with a neighbor can mean hell to pay; yet we easily let others encroach on our lives—worse, we often pave the way for those who will take it over. No person hands out their money to passersby, but to how many do each of us hand out our lives! We're tight-fisted with property and money, yet think too little of wasting time, the one thing about which we should all be the toughest misers."

—SENECA, *ON THE BREVITY OF LIFE*, 3.1–2

"It's not at all that we have too short a time to live, but that we squander a great deal of it. Life is long enough, and it's given in sufficient measure to do many great things if we spend it well. But when it's poured down the drain of luxury and neglect, when it's employed to no good end, we're finally driven to see that it has passed by before we even recognized it passing. And so it is—we don't receive a short life, we make it so."

—SENECA, *ON THE BREVITY OF LIFE*, 1.3–4A

December 3rd   What practical problems am I solving with this philosophy?

MORNING REFLECTION

EVENING REFLECTION

December 4th   What do I truly own?

MORNING REFLECTION

EVENING REFLECTION

December 5th   What unpleasant thoughts can I face and use to my advantage?

MORNING REFLECTION

EVENING REFLECTION

December 6th   What can I do to *live* now, while I still can?

MORNING REFLECTION

EVENING REFLECTION

December 7th   Can I love the hand Fate deals me?

MORNING REFLECTION

EVENING REFLECTION

December 8th   Are there any feelings I need to face?

MORNING REFLECTION

EVENING REFLECTION

December 9th   Are you saying no enough?

MORNING REFLECTION

EVENING REFLECTION

WEEK L
KEEP THE RHYTHM

Marcus Aurelius must have known that as emperor he was part of a grand and great history. As a philosopher, he also knew that all people are part of a rhythm pulsing through both history and their own lives, and he liked to remind himself to not lose that beat. Return to your philosophy, he would tell himself when he drifted. Don't give in to the distractions. In fact, he tried constantly to return to it. That kind of awareness (*prosochē*, paying special attention) is something he learned from reading Epictetus, who told his students that while none of us can be perfect, we can catch ourselves when we begin to slide, when we drift from where we should be. Can you feel that rhythm this week? Can you point to examples of when you really felt locked into it?

> "Walk the long gallery of the past, of empires and kingdoms succeeding each other without number. And you can also see the future, for surely it will be exactly the same, unable to deviate from the present rhythm. It's all one whether we've experienced forty years or an aeon. What more is there to see?"
>
> —MARCUS AURELIUS, *MEDITATIONS*, 7.49

> "When forced, as it seems, by circumstances into utter confusion, get a hold of yourself quickly. Don't be locked out of the rhythm any longer than necessary. You'll be able to keep the beat if you are constantly returning to it."
>
> —MARCUS AURELIUS, *MEDITATIONS*, 6.11

> "When you let your attention slide for a bit, don't think you will get back a grip on it whenever you wish—instead, bear in mind that because of today's mistake everything that follows will be necessarily worse. . . . Is it possible to be free from error? Not by any means, but it is possible to be a person always stretching to avoid error. For we must be content to at least escape a few mistakes by never letting our attention slide."
>
> —EPICTETUS, *DISCOURSES*, 4.12.1; 19

December 10th   What are you getting in return for the time you spend so freely?

MORNING REFLECTION

EVENING REFLECTION

December 11th   Are you living with dignity and courage?

MORNING REFLECTION

EVENING REFLECTION

December 12th   Will I keep the rhythm of life, no matter the interruptions?

MORNING REFLECTION

EVENING REFLECTION

December 13th   Can I be grateful for the time I've been given?

MORNING REFLECTION

EVENING REFLECTION

December 14th   What will my life be a testament to?

MORNING REFLECTION

EVENING REFLECTION

December 15th   Am I going to get a little bit better today?

MORNING REFLECTION

EVENING REFLECTION

December 16th   What am I doing to build my self-confidence?

MORNING REFLECTION

EVENING REFLECTION

∾

WEEK LI
STAKE YOUR CLAIM

W e like to collect the sayings of great writers or of leaders we admire—they often become mantras for us on the path of life, providing guidance and assurance. But as Seneca reminds us, truth hasn't been monopolized. We need to spend some time and effort each week formulating our own wisdom, staking our own claims based on our study, practice, and training. That's what this journal is about. Reflecting on the Stoic wisdom and adding our own to it. Seneca urged us to blaze our own trail and to take charge and stake our own claim. Well, let's do it. Let these pages reflect the insights you have learned by your own experiences. Let the inspiration you've taken from the Stoics create your own exercises, reminders, and perspectives.

"For it's disgraceful for an old person, or one in sight of old age, to have only the knowledge carried in their notebooks. Zeno said this . . . what do you say? Cleanthes said that . . . what do you say? How long will you be compelled by the claims of another? Take charge and stake your own claim—something posterity will carry in its notebook."

—SENECA, *MORAL LETTERS*, 33.7

"Won't you be walking in your predecessors' footsteps? I surely will use the older path, but if I find a shorter and smoother way, I'll blaze a trail there. The ones who pioneered these paths aren't our masters, but our guides. Truth stands open to everyone, it hasn't been monopolized."

—SENECA, *MORAL LETTERS*, 33.11

"Don't act grudgingly, selfishly, without due diligence, or to be a contrarian. Don't overdress your thought in fine language. Don't be a person of too many words and too many deeds. . . . Be cheerful, not wanting outside help or the relief others might bring. A person needs to stand on their own, not be propped up."

—MARCUS AURELIUS, *MEDITATIONS*, 3.5

December 17th How well do I really know myself?

MORNING REFLECTION

EVENING REFLECTION

December 18th The end for us all is clear, but is my purpose?

MORNING REFLECTION

EVENING REFLECTION

December 19th   What can I focus on that is much, much bigger than me?

MORNING REFLECTION

EVENING REFLECTION

December 20th   What am I really so afraid of?

MORNING REFLECTION

EVENING REFLECTION

December 21st   How can I make the most of today—and in doing so, my life?

MORNING REFLECTION

EVENING REFLECTION

December 22nd   What wisdom will I create today?

MORNING REFLECTION

EVENING REFLECTION

December 23rd   If I relaxed my tight grip on life, what would happen?

MORNING REFLECTION

EVENING REFLECTION

WEEK LII
TURN WORDS INTO WORKS

arcus spent a great deal of time on his journals, yet within their pages we find him admonishing himself to throw them away, to never read their pages. Why? Because he didn't want them to be an excuse from the essential tasks at hand. The art of living will never be found anywhere but in our own efforts to be a good person. Never forget that is the aim of this journal. It is not to fill up pages with pretty thoughts but to inspire you to take action, to turn the words, as Seneca said, into works. In that we have the perfect place to end this year, with the ultimate Stoic prompt: Get active in your own rescue.

"Stop wandering about! You aren't likely to read your own note-books, or ancient histories, or the anthologies you've collected to enjoy in your old age. Get busy with life's purpose, toss aside empty hopes, get active in your own rescue—if you care for yourself at all—and do it while you can."

—MARCUS AURELIUS, *Meditations*, 3.14

"You have proof in the extent of your wanderings that you never found the art of living anywhere—not in logic, nor in wealth, fame, or in any indulgence. Nowhere. Where is it then? In doing what human nature demands. How is a person to do this? By having principles be the source of desire and action. What principles? Those to do with good and evil, indeed in the belief that there is no good for a human being except what creates justice, self-control, courage, and freedom, and nothing evil except what destroys these things."

—MARCUS AURELIUS, *Meditations*, 8.1.(5)

"All study of philosophy and reading should be for the purpose of living a happy life . . . we should seek precepts to help us, noble and courageous words that can become facts . . . we should learn them in a way that words become works."

—SENECA, *MORAL LETTERS*, 108.35

December 24th   Can I consume less to make more room for virtue?

MORNING REFLECTION

EVENING REFLECTION

December 25th   Where can I find reinvigoration and balance?

MORNING REFLECTION

EVENING REFLECTION

December 26th   Where am I wasting life?

MORNING REFLECTION

EVENING REFLECTION

December 27th   Is my soul stronger than my body?

MORNING REFLECTION

_____

_____

_____

_____

_____

_____

_____

_____

EVENING REFLECTION

_____

_____

_____

_____

_____

_____

_____

_____

December 28th   In a hundred years, who will remember or be remembered?

MORNING REFLECTION

_____

_____

_____

_____

_____

_____

_____

EVENING REFLECTION

December 29th   What am I grateful for?

MORNING REFLECTION

EVENING REFLECTION

December 30th   How can I bring a calm mind to tough situations?

MORNING REFLECTION

_____

_____

_____

_____

_____

_____

_____

_____

EVENING REFLECTION

_____

_____

_____

_____

_____

_____

_____

_____

December 31st   How will I turn these words into works?

MORNING REFLECTION

_____

_____

_____

_____

_____

_____

_____

EVENING REFLECTION

MORE STOIC PROMPTS

While this journal was designed to be the ultimate companion for *The Daily Stoic*, and *The Daily Stoic* was designed to be read as many times as a reader would like, you might well be looking for even more prompts and Stoic readings, especially if this is your second go around with the journal. That is something we are happy to provide.

First, we send out a free e-mail every single day of Stoic wisdom at DailyStoic.com. If you haven't signed up yet, you absolutely should!

Second, if you're looking for some classic and modern Stoic texts to journal along to, we have some recommendations:

- *Meditations* by Marcus Aurelius (we strongly recommend the Gregory Hays translation for Modern Library)
- *Letters of a Stoic* by Seneca (the abridged Penguin Classics edition is wonderful and there is also a full—and free—e-book edition put out by Tim Ferriss)
- *Discourses and Selected Writings* by Epictetus (again, hard to do better than Penguin Classics)
- *The Inner Citadel: The Meditations of Marcus Aurelius* by Pierre Hadot (this is a wonderful deep dive into Marcus Aurelius's philosophy and what makes him tick)
- *The Moral Sayings of Publilius Syrus: A Roman Slave* by Publilius Syrus (another slave turned philosopher whose pithy epigrams will give you something to write about each day)

If you want to learn more about Stoic exercises and practices, and their purpose, we like the following sources:

- Chapter 3 in Pierre Hadot's *Philosophy as a Way of Life: Spiritual Exercises from Socrates to Foucault* (Wiley-Blackwell, 1995)
- Chapters 15–16 in Richard Sorabji's *Emotion and Peace of Mind: From Stoic Agitation to Christian Temptation* (Oxford University Press, 2000)

- Part Two of Donald Robertson's *The Philosophy of Cognitive Behavioural Therapy: Stoic Philosophy as Rational and Cognitie Psychotherapy* (Karnac Books, 2010) or his equally excellent *Stoicism and the Art of Happiness* (Hodder & Stoughton, 2013)
- Part III of Massimo Pigliucci's *How to Be a Stoic: Using Ancient Philosophy to Live a Modern Life* (Basic Books, 2017)

For a broad selection of Stoic reading beyond the titles above, we have compiled the following list, which is continually being revised and added to at www.dailystoic.com/books-on-stoicism:

- James B. Stockdale's *Courage Under Fire: Testing Epictetus's Doctrines in the Laboratory of Human Behavior* (Hoover Institution Press, 1993)
- James Romm's *Dying Every Day: Seneca at the Court of Nero* (Vintage, 2014)
- Rob Goodman and Jimmy Soni's *Rome's Last Citizen: The Life and Legacy of Cato, Mortal Enemy of Caesar* (St. Martin's Griffin, 2014)
- Tom Wolfe's *A Man in Full* (Dial Press, 2001)
- William B. Irvine's *A Guide to the Good Life: The Ancient Art of Stoic Joy* (Oxford University Press, 2008)
- Alain de Botton's *The Consolations of Philosophy* (Vintage, 2001)
- Nassim Nicholas Taleb's *Antifragile: Things that Gain from Disorder* (Random House, 2014)
- James Miller's *Examined Lives: From Socrates to Nietzsche* (Picador, 2012)
- Nancy Sherman's *Stoic Warriors: The Ancient Philosophy Behind the Military Mind* (Oxford University Press, 2007)
- John Sellar's *Stoicism* (University of California Press, 2006)
- R. W. Sharples's *Stoics, Epicureans, and Skeptics: An Introduction to Hellenistic Philosophy* (Routledge, 1996)
- M. Andrew Holowchak's *The Stoics: A Guide for the Perplexed* (Bloomsbury Academic, 2008)
- F. H. Sandbach's *The Stoics* (Hackett Publishing Company, Inc., 1994)

- Margaret Graver's *Stoicism and Emotion* (University of Chicago Press, 2009)
- Brad Inwood's *The Cambridge Companion to the Stoics* (Cambridge University Press, 2003)
- Ronald Pies's *Everything Has Two Handles: The Stoic's Guide to the Art of Living* (Hamilton Books, 2008)
- Jules Evans's *Philosophy for Life and Other Dangerous Situations* (New World Library, 2013)
- Lawrence C. Becker's *A New Stoicism: Revised Edition* (Princeton University Press, 2017)
- Emily Wilson's *The Greatest Empire: A Life of Seneca* (Oxford University Press, 2014)

Interested in learning even more about stoicism? Visit DailyStoic.com to sign up for a daily email, engage in discussion, get advice, and more.

Join millions of other readers with these #1 bestsellers!

Portfolio/Penguin
An imprint of Penguin Random House LLC
375 Hudson Street
New York, New York 10014

Most Portfolio books are available at a discount when purchased in quantity for sales promotions or corporate use. Special editions, which include personalized covers, excerpts, and corporate imprints, can be created when purchased in large quantities. For more information, please call (212) 572-2232 or e-mail specialmarkets@penguinrandomhouse.com. Your local bookstore can also assist with discounted bulk purchases using the Penguin Random House corporate Business-to-Business program. For assistance in locating a participating retailer, e-mail B2B@penguinrandomhouse.com.

Library of Congress Cataloging-in-Publication Data

Names: Holiday, Ryan, author.
Title: The daily stoic journal : 366 days of writing and reflection on the art of living / Ryan Holiday.
Description: New York : Portfolio, 2017.
Identifiers: LCCN 2017060837 | ISBN 9780525534396 (hardcover)
Subjects: LCSH: Stoics. | Authorship. | Diaries—Authorship.
Classification: LCC B528 .H653 2017 | DDC 188—dc23
LC record available at https://lccn.loc.gov/2017060837

Printed in the United States of America
6th Printing

Book design by Daniel Lagin